Educational Leadership

◆ A REFERENCE HANDBOOK

Other Titles in
ABC-CLIO's
CONTEMPORARY EDUCATION ISSUES
Series

African American Education, Cynthia L. Jackson
The Assessment Debate, Valerie J. Janesick
Bilingual Education, Rosa Castro Feinberg
Charter Schools, Danny Weil
Migrant Education, Judith A. Gouwens
Special Education, Arlene Sacks
Student Rights, Patricia H. Hinchey
Teacher Training, Dave Pushkin

FORTHCOMING

Alternative Schools, Brenda J. Conley
Diversity and Multicultural Education, Peter Appelbaum
Native American Education, Lorraine Hale
School Vouchers and Privatization, Danny Weil

Educational Leadership

A REFERENCE HANDBOOK

Pat Williams-Boyd

A B C ☰ C L I O

Santa Barbara, California • Denver, Colorado • Oxford, England

© 2002 by Pat Williams-Boyd

Library of Congress Cataloging-in-Publication Data

Williams-Boyd, Pat.
  Educational leadership : a reference handbook / Pat Williams-Boyd.
    p. cm. — (Contemporary education issues)
Includes bibliographical references (p.) and index.
  ISBN 1-57607-353-X (alk. paper); 1-57607-751-9 (e-book)
  1. Educational leadership—United States—Handbooks, manuals, etc. 2.
School management and organization—United States. 3. Community and
school—United States. I. Title. II. Series.
  LB2805.W517 2002
  371.2—dc21

                                                        2002000395

This book is also available on the World Wide Web as an e-book.
Visit www.abc-clio.com for details.

08 07 06 05 04 03 02   10 9 8 7 6 5 4 3 2 1

ABC-CLIO, Inc.
130 Cremona Drive, P.O. Box 1911
Santa Barbara, California 93116-1911

This book is printed on acid-free paper ∞.
Manufactured in the United States of America

To the two people whom I love most in this world
Mom and Dad, Blanche and Dell Williams
Who believed in the power of learning
To change lives

☙ Contents

●◆ Series Editor's Preface

The Contemporary Education Issues series is dedicated to providing readers with an up-to-date exploration of the central issues in education today. Books in the series will examine such controversial topics as home schooling, charter schools, privatization of public schools, Native American education, African American education, literacy, curriculum development, and many others. The series is national in scope and is intended to encourage research by anyone interested in the field.

Because education is undergoing radical if not revolutionary change, the series is particularly concerned with how contemporary controversies in education affect both the organization of schools and the content and delivery of curriculum. Authors will endeavor to provide a balanced understanding of the issues and their effects on teachers, students, parents, administrators, and policymakers. The aim of the Contemporary Education Issues series is to publish excellent research on today's educational concerns by some of the finest scholar/practitioners in the field while pointing to new directions. The series promises to offer important analyses of some of the most controversial issues facing society today.

Danny Weil
Series Editor

▪❖ Preface

Educational leadership for the twenty-first century reflects a shift to an unprecedented commitment to community. No longer is authoritarian, top-down compliance the most effective way of governing a school. This book examines the shift in authority from the district office to the individual school, a shift from the principal as authority-manager to a variety of constituents who share the school's governance. New Era leaders are students, teachers, families, community members, school boards, politicians, and corporate and philanthropic foundations.

This book examines the major questions of how leadership distributed throughout a community might look, how collaborative relationships might be forged, and how the school can be perceived as a rich environment of collegiality, shared authority, and authentic partnerships. In addition, it discusses how leaders mobilize people for change, what the critical issues are that leaders confront, what leaders do and how they do it, what an effective leader might look like, and how effectiveness may be measured. The text also discusses the moral and ethical responsibilities that stakeholder leaders must exercise when equitably educating all the nation's young people.

Finally, because leaders initiate, support, and conduct school reform, the text offers a critical presentation of twenty leading reform models. Also included are valuable reform resources for foundation funding and annotated lists of organizations, leadership workshops and institutes, websites, and print and nonprint materials.

● Acknowledgments

This book is born of the love, encouragement, mentorship, and leadership of many people:

- ● To the students, parents, faculty, and staff of Central Junior High School, Lawrence, Kansas, 1976–1996, thank you for sharing your lives, your enthusiasm, your willingness to take chances, and your vibrancy as you were daily, authentically engaged in the business of learning
- ● To Dan Weil, writer, academic, teacher, and visionary for his persistent encouragement and support
- ● And to Dr. Valerie Janesick, artist, scholar, author, educator, colleague, and Renaissance woman, for her selfless and abiding mentorship, experienced in the truest and fullest sense of the word, thank you

Chapter One

•€ Overview

People throughout history have championed their leaders, men and women who have in time of political, social, cultural, or religious crisis been deemed passionate about their beliefs, powerful in their abilities, effective in their performances. People such as Gandhi, Winston Churchill, Cesar Chavez, Golda Meir, Martin Luther King, John Fitzgerald Kennedy, Eleanor Roosevelt, John Dewey, and Susan B. Anthony leap from the pages of the past to inspire the present and shape the future. These are people who define a movement or a social cause. They are people who push the frontiers of understanding and knowledge; people to whom others look for examples of higher ideals, nobler moral values, more democratic principles; people who heroically incite others to confidence and to action.

On an educational level, phrases like "dynamic leader," "strong leader," or "visionary leader" are used when answering the question of why a particular school succeeds while another struggles. Our desire to see someone "rally the troops," "take charge of the situation," and "get the job done" is typically American. Even more typical is the search for someone who will come into the school district or the school and see the bigger picture, be responsive to taxpayers, raise student test scores, prepare students for higher education or the work world, and ready them to step into their democratic roles and the competitive economic world market. Administrators today are often hired not only because of their perceived expertise, but because of their ability to lead a school district in taking effective action.

CONSTRUCTING THE PAST: WHERE WE'VE BEEN

In the early years of American schooling, the school board made decisions about the operation, finances, and personnel of a public school. However, schools quickly grew in both size and complexity, and the political model of leadership was replaced by the bureaucratic model, whereby decision making and general school operation became the provinces of professional administrators (Seyfarth 1999, 6).

Large urban areas in the nineteenth century adopted the bureaucratic model to ameliorate political graft and to improve the daily operation of growing schools. Schools were standardized to the extent that employees were evaluated based on compliance with standards rather than on student learning outcomes. Rules, regulations, operations, and school procedures were all uniform and, as a result, impersonal (Guthrie 1990).

As school employees were challenged to become specialists, the "principal teacher" arose in the later part of the nineteenth century. Seen as an instructional leader, this individual reported to the superintendent on the work of the school's teachers. However, because schools continued to grow rapidly, the tasks of the principal teacher became much more diverse. The position now required managing the operation of all facets of the school, including building maintenance, personnel hiring, and finances. The "principal" assumed an additional mantle of political activist, for he "sought to sense and transform public expectations into formal decisions and authoritative actions" (Seyfarth 1999, 7).

At the opening of the twentieth century, business executives and professionals continued to exert growing influence on city school boards. "In their attempt to counter criticisms that the schools were inefficient, superintendents and university education experts rushed to borrow language and concepts from business, and 'businesslike' became almost synonymous with 'scientific'" (Tyack and Cuban 1995, 114). School leaders became managers as they developed time- and cost-efficient tasks for the workers, who were teachers and students.

However, during the Great Depression, when businesses suffered, the rush to emulate corporations briefly subsided, only to rise again in the 1960s and 1970s. To increase social efficiency, people offered new businesslike prescriptions for teaching in the classroom, managing the school, and budgeting in the district. With pressure on district school leaders to produce more effective products—students who would be cost-efficient contributors to the competitive world economy—many school boards adopted such corporate models as the Program Planning and Budgeting System (PPBS). Through this system, school goals and objectives were developed based on program costs as measured against results.

During the same period, policy makers and executives outside the school believed that corporate organization and standardized conduct could raise the scores of low-achieving students. But those engaged directly in the classroom felt that teaching and learning were reduced to drill-and-practice, with little attention paid to teacher expertise, thinking skills, depth of understanding, or the individual progress of students.

At the start of the twenty-first century, as the United States has moved from an industrial economy to a knowledge-based economy, we cannot ignore the power and influence that the business world, and in particular corporate individuals, have had on the broader culture. We are challenged by images of an Iacocca rescuing a failing corporation or of a Gates continually creating new business. Superintendents of low-achieving school districts are often replaced by chief executive officers (CEOs) taken directly from the corporate world or from the ranks of retired military personnel.

Proponents of authoritative, standardized, corporate-model leadership emphasize the dramatic effect one person may temporarily have on schools, but they ignore the more enduring and important work of a school team (Mitchell and Tucker 1992). The critical day-to-day work of the school, fundamental changes that produce long-range effects, and the dynamics of change and of leadership as processes become overshadowed by the spotlight placed on a single charismatic leader.

Yet with the overwhelming emphasis placed on schools being run as businesses, we might ask whether there are commonalities between the corporate and educational worlds that would help us define educational leadership, or whether there is a process at work that sets apart the leadership of America's schools.

COMPARING THE CORPORATE AND THE EDUCATIONAL

Although there are apparent similarities between the corporate boardroom and the school board meeting room, and between the CEO and the superintendent/principal, there are both subtle and dramatic differences. There are differences between the school and the factory, between products and pupils, differences that mandate a new type of leadership shaped by the community's hopes that lie with their children's education.

Ramsey (1999) lists several clear distinctions between school administrators and corporate leaders. He states that school leaders

➣ Lead organizations with no clear and consistent mission

- Contend with chronic uncertainty and lack of control regarding funding and funding sources
- Are often unsure who their clients are (taxpayers, parents, policy makers, students)
- Make daily decisions while engaged with different constituencies as opposed to being able to objectively make decisions in isolation
- Answer to multiple and varied constituencies
- Exert a wider span of control and affect a broader part of the community
- Strive for gains/outcomes (as they affect students' lives) that are often not immediately measurable
- Operate in a highly political environment and must report directly to a publicly elected board
- Have more "bosses" than does the CEO
- Must possess and use both management and leadership skills
- Function in a work setting in which everyone sees themselves as experts (5, 6)

Like management in the business or corporate worlds, management of schools is demanding. However, in schools true leadership is even more complex and shaped by personal contexts.

What, then, do we mean by educational leadership? It is among the hardest terms to define and agree upon, particularly among educational researchers.

SETTING TWENTY-FIRST-CENTURY EDUCATIONAL LEADERSHIP IN CONTEXT: WHERE WE ARE

Today, educational leaders are challenged to educate a growing and diverse student population; to be responsive to the needs of an expanding underclass; to address broader needs of students and their families; to implement teaching and learning strategies that will prove effective both for students and taxpayers; and to engage in sound, data-driven practices.

Yet because educational leadership cannot be separated from the sociopolitical, cultural, historical, or ideological environments in which it exists, defining the term is often like touching the smoke from a fire. To understand leadership, which both mirrors society's values and provokes the educational context, is to understand the future of schooling. In other words, how we choose to define educational leadership has implications for social interactions, for students' socialization into the larger culture, for the very formation of citizens. It will affect society's growth and health as it addresses issues of class, gender, race, ethnicity, and religion (Grace 1995).

Defining New Era Leadership

In 1991, Moss defined educational leadership as both a process and a property. The process of leadership involves directing the work of the teachers. The property of leadership refers to common traits or characteristics shared by effective leaders. Mitchell and Tucker (1992) characterized leadership as a way of thinking, a sense of spirit founded in overlapping environments—our own, that of the profession, and that of the educational process itself. Some have equated leadership with role responsibility, seeing the principal as the educational leader. Holzman (1992) maintained that the literature written about effective schools "is virtually a paean to the virtues of the principal as [a] 'strong' leader." Others have defined leadership in terms of metaphors: the principal as manager or instructional leader, the superintendent as the decision maker or problem solver. Researchers continue to contrast leadership that is management-oriented with leadership that empowers people.

Of the over 400 definitions of leadership argued in the literature, the definitions that have recently emerged are expressed through the concepts of power and community. At the beginning of the 1990s, Sergiovanni (1992) began to frame this shift in definitions in terms of a question: "Should schools be understood as formal organizations or as communities?" Although there are aspects of both formal organizations and communities in schools, the dominance of one perspective or the other reflects assumptions about positional relationships, ownership of knowledge, privilege, cultural norms, and values (discussed below).

Bolman and Deal (1997) defined leadership as an interactive relationship between leaders and followers. Its cultural, gender, class, or ethnic components aside, leadership is best characterized by influence and identification. Leading speaks to both the ability to frame a communal sense of meaning and to engage constituents in purposeful action.

Leadership, then, is a collaborative process of engaging the community in creating equitable possibilities for children and their families that result in academic achievement. The new notion of leadership dreams of changing the world rather than maintaining it (Giroux 1993). It celebrates embrace of others, champions differences, and nurtures young minds toward seeking questions and posing solutions. It is a notion of stewardship that seeks a higher moral purpose and a more communal humanity born of shared vision and common purpose. It dreams of things that do not yet exist and asks, "Why not?"

Contrasting New Era Leadership with Previous Experience: Where We're Going

Discussion of the values and attitudes of leadership is new. So is the notion that educational leadership is exercised by others in the community than the principal or the superintendent. Collaboration and attention to actual teaching and learning have replaced the overemphasis on process and skills.

It is important to be aware of those characteristics and styles of leadership that result in effective schools. Sergiovanni (1992) maintains that the study of leadership has historically addressed only "levels of decision making, assessing the consequences of their variations for followers' satisfaction, individual compliance and performance, and organizational effectiveness" (2). In other words, it has addressed form and process over substance and function. It represents a managerial mode of top-down authority that replaces results with the "right" methods. It is concerned with

> doing things right rather than doing the right things. In schools, improvement plans become substitutes for improvement outcomes. Scores on teacher-appraisal systems become substitutes for good teaching. Accumulation of credits in courses and in-service workshops becomes a substitute for changes in practice. Discipline plans become substitutes for student control. Leadership styles become substitutes for purpose and substance. Congeniality becomes a substitute for collegiality. Cooperation becomes a substitute for commitment. Compliance becomes a substitute for results. (Sergiovanni 1992, 4)

It has taken nearly two centuries to break out of this top-down mode of governance. The three-pronged view of principal leadership— political activist, manager, and instructional leader—has brought us into the 1990s. With increased emphasis on accountability for student achievement and on collaborative decision making, the role of the principal has begun to shift in ways Sergiovanni describes above. Because school funding has not kept pace with budgetary demands; because over one-third of the current teaching population will retire in the next five years; and because the student population is increasingly from families of lower socioeconomic levels who speak English as a second language, educational leadership has begun to shift from the top-down mode to the more linear community-oriented model.

EDUCATIONAL LEADERS—LEADERS IN EDUCATION: WHO IS LEADING?

Although for the foreseeable future principals will be the focal point of school accountability and therefore leadership, the models of leadership discussed in chapter 3 are converging into the notion that "the essence of leadership is achieving results through people" (Smith and Piele 1997, xiii). Rather than simply exercising authority to make subordinates comply with their wishes, principals are beginning to function as the peers of teachers, supporting their professional expertise and collaborating with them on school-based decisions.

During the past century, the teacher was responsible for student achievement in the classroom; the principal was accountable for the ongoing success of the school; the superintendent was answerable to the locally elected school board about the operation of the school district; and the state was responsive to federal mandates. Today we discuss leadership in light of three main notions:

1. Shared governance is a bridging of these separate domains of responsibility and opportunity.
2. Systems thinking is the ability to perceive the "hidden dynamics of complex systems, and to find leverage" (Senge 2000, 415).
3. Engagement. New era leadership uses the language of engagement, the ability to perceive and frame difficult problems and then to mobilize individuals and constituent groups toward a common action.

Who, then, are these leaders in education, this constituent group, this broad community of leaders?

As schools are increasingly concerned with public engagement, the audiences to whom traditional school leaders were once merely answerable are beginning to become direct participants in the processes and progress of the school itself. While legislators on the local, state, and national levels still exercise great influence on schooling, others are also becoming partners in the leadership of the school. They include administrators at all levels, teachers, parents, students, school boards, taxpayers, local businesses, corporations, universities, state educational agencies, and the general service community.

An Example of Heightened Partnership

In a northern California school district, what is known as the Collaborative pools resources and expertise in the service of students and their families. Constituent groups came together to form the Collaborative, which includes the following categories of stakeholders:

- *Education*
  - Unified school district
  - Individual schools
  - County Office of Education
  - Colleges and universities in California
- *County service agencies*
  - County public health services
  - Family Service Agency
  - County Medical Center
  - Department of Public Health
  - Department of Social Services
  - County drug and alcohol programs
  - County Family Health Center
- *Other public stakeholders*
  - County Housing Authority
  - City police department
  - Law enforcement and district attorney's office
  - Probation department
- *Private nonprofit community stakeholders*
  - California Early Intervention Program
  - Center for Human Services
  - Salvation Army Red Shield Center
  - Haven Women's Center
  - Private mental health, dental, and medical personnel
- *Direct constituents*
  - Students and families (Williams-Boyd 1996, 102–103)

Although this may be an example of the most intense sort of collaboration—a model of joint leadership and provision called "full-service schools"—other schools across the country are beginning to reach out and engage stakeholders as peer leaders. (More in-depth discussion of leadership collaboration follows in chapter 3.) Joint councils made up of parents, students, administrators, teachers, university personnel, and members of the health and social services communities are emerging in disenfranchised neighborhoods. A variety of services—

often referred to as school-linked services—are becoming available through the school sites in these neighborhoods.

In Michigan, Florida, Texas, New York, Kentucky, West Virginia, and Kansas, collaborative leadership means shared leadership. In other states, roundtable councils bring together school boards, teachers, administrators, legislators, parents, students, members of the chamber of commerce, and university personnel for both discussions and exercising leadership. At still other school sites, through partnerships with corporate and philanthropic foundations (some listed in chapter 6), resources and talent become synergistic forces for the common good.

In what is often referred to as "distributed leadership," the constituent groups and their work are delineated as shown in Table 1.1.

Let us look more carefully at each of the stakeholder groups who are playing distinctive leadership roles in New Era education. And let us begin with "practice"—the classroom—and move outward. We will start with an underestimated group of potential leaders, the students. For although the vast majority of writings on educational leadership begin with the principal and end with the superintendent, with an occasional nod at the school board, New Era leadership invites and mobilizes all people in the school community.

PRACTICE LEVEL

Students

In the 1990s an extensive study identified forty critical attributes that would allow students to better maximize their potential and resist engaging in at-risk behaviors like drug and alcohol abuse, gang involvement, and dropping out of school. Among those attributes are

- Adult role models
- School engagement
- Bonding to school
- Sense of purpose
- Caring school environment

The research further indicated that the typical student possessed only eighteen of these forty attributes, contributing to student disaffection and failure. In schools that have provided leadership opportunities for students, many of these critical attributes have been addressed and students have experienced vital connections, leading to newfound successes.

Table 1.1
Distributed Leadership

Leadership Role	Leadership Function
Policy Level	
Legislators at various levels, chief state school officers, state superintendents, state boards of education, local boards of education	➠ Set standards and benchmarks of performance ➠ Monitor and assess performance ➠ Administer rewards and sanctions ➠ Adjudicate issues of process, design, and implementation of programs and issues that are noninstructional
Professional Level	
Researchers, recognized practitioners, staff professional developers	➠ Develop, pilot, and assess new standards and new teaching and learning practices ➠ Provide in-service and preservice training ➠ Conduct cutting-edge staff development ➠ Respond to needs of entire school systems on issues of best practice
System Level	
District superintendents, assistant superintendents, support personnel	➠ Mandate systemwide improvement strategies ➠ Design incentive frameworks for principals, teachers, staff ➠ Allocate district resources to individual schools ➠ Recruit and evaluate building principals ➠ Act as ombudsman or buffer for relational issues concerning teachers, principals, students, and families
School Level	
Principals, assistant principals, support staff	➠ Design or implement school improvement strategies ➠ Recruit, hire, and evaluate faculty and staff

	↠ Distribute resources for teaching and learning
	↠ Seek partnerships with and investment of community stakeholders
	↠ Secure outside funding in the form of grants for the work of the school
	↠ Unify the vision of the entire neighborhood school community
	↠ Buffer exchanges between faculty, staff, students, and family
	↠ Provide an environment of community and shared governance

Practice Level

Teachers, support staff, professional developers	↠ Influence the collegial environment of the school
	↠ Respond to the learning needs of the students
	↠ Design, conduct, participate in, and evaluate professional development
	↠ Participate in or serve as chairs of building and district instructional committees
	↠ Engage the family in the work of the classroom and the school
	↠ Participate in recruitment and hiring of new teachers and in the dismissal of those who violate their contracts
	↠ Mentor, support, and evaluate the work of colleagues

Source: Adapted from Richard F. Elmore, "Leadership of Large-Scale Improvement in American Education" (paper presented to the Consortium on Policy and Research in Education, Harvard University, Cambridge, MA, September 1999), 40.

Typical Student Leadership Opportunities. Structured opportunities for student leadership frequently take the form of specific roles in school organizations, such as

➡ National Honor Society
➡ Various service clubs or organizations, e.g., the school's newspaper or yearbook, booster club, photography club, music and drama organizations, diversity groups, Y-Teens (a youth branch of the YWCA), pep club, chess club
➡ Various academic clubs, e.g., foreign language clubs, biology or other science clubs
➡ Competitive academic groups, e.g., Science or Math Bowl, debate and forensic teams, music competitions
➡ Community volunteer work through the school, such as the National Youth Service Day program
➡ Girls/Boys State, a national program that gives young people direct experience in government
➡ Student government

In many middle schools and high schools, students who have been chosen by their peers express the "student voice" in the daily operation of the school by participation in the student council. The extent to which this participation represents authentic leadership that moves others to action, or is more symbolic and represents a token gesture on the part of the adult population, varies from school to school. The intention is usually to offer leadership experiences for young people and to provide them opportunities to feel as if they could affect the school culture.

Student Government. Structured opportunities like student councils, where each class may elect a representative to the larger all-school council, present some limited occasions for leadership development. Often, student councils engage in a community project during the holiday season, such as adopting a family in need. In other instances, they may take on a social issues project such as recycling paper throughout the school, adopting part of the rain forest, or keeping a mile of a nearby highway clean for the duration of the school year. In still other instances, an elected school representative may sit as an observer on the local school board.

One of the more effective programs for students is the California Association of Student Councils (CASC), which sponsors camps, conferences, and volunteer activities locally, statewide, and internationally. CASC provides training in leadership, communication skills, and conflict management. It also instills in students a sense of personal, local, and global responsibility. Its sister project with Russia, the Association of Young Leaders, or AYL, connects students from both countries as they engage in leadership development. Students are mentored in the organization of conferences, curriculum training, and local and state projects.

CASC represents the ideal of student council involvement. Yet it includes only a small proportion of a given student population.

Expanded Opportunities. There are individual initiatives that show great promise in offering leadership opportunities to a wider group of students. Leadership High School in San Francisco uniquely prepares a diverse student population to become effective leaders in their communities. All students engage in team building and communication-skills training, student-directed extracurricular activities, and various leadership opportunities, as well as rigorous academic study. Leadership High requires active parent/guardian commitment in the form of thirty hours of volunteer time per year. The home, neighborhood, and school environments join to foster a sense of advocacy and concern for each student.

Many other initiatives nurture the leadership capacity of students through work in the community. The Vietnamese American Youth for the Future (VAYF) Youth Leadership Project offers ongoing seminars and an intensive ten-week training during which youths examine themselves, their family values, and their leadership capacity in the community.

The New York City Leadership Institute provides leadership training for young people as they live and work on the Upper West Side of Manhattan. The Appalachia Leadership Institute combines leadership training and spiritual development with service to the community such as painting homes for senior citizens and people in need. Similar projects and institutes are found in Jamaica and Mexico.

The Florida Student Leader: The Forum for America's Emerging Leaders is published for high school students by Oxendine in Florida. *The Florida Student Leader* and Oxendine's sister publication, *Florida Leader: The Magazine for Florida College Students,* are regarded as premier magazines for college-bound high school students and college students. In 2000, its eighteenth year, the *Florida Leader* published three thematic issues in the 2000 academic year; the issues addressed ""What Florida Students Think," "Best of Florida Schools," and "Student of the Year." The magazines included interviews, publicity for projects and leadership programs, and recruitment ideas. The high school companion magazine featured articles on college leadership ideas, fundraising suggestions, and possible solutions to challenges faced by peer leaders, such as negativism, apathy, or lack of student participation.

National Student Leadership. Canada has organized its development of student leadership into the Canadian Association of Student Activity Advisors (CASAA). Junior high school and senior high school student leadership sponsors have joined together to promote the growth of both sponsors and student leaders through developing and sharing information, resources, and talent. Representing all provinces and territories in Canada, the association holds two national conferences yearly that address both student leadership development and the ongoing needs of sponsors. *Above and Beyond,* CASAA's newsletter for advisors and student leaders, addresses such topics as the importance of cocurricular activities; the knowledge, skills, and attitudes necessary for the development of student leaders; ways in which student leaders may ameliorate the effects of crime and violence; and common concerns that join students with their communities.

Cultural Student Leadership. The face of leadership is as diverse as our country. Though leadership in predominantly white, middle-class schools has a leader-follower character, the notion of leadership may look very different through other cultural eyes. To Native Americans, or First Americans, a true leader should be a servant of others in the community. The tension these often unvoiced perspectives create is mitigated only by careful teaching of both cultures. Through such initiatives as the National Indian Youth Leadership Project, young people are taught leadership skills compatible with their indigenous values and beliefs. While addressing the total health and growth of the individual, the attributes, attitudes, and experiences valued by the cultural community are nurtured and developed.

Service-Learning. Students in nearly a third of the nation's schools are engaging in another form of leadership development called service-learning. Although teachers have frequently involved their students in community activities, academic service-learning systematically links thoughtful service to the community with the classroom curriculum. Service-learning

- Establishes strong links between the school and the community
- Provides students with experiences in assessing, designing, and implementing plans to meet authentic community needs while at the same time addressing academic goals
- Stimulates, through a process of reflection, the use of academic teachings in the lives of community members
- Develops, through experience, the dynamic of active egalitarian participation

Interest in academic service-learning and its effects on students' lives has grown rapidly. The National and Community Service Trust Act of 1993 provided funds for every state to include service-learning in their schools. And by the year 2000, the Department of Service-Learning of the Corporation for National Service provided some $20 million in funding for local service-learning efforts through its Learn and Serve America initiative. The National Commission on Service-Learning's Learning in Deed: Making a Difference through Service-Learning builds on the W. K. Kellogg Foundation's decade-long support for K–12 service-learning opportunities. Learning in Deed's K–12 Service-Learning Leadership Network brings together organizations, coalitions, leaders, and students through sharing information and resources, through conferences and workshops, and through purposeful and focused collaboration.

Examples of Academic Service-Learning. There are as many different service-learning projects as there are people who participate in them. Some possible examples include

- A middle-level science class that tests water samples of the local watershed and in the process of data collection attempts to restore the natural environment of the source. Students may write letters to environmentalists and public officials. They may give a presentation to the city commission and explain their findings, their efforts, and the responsibilities of the local government.
- In their study of equations, a high school algebra class may work with a local elementary school in building new playground equipment. The high school students enlist the help of the elementary school students and parents in presenting their preferences in equipment. They then use their understanding of algebraic formulas to design cost-effective equipment as they work with the local lumberyard or a volunteer architect.
- An elementary school class is studying fractions and the budgeting of money. They meet a group of senior citizens at the local grocery store and help them select their groceries, take note of bargains, keep track of the money they spend, push the grocery cart, and help with checkout and bagging of purchases.

In each instance, responsible and just relationships were established. Civic pride and involvement, self-efficacy, leadership skills, and learning were realized in an integrated, coordinated, and intentional fashion.

Yellow Light. In the face of a nation engulfed by the standards movement, service-learning brings a principled, activist perspective to the voluntary engagement of young people in authentic problem solving and civic leadership. Caution, however, should be exercised when well-meaning policy makers, on whatever level, begin to mandate service-learning as just one more quick fix to far more complex problems. Just as standards do not eradicate curricular failure, service-learning is not an antidote to discrepant, unequal treatment and social alienation.

Green Light. When schools, teachers, and students do choose to become involved in service-learning, however, the evidence for positive effects on young people has been dramatic:

1. Personal outcomes
   - Personal growth
   - Greater social responsibility
   - Interpersonal growth
   - Self-efficacy
   - Reduction in behavioral problems
   - Decrease in at-risk behaviors
   - Greater sense of empathy
   - Greater cognitive complexity
2. Civic responsibility
   - Heightened community awareness
   - Self-efficacy
   - Deeper understanding of the complexities of political, moral, and sociocultural contexts and the effects they can have
   - Augmented sense of community responsibility
   - Broader understanding of government
   - More active participation in society
3. Academic learning
   - Average to above-average gains on achievement tests and daily homework
   - Strong correlation between service-learning and higher standardized test scores (Civic Literacy Project, 2000)
   - Increase in grade point averages
   - Improved problem-solving skills
   - Increased interest in academics
   - Increased attendance
   - Students report themselves as more motivated
4. Career exploration and expectations
   - More knowledgeable about opportunities

- ➥ More realistically prepared
- ➥ Positive work skills
5. School environment
    - ➥ More mutual respect between students and teachers
    - ➥ More collegial atmosphere and sense of connection
    - ➥ Stimulates professional discussion about most effective and appropriate ways to motivate and teach students
6. Community engagement
    - ➥ Community experiences students as valuable and caring young citizens (Billig 2000, 660–662)
7. Leadership development
    - ➥ Shift in relationship between teacher and student from follower-leader to one of collegiality and respect
    - ➥ Trust in both the process and the outcome: Student leadership development necessitates accepting responsibility for consequences rather than the teacher rescuing the student. This does not imply a sink-or-swim mentality but experiential learning that is facilitated rather than directed.
    - ➥ Experience in the continual changes of working with people outside the classroom
    - ➥ Experience of actually "making a difference" in someone else's life (Des Marais, Yang, and Farzanehkia 2000, 680)
    - ➥ Respect for the student as a valuable, viable, and active citizen in the democracy

Conclusion. Despite the blatant disregard of students in the educational leadership literature, they are a powerful force for doing just and worthy things in the nation's schools. And although they may sit behind desks, they are now being given the opportunity to rise up and walk as leaders in their communities. Whether students are limited to the traditional leadership roles of the previous generation, or whether they are freed to create their own leadership opportunities through service-learning, the vitality, commitment, and energy of youth are once again focused on participatory democracy. "By engaging actively as citizens, students today shed the passive mantle of dependence for the more active roles of contribution and influence" (Kielsmeier 2000, 652).

This is a kind of leadership whose words are spoken in many dialects, whose energies represent diverse cultural, spiritual, and ethnic values, and whose actions are played out on the court of the common good. The neighborhood becomes the classroom; the student becomes a partner-teacher; and the greater community becomes richer.

The Family: Parents/Guardians as Partner-Leaders

As recently as the 1970s, educational professionals expected parents/ families to passively accept and quietly support the decisions of the school. Communication between the school and the home was infrequent and often negative. Parents were usually apprised of the events of the school during parent-teacher conferences or rather perfunctory Parent-Teacher Association (PTA) or Parent-Teacher Organization (PTO) meetings, usually conducted by the principal. Parents were asked to bake pies for fundraising projects, chaperone field trips for students, and encourage their children to do their homework.

Special Education Leads the Way. But with the Family Educational Rights and Privacy Act (1974), which pioneered parental access to their children's records, came a shift in the regard with which parents were held. In 1975 the Individuals with Disabilities Education Act (IDEA), or PL94-142, superseded the previous act by structuring parent support and involvement around the Individual Educational Planning (IEP) meetings held for particular students. Parents became active decision makers as a result of this revolutionary law. Congress now saw the family, at least for students with disabilities, as an equal participant with the school in determining what services needed to be provided and what the outcomes for the student should be. By redefining service recipients to be the family, PL99-457 subsequently placed more emphasis on the role of the parents. Technically, the IEP was replaced by the Individualized Family Service Plan (IFSP). Practically, though, parents' participation was still marginalized.

The Education Consolidation and Improvement Act of 1980 emphasized parental involvement in Title 1, the original federal compensatory education program. But it is important to note the use of the word "involvement" rather than "ownership" or "investment" on the part of parents. The bureaucratic and authoritarian control of the last thirty or forty years is evidence that families were allowed to visit the school but were not extended opportunities to become involved on a more active basis.

From Controlled to Collaborators. However, researchers and practitioners in movements such as the full-service schools initiatives (which link and provide health and human-service delivery at the school) observe that federal policy spurs local initiatives. In full-service schools initiatives, "top-down" administrators are encouraged to foster ways of providing services and reforming schools from the "bottom up" rather than by trying to change the system through stricter controls by removed administrative offices (First, Curcio, and Young 1994).

This shift has moved parents/families from passive supporters to engaged collaborators. Schools have begun to understand a point often made in research: that the single most critical factor in a child's educational success is authentic parental involvement.

Legislated Involvement. California was the first state with both a state board of education policy on parent involvement and a state law mandating parent involvement in all school districts. Based on research, the state board outlined five types of parent involvement that its school districts should implement. Because this represented an evolution in both parent involvement and parents as leaders, the board's principles and some ways in which they were realized in the schools are listed below:

1. Help parents develop parenting skills and foster conditions at home that support the child's efforts in the learning process (addressed through parenting classes and family wellness, thus still addressing the deficits the family exhibits)
2. Provide parents with knowledge of techniques to assist their children in learning (e.g., Parent Partners program, parent activity calendar, family math nights)
3. Provide access to community and support services for children and families, and coordinate them (e.g., multicultural family involvement, Community of Caring program, HOPE infant program)
4. Promote clear, two-way communication between the school and parents about children's progress (e.g., parent education programs, parent involvement programs, parent information centers)
5. Support parents as decision makers and develop their leadership, governance, advisory, and advocacy roles (e.g., guidance committees, board/school site council interaction)

In 1988 the California Department of Education's Parent and Community Education Office was assigned the responsibility for providing statewide leadership and support for parent involvement efforts in school districts. In January of 1989, the California State Board of Education wrote in its "Policy of Parent Involvement":

> A critical dimension of effective schooling is parent involvement. Research has shown that students learn better if, in addition to being provided a good instructional program, they receive the continuing support of parents and other adults . . . The inescapable fact is that consistently high levels of student successes are unlikely without long-term family support and reinforcement of the school's curricular goals. (Honig et al. 1995)

Two years later, Assembly Bill 322 supported parent involvement policies and programs as a requirement of the federal amendments to the 1965 Elementary and Secondary Education Act. This bill made implementation of parent involvement necessary for receipt of funds for state school improvement and economic impact aid.

Nationally. As concern for greater family investment in schools moved from the state to the national level, the National PTA was successful in its efforts to include parent involvement in the eight National Education Goals of 2000: "Every school will promote partnerships that will increase parental involvement and participation in promoting the social, emotional, and academic growth of children." Utilizing over thirty years of research, the National PTA set voluntary standards for parent/family involvement programs based on Joyce Epstein's work noted below:

Standard 1: Communicating—communication between home and school is regular, two-way, and meaningful

Standard 2: Parenting—parenting skills are promoted and supported

Standard 3: Student learning—parents play an integral role in assisting student learning

Standard 4: Volunteering—parents are welcome in the school, and their support and assistance are sought

Standard 5: School decision making and advocacy—parents are full partners in the decisions that affect children and families

Standard 6: Collaborating with community—community resources are used to strengthen schools, families, and student learning (National Parent-Teacher Association 1998)

These standards not only helped to guide national policy, they also reflected and stimulated research on family involvement projects and their implementation across the country.

Attitudinal Shift. There are many reasons to engage parents in the work of the school. They range from improving the school environment, providing reciprocal services, and nurturing leadership to assisting school personnel with the increasing and overlapping roles the school is asked to assume. Yet it is critical that involvement leads to the kind of leadership that will ultimately help improve students' academic performance. At the same time, parents and families are being reeducated about their own expertise, abilities, and skills. Likewise, school personnel are reshaping their thinking about control and turf battles.

The essence of family involvement that leads to leadership rests in beliefs in ownership, in the strength and power of authentic collaboration, in equality of voice, and in a generative rather than prescriptive process. It also rests in beliefs in the family's potential to positively affect their child's education, in the long-term continuity of the program, and in the family's sovereign right of place within the school. The degree to which families trust the school and the amount of respect school personnel have for the family and their expertise affect whether family involvement leads to leadership. Here lies the distinctive difference between allocation (the school acting according to its perceptions of what is needed) and true collaboration (the flattening of the hierarchy and an opportunity for the family to achieve access and equity). The family must believe in the honesty and integrity of the school's invitation.

From Bystander to Collaborator. Schools have involved parents in various ways. Figure 1.1 shows an upward spiraling of engagement from static supporter to advocate.

It is the intent of parent leadership initiatives to engage people in the spiral, encouraging them to continuously move up toward the role of advocate, not only for their children but for all students. In large measure, the parents' beliefs determine whether a family moves from one position to another, as does the quality of the family's experience with the school.

Practical Application. Many new understandings, approaches, and models for family, school, and community partnerships have been based on the seminal work of Joyce Epstein of Johns Hopkins University. In her research, she carefully uses the term "partnership" to indicate the equality in both role and voice of all stakeholders, a relationship mandatory to parent/family leadership.

Based on research on effective programs in elementary, middle, and high schools, Epstein found significant commonalities in the levels of involvement and the subsequent results for students. Because this work has been so frequently used as a basis for developing parent leadership capacity in schools, and because it is vividly seen in the national standards set by the National PTA, I summarize Epstein's "Framework of Engagement" here:

Type 1: *Parenting*—assist families in home support of the child as a student
Examples:
➻ Home visits and contacts at transition points (elementary to middle school)

Figure 1.1
Stages of Positional Parental Investment

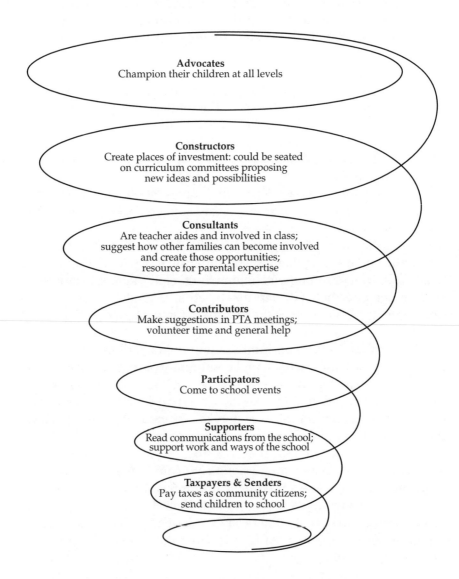

Advocates
Champion their children at all levels

Constructors
Create places of investment: could be seated
on curriculum committees proposing
new ideas and possibilities

Consultants
Are teacher aides and involved in class;
suggest how other families can become involved
and create those opportunities;
resource for parental expertise

Contributors
Make suggestions in PTA meetings;
volunteer time and general help

Participators
Come to school events

Supporters
Read communications from the school;
support work and ways of the school

Taxpayers & Senders
Pay taxes as community citizens;
send children to school

Source: From P. Williams-Boyd, "A Case Study of a Full-Service School: A Transformational Dialectic of Empowerment, Collaboration, and Communitarianism" (doctoral diss., University of Kansas, 1996).

➤ Brochures, workshops, videos, and communication, with suggestions and hints on how to support their child's learning at home

Benefits for students:

➤ Awareness of importance of school and of coordinated efforts by the school and home

➤ Balance of types of student activities outside of school

➤ Development of lifelong values and beliefs about self and the world

Type 2: *Communicating*—increasing the clarity and effectiveness of two-way communication between school and home on the school's programs and the student's progress

Examples:

➤ Conferences with student, parent, and teacher—often student-led

➤ Regular notice of concerns, recognition, and information

Benefits to students:

➤ Increased ownership of their own learning

➤ Participation in the learning partnership

Type 3: *Volunteering*—soliciting and organizing family help

Examples:

➤ Establishment of a parent room or designated space for volunteer parents to work and provide services to other parents as well as to students and school personnel

➤ Establishment and maintenance of neighborhood parent teams, phone trees, community watches for school safety, information, and ideas

Benefits to students:

➤ Augmented learning experiences such as those provided by parent-tutor or mentor

➤ More experiences with a variety of adults serving the students in varied ways

Type 4: *Learning at home*—extend the classroom, with suggestions about how to help the child with homework, projects, or other school-related tasks

Examples:

➤ Succinct and understandable information about subject-area skills and attitudes all students should have

➤ Consistent notification of homework, student progress, and how to monitor it

➤ Learning packs that students may check out at designated times or during extended vacations

    •• Content-focused school events for the whole family—
math or science night, English evening

Benefits to students:

    •• Increased completion of homework and projects

    •• Increased knowledge, skills, attitudes, and assessment
performance

    •• Improved attitude toward school and learning

    •• Blurring of boundaries between learning at home and
learning at school—school is more like home and home is
more like school

    •• Adult role models seem more like kin—teachers are more
like family, families are more like teachers

Type 5: *Decision making*—including parents in school decisions,
governance, and leadership

Examples:

    •• Engaged PTA or PTO authentically conducted by
parents—nurtures parent leadership both in large
groups and on such committees as personnel hiring,
curriculum, safety, student activities, and program
construction

    •• Advocacy groups that speak for school reform, projects,
resources, and allocations

    •• District-level committees and councils representing the
school and the family

    •• Neighborhood webs engage all parents in the work of the
school

Benefits for students:

    •• Awareness of the family's role and voice in education and
its governance

    •• Benefits from particular parent representation and advo-
cacy

    •• Comprehension that the student and family have undeni-
able rights as well as responsibilities, and that education
involves work and conflict

Type 6: *Community collaboration*—identifying, coordinating,
and integrating the resources of the community on behalf of the
student

Examples:

    •• Brochures, videos, presentations, and workshops; infor-
mation on social, health, and human services offered in
the community

    •• Information on community activities that would comple-

ment and extend learning skills, during both the school
year and the summer

•• Linkage of health, social, and human services through the
school—access information that presents the school as a
liaison to professional services

•• Linkage of health, social, and human services on the
school campus—a one-stop shopping of sorts that coordinates and integrates all services for the student and
family at the school

•• Service to the community through service-learning projects; special projects such as recycling, the adoption of
senior citizens, involvement in Habitat for Humanity,
which builds homes for those in need; and concerts, programs, and exhibits by the fine arts students

Benefits to students:

•• Specific benefits of coordinated or linked services

•• Enriched experiences that apply and challenge talents
and skills

•• Practical awareness of career possibilities (Epstein 1995b,
701–712)

Challenges. Admittedly, the path upward toward advocacy or to
type 6 is not without bumps. Thoughtful inclusion of all families in all
designated activities is very important. Equity of access as well as opportunity is as critical to the family as it is to the student and the school.
Program initiators, whether parents or school personnel, need to provide training, opportunities for leadership and participation, and activities that enable all families—whatever their ethnicity, class, backgrounds, or work schedules—to participate. Concerns about resources,
allocation, control, and turf must be resolved before relationships can
yield the kind of results spoken of above. The school staff must see
themselves as facilitators of learning and embrace each student-family
within the context of its own culture and community. Teachers must
confirm and reaffirm the positive role that all families, regardless of
their level of education, economic attainment, or resources, play in the
academic life and development of the child.

Practical Suggestions. Karen Rasmussen (1998) interviewed families, teachers, and administrators who collectively offered the following
adapted tips for effective and successful school-family partnerships:

•• Make school user-friendly and welcoming

•• Design specific ways to involve parents in schools—many

parents don't know what they can do in the school; some were unsuccessful in their own school experiences; and most haven't been in school since they were students

➤ View parents as equal partners with educators in decision making

➤ Resist educational jargon, which parents may be unfamiliar with

➤ Schedule meetings flexibly around all parents' work schedules

➤ Respect parents' perspectives and expertise

➤ Cultivate an engaged, cooperative, and collaborative atmosphere

➤ Keep parents "in the loop" of information and communication

➤ Celebrate diversity and family participation

Sample Projects. Kentucky's 1994 program, Parents and Teachers Talking Together, expanded into a broader initiative called the Commonwealth Institute for Parent Leadership. It develops parents' capacity for leadership through examination of Kentucky's schools and the ways parents may effect change, and through training in organizational strategies, group process skills, and collaboration. Participants design and implement projects that engage other parents in their school and community (for example, the Prichard Committee for Academic Excellence).

Connecticut's Parent Leadership Training Institute (PLTI) develops family leadership with a focus on positive outcomes for student learning and civic engagement. This intergenerational initiative, used in eight other states, targets the family's perception of leadership ability and the development of skills at coalition building. It also focuses on the law and legislation, public speaking, problem solving, assessment strategies, and working in diverse environments. It assists members of the family in becoming change agents, advocates, and leaders for children and other families on all levels.

There is much to learn from the pioneering work of special education. Wisconsin's statewide Parent-Educator Initiative: Parent Involvement in Education for Children with Disabilities is an example of collaborative leadership development. Designated school leaders and parent/family leaders are jointly trained in developing, discovering, and procuring resources on behalf of children. Through a variety of workshops, networking, information sharing, and projects, cooperative and collaborative leadership is developed in practical and tangible ways.

ABC Unified School District in Cerritos, California, fosters and values family leadership in a variety of ways. During the annual Parent Leadership Conference, parents share ways in which they may help each other and their children to maximize the school experience. Monthly workshops, community groups, newsletters, and work sessions focus on topics ranging from communication skills and conflict resolution strategies to support of exceptionalities and the use of technology.

At Leadership High School in San Francisco, admittance to the school carries a formal commitment from the parents/family to volunteer thirty hours per year to the school. Participation varies from being a club facilitator, tutoring, or serving as a leadership speaker to sponsorship of laboratory exercises in the community.

Community Unit School District 300 in Illinois follows a shared governance model in decisions of the school. Parent/family teams are trained in collaboration, consensus building, holding a shared vision and maintaining ongoing improvement. The results have been dramatic. Applying the findings of research, schools have made shifts in teaching, learning, structure (e.g., moving to block scheduling, changing from a junior high to an authentic middle school), and program (e.g., multi-age classrooms, dress codes, high school graduation requirements).

But the shift hasn't been easy. Says parent volunteer June Cavarretta,

> Shared decision making has meant jarring people out of their comfort zones; principals who have called the shots for years; teachers and curriculum specialists who consider themselves the experts; and parents whose attitudes toward schools range from complacency to combativeness. Equally challenging is bringing students into a collaborative process that may ultimately change how they experience school. (Cavarretta 1998, 14)

And yet she concludes that of all her volunteer experiences, this has been the most meaningful:

> My experience seeing my children move through the school system underscores a critical factor in school improvement efforts, that of parental urgency. Children slip through schools quickly. Parents don't have a lot of time to wait for schools to get it right. We want it right for our kids, and we want it that way now. (Cavarretta 1998, 15)

Conclusion. Research suggests that when the family is involved in the work of the school, when the capacity for parental leadership is given adequate attention, when good parenting grows into child advocacy, taxpayers are more willing to support the school. Moreover, the overall health of the community improves, students' experiences in school are improved holistically, and the connections and collaboration established serve to better not only the school but the community and commitment to it. New partnerships mean renewed life. Shared governance means shared responsibility. And shared ownership improves the well-being of all the nation's children.

Teachers

Belief Systems. "Aside from the family, education is the most person-centered of all institutions," write Combs, Miser, and Whitaker (1999, 10) in a thoughtful text on leadership. The research of Combs, Miser, and Whitaker suggests that it is not the correct teaching methods or the amount of content knowledge that enable teachers to be effective in the classroom, but rather their beliefs—beliefs about themselves as valued professionals, about their students as capable and talented, about their work environment as one conducive to growth, and about the profession as dynamic and interactive. According to Combs, Miser, and Whitaker, person-centered leadership is understood "in terms of the belief systems of leaders and the belief systems of those they want to lead" (1999, 13).

Expertise. Contrary to Combs, Miser, and Whitaker, noted researcher and educational leader Linda Darling-Hammond argues that teacher expertise (that is, what teachers both know and are able to do) accounts for the greatest variance in student performance (Darling-Hammond and Loewenberg Ball 1997a). If that is the case, the engagement of teachers as leaders is critical, but only when they have a voice in the direct work of the school, including on goal-setting, personnel hiring, environmental decision making, and instructional operation. This is the business of shared governance.

A Marriage of Both. Perhaps teacher leadership is about both beliefs and expertise. Leadership is about relationships. Teaching is about relationships. Both focus on instructional improvement. Those people who have the most direct impact on students are teachers, people driven by their commitments to quality and performance, to compassion and caring, to a belief in the integrity of each individual student. People who know that powerful teaching is born in the knowledge of who students are and what motivates and captivates them; people who are trained in the craft of the profession and who hone its art; people who constantly seek new knowledge; people who are often isolated both in the physical space of the building site and in the opportunity to use their skills; people who desire the opportunity to join the community of leader-learners. For leadership is both an opportunity and a choice, an opportunity to shape the future and to participate in the changes necessary to sustain health and growth. When teachers who are held most directly accountable for the academic success of students are given the opportunity to participate in shared governance, in the decisions of the school, their sense of ownership and professional integrity are enhanced.

Structured Examples of Teachers as Leaders. Teachers are at the heart of school change, student success, and educational leadership. They lead by example. And they influence others by their creativity, commitment, and dynamic energy. They implement new instructional strategies that reflect a deep understanding of the diversity of student needs and talent. They embrace only that which will have abiding and enduring effects on their students, and rigorously resist fads, no matter how flashy.

When teachers are given the opportunity to exercise their professional talents beyond the classroom, everyone benefits. All too often, outstanding teachers leave the public school because use of their leadership capabilities and professional skills has been limited only to a single classroom. Increasingly, however, schools that understand the breadth of teacher-leader talent are beginning to provide opportunities for teachers to participate in a variety of leadership roles. These opportunities include

- ➡ Member of School Improvement Teams (SITs) comprised of parents, teachers, and administrators. SITs collectively set the school's agenda on goals and outcomes for the coming year. They assist in making curricular and program decisions and collegially guide the ongoing work of the school.
- ➡ Chair or member of the school's Leadership Council, which is usually different from the SIT in that it does not address curricular issues.
- ➡ Member of district textbook selection committee.
- ➡ Facilitator of study groups.
- ➡ Mentor for new teachers.
- ➡ Member or chair of district content-area committees that develop curriculum based on state standards and benchmarks for that particular subject area for all schools in the district; represent the faculty on issues of curriculum and instruction.
- ➡ Chair or coordinator of school or district discipline committee

—selects a discipline or classroom management program and tracks its ongoing effectiveness; also often participates at the building or district level in peer mediation programs or conflict resolution programs for students.

•• Faculty representative to PTA, acting as a conduit of information for both faculty and parents.

•• Trainer for self-initiated or school-adopted special programs such as Writing Across the Curriculum, the Think Write program, new technology applications or uses of computers in the classroom, or the Science for All program.

•• Staff developer. In a variety of areas of expertise developed through both work in the classroom and graduate work, faculty engage colleagues at school and districtwide in valuable professional development.

•• Team leader. In schools, particularly middle schools that have moved to full interdisciplinary teaming (a small number of students are shared by a team of subject-area teachers), the team of teachers, guided by a peer, makes all curricular and program decisions for their team of students.

•• Curriculum specialist. Participates in the selection of school-wide reading programs such as Success for All, Reading for Real, Real Reading in the Middle, or the Accelerated Reader; participates in their implementation and evaluates their effectiveness.

•• Conference speaker. Represents the work of the school through presentations at national and statewide educational conferences.

•• District representative. Participates in or chairs the district-wide Professional Development Council, which brings together central administrators (superintendent, assistant superintendent) with representative principals and selected faculty and staff from all the district's schools to discuss issues, examine problems, and pose solutions on a broader scale.

•• Policy participant. Sits on local, state, and national association boards to help set policy affecting the teaching profession in general and to help make decisions about such specific topics as accreditation, scholarship and grant opportunities, environmental or health concerns at schools, and the allocation of ancillary resources.

Unstructured Examples of Teachers as Leaders. There are many instances during the school year when teachers step forward and assume leadership roles in a less structured format. Often these teachers are respected by their colleagues for their expertise, wisdom, support, or willingness to engage in a critical dialogue and to reflect, enhancing the growth of the school. They emerge in faculty meetings, in content-area meetings, or when there is a particular need or even a crisis in the school. Yet they quite often are content to be in the shadows, assisting the teacher-leaders in their work, invaluably working with students, parents, and colleagues. They seek neither power nor privilege, neither leadership nor recognition. They are nonetheless critical to the health of the school and to the growth of leadership in the school community.

The View from Colleagues. Often those most respected as teacher-leaders assume leadership roles in addition to teaching in their classroom. The perception "she's one of us and therefore understands what we experience" serves to give more credence to statements she makes at a staff development workshop or to a suggestion that colleagues take on yet more work of the school. There is an earned credibility because of a mutuality of participation and place, both in the profession and at the school. There is a sense of sharing the work at the school, and a daily validity check on site by colleagues of the knowledge and skills of the teacher-leader. They have the "capacity to facilitate problem solving in the immediate instructional worlds of their peers, which permits them to influence directly the teacher group's collective efficacy" (Donaldson 2001, 103). Teacher-leaders bring to their roles the ability to fluidly and intentionally build relationships based upon the trust already established with colleagues, a crucial reciprocity.

Yet there are additional challenges. In a very insightful issue of the *Journal of Staff Development* devoted to teacher leadership, teacher Mike Lodico states, "I found I had to re-define myself in relation to my colleagues. Teacher-leaders don't have position power. We can't say: 'Do it or I'll tell the principal.' Teacher leadership is an undefined role as opposed to a principal or assistant principal" (Lodico 1999, 20). And teacher-leader Eden Combes adds, "I have to learn how to reach consensus and gain support" (Combes 1999, 13).

The View Inside Out. Traditionally, curriculum specialists—those people whose specific area of expertise is instructional strategies and learning practices—are hired by school districts to service all the schools through the central office. They offer staff development workshops to update teachers on the most effective practices. But all too often these well-intentioned and often well-trained people dart into the school, present an hour-long workshop either on a district-initiated topic or on a perceived faculty need, and then return to the central administration building. In their wake is teacher frustration, not only because of the added demands and expectations, but more importantly because of the lack of connection between the specialist and the culture of the school and the expertise of the staff.

Douglas County schools in Colorado offered a very rich and robust alternative to the curriculum specialist that they called the Building Resource Teacher (BRT). The BRT is released from teaching duties and instead serves as an in-house mentor, coach, and resource provider. "BRTs provide observation and feedback sessions, teach demonstration lessons, procure staff development resources, and give teachers at each school access to expert knowledge on teaching practice. BRTs also work with principals, parents, and teacher assistants, enhancing communications between the district office, the school site, and the community" (Hayes, Grippe, and Hall 1999, 18).

Douglas County schools carefully developed the position of BRT as an on-site teacher-leader, and monitored the effectiveness of the program over a three-year period. The program has been embraced by both novice and career teachers. Because BRTs were given a wide berth to respond to the needs of the particular buildings in which they were situated, the organic development of this leadership position was seen to come from the entire faculty.

Rewards. Although not all teachers desire to be teacher-leaders or even BRTs, when teachers are given opportunities, ownership of the ongoing growth of the school looks very different. The intrinsic rewards of such opportunities far outweigh the sometimes unprovoked jealousies of a few fellow teachers. Teacher-leaders demonstrate a renewed energy in the classroom. They develop a bigger picture of the work of the school, the district, and the profession.

Growth. Rather than growing unidimensionally—only in the classroom—teacher-leaders mature in a multidimensional manner through applying their expertise, showing concern for their students and colleagues, and experimenting with their creative ideas. Deci and Ryan (1985) suggest that teachers' sense of their own competence and connection spurs their growth, which benefits their students, their school, the community, the profession, and themselves.

Caution. As policy makers, administrators, university professors, and teachers strive to create and participate in opportunities for teachers as leaders, there are some roadblocks that must be surmounted. The challenge posed by the unlimited demands placed on teacher-leaders, as colleagues become excited about innovative strategies, is accentuated by the reality of limited time. It is wise for others to be mindful of excessive paperwork and the need to use people's time to its best advantage. The use of the teacher-leader's time for sorting mail or running off handouts for students and colleagues occurs frequently but is ill spent. And the thoughtful administrator, mentor, or guide for the teacher-leader must be aware of the teacher-leader's tendency to try to be all things for all colleagues.

Critical attributes. Teacher-leaders both possess craft knowledge and show artistry in conducting their relationships. In particular, they

- Are skilled in the particulars of their content area as well as in the strategies and methodologies of the profession in general
- Are voracious learners, constantly seeking new ideas that can improve instruction and learning
- Consistently place students at the center of their work and attention
- Maintain an abiding belief in the potential and integrity of each student
- Are advocates for the overall well-being of the student and the family
- Are committed to the success of all students
- Are aggressive listeners—with colleagues, students, families, the outside community—and more intent on understanding than on being understood
- Are thoughtful risk-takers who are not afraid to fail
- Are problem solvers as well as generators of ideas—insightful, thoughtful, and sensitive
- Value growth and relationships, and lead by example
- Are tenacious in their work in the classroom and in extracurricular activities
- Are innovators who creatively motivate all students
- Foster collegiality with fellow teachers, and support and encourage them
- Are rarely content with their work, for they constantly seek new challenges
- Are role models for the profession, colleagues, families, and students

Gender and Teacher-Leaders. There has been reference made in the literature to issues of gender and the dynamics of teacher-leadership:

> An asset that many women teacher-leaders can bring to relationship-building is, in the view of a growing number of writers, a natural leadership style that emphasizes the interpersonal and emotional dimensions . . . Women who naturally foster connectedness are likely to be

leaders if their inclination toward relationship-building feeds into purposeful action. (Donaldson 2001, 69)

Writers such as Nel Noddings (1984), Sally Helgesen (1995), and
Connie Titone and Karen Maloney (1999) all place value on the feminine
presence and interconnectedness spoken of in the early research by Carol
Gilligan (1982). And although there may well be masculine and feminine
styles of leadership (as addressed in chapter 3), the evidence to support
the value of relationship-building by both genders is well recognized.

Conclusion. There resides in the country's schools an untapped
natural source of vibrant and vital leadership. In a school whose daily
operation is based on trust, loyalty, and openness to new ideas, the potential for growth and student success will flow naturally. When teachers
are unified in the pursuit of a common goal—the success of every young
person in the school—the framework for burgeoning leadership has
been established.

Where administrators still value the conventional "let's not rock
the boat" kind of school, the risk-taking involved in engaging teachers
as leaders will not be experienced. A revealing 1993 study (Wilson)
found that teacher-leaders recognized administrators were guided by
different tasks than they were. But where principals organized the
school around authority-based directives in which everyone "knew
their place," teacher-leaders found fewer possibilities for growth. Yet
because teachers are characteristically guided by the tenets of collaboration and cooperation, confrontations with principals were rare.
Teachers exhibited a respectful "as-you-choose" attitude. Wilson's
study offered the following interesting comments from teachers about
leaders:

- The label of "leader" sets a person apart from peers and
  diminishes his or her ability to bring about change.
- Leadership is a role played by one person in a group. The role
  seduces the leader into believing that he or she is the mouth-
  piece of the group. Given a strong group of competent people, a leader may not be necessary.
- Secondary teachers value their autonomy and do not wish to
  lead or be led.
- As a group, teachers should exercise more control over the
  initiation and the implementation of change.
- Participatory decision making is critical. Any teacher who
  wishes to participate in a particular decision should be encouraged to do so. (Wilson 1993, 24–25)

These are indeed nontraditional observations of leadership. Yet shared governance again emerges as a theme. However, the typical school culture does not encourage and often does not even allow creativity, individuality, or exceptional teacher commitment that does not fit the mold of the school. Teachers realize that schools value conformity more than innovation. And unfortunately, teacher-leaders often leave public schools, not because of what is commonly referred to as "teacher burnout," but because of denied opportunity.

Where administrators have embraced teachers as peers and have nurtured their growth, teachers have become formal leaders in many of the ways noted above. Informal teacher-leaders insist on high standards in their daily performance, and in knowledge, beliefs, and practice. Many researchers maintain that these are the key players in the effective work and environment of the school (Darling-Hammond and Loewenberg Ball 1997b). Yet when these same people are asked who the leaders in the school are, for the most part they will not point to themselves but rather to the administrators—the principal and the vice principal.

SCHOOL-LEVEL ADMINISTRATIVE LEADERSHIP

The significance of the designated leader in the school cannot be minimized, although the role has begun to assume a new shape. When the appointed leader, in this case the building principal, shares leadership with the faculty and supports their own leadership, a rich and robust professional environment becomes possible, one that involves risk-taking and the sharing of opportunity.

A 1972 Senate report expressed the importance of the building principal in establishing the learning environment for the entire community of learners: "If a school is a vibrant, innovative, child-centered place; if it has a reputation for excellence in teaching; if students are performing to the best of their ability, one can almost always point to the principal's leadership as the key to success" (U.S. Senate Select Committee on Equal Educational Opportunity 1972, 305).

It is the principal rather than the role itself who sets the tone of professionalism, mutual respect, growth, high expectations, and shared ownership in the school. Those principals who can maximize the opportunities for leadership understand the uniqueness of the school as an institution, which is quite unlike a corporate or other business venture. They understand that schools continually engage adults and children in the disequilibrium that is called learning. They know that schools reflect individual neighborhoods and are seen as centers of promise and forums for mediation even within the most impoverished communities, that schools as neighborhood institutions are centers for a common good, based on the legitimacy of the democratic ideal. They perceive that those who are engaged in the work of the school have common purposes, shared or mutual visions, and ideas for growth. And they build healthy schools by tapping the youthful energy, vitality, motivation, enthusiasm, enjoyment, and commitment of the people within that school and the greater community.

Historically, the principal's work was focused on managing the process and functions of the school. Principals were hired in the 1920s when schools became too large for teachers to both teach and manage them. Principals were responsible for bringing the "latest" educational practices, organization, and curriculum to the teaching faculty. Sergiovanni (1995) cites a 1937 acronym POSDCoRB for the business of administrative functioning. It stands for planning, organizing, staffing, directing, coordinating, reporting, and budgeting. In essence, the principal was the administrative manager. This model worked until the 1950s, when economic affluence seemed promised to all but was denied to some. Schools were now called to task for not educating "all" children; some critics noted the discrepancies in schooling between minorities and the lower socioeconomic populations. In 1955 the American Association of School Administrators responded by adding to the list of tasks encompassed by the acronym POSDCoRB "stimulating and evaluating staff. Accountability."

Donaldson (2001, 35) contrasts the more traditional leadership model with the reality of the everyday school (see Table 1.2).

Proficiencies. During the 1990s, these processes were spoken of as proficiencies and competencies. Sergiovanni (1995, 4) lists examples of the ten categories of behavior that the National Association of Elementary School Principals (NAESP) said were evident in "expert" principals:

- *Leadership Behavior*
  - Inspire all concerned to join in accomplishing the school's mission
  - Apply effective human relations skills
  - Encourage the leadership of others
- *Communication Skills*
  - Persuasively articulate their beliefs and effectively defend their decisions
  - Write clearly and concisely so that the message is understood by the intended audience
  - Apply facts and data to determine priorities

Table 1.2
Teacher-Principal Contrast

Traditional Leadership	*School Reality*

Designated leaders with formal authority and schoolwide roles
  ➼ Hired by superintendent and school board
  ➼ Determine and enforce school policies, purposes, priorities, and goals
	Educators earn each other's respect and authority; positions are equal
	  ➼ Informal authority guides practice
	  ➼ Autonomous teachers often feel marginalized in the exercise of professional ability
	  ➼ Teachers exercise authority and control in classroom

Leaders with general expertise
  ➼ Exercise quality control
  ➼ Determine plans and make decisions
  ➼ Own information and manage its distribution
	Faculty and staff demonstrate particular expertise on teaching, learning, and students
	  ➼ Often feel "out of the loop" of information
	  ➼ Teacher decisions exert greater effect on the students

Leaders manage a standardized system
  ➼ Control behavior, allocation of resources, and opportunities
  ➼ Structure curriculum and assign tasks
  ➼ Measure and evaluate faculty, staff, and goals
	Professionals adapt to student-school needs
	  ➼ Are flexible, shaping curriculum to student needs and available resources
	  ➼ Structure work according to differences in student learning
	  ➼ Protect professional autonomy

Leaders control school, staff, students, and exchanges
  ➼ Follow hierarchical structure
  ➼ Are driven by the system of practice following organizational goals
  ➼ React to events
	Teachers control work of the classroom
	  ➼ Collaboration is voluntary and arbitrary
	  ➼ Relationships—with team, colleagues, students, families, and community—are most important

Source: Adapted from Gordon Donaldson, *Cultivating Leadership in Schools: Connecting People, Purposes, and Practice* (New York: Teachers College Press, 2001), 35.

- *Group Processes*
  - Involve others in setting short- and long-term goals
  - Apply validated principles of group dynamics and facilitation skills
  - Understand how to resolve difficult situations by use of conflict resolution
- *Curriculum*
  - Understand the community's values and goals and what it wants the curriculum to achieve
  - Set forth, as a continuum, the skills and concepts the curriculum is designed to provide
  - Monitor the curriculum to ensure that the appropriate content and sequence are followed
- *Instruction*
  - Understand and apply the principles of growth and development
  - Regularly assess the teaching methods and strategies being used at the school to ensure that they are appropriate and varied
  - Understand and apply validated principles of teaching and learning
- *Performance*
  - Set high expectations for students, staff, parents, and self
  - Appropriately match particular learning styles with particular teaching styles
  - Enhance student and staff strengths and remediate weaknesses
- *Evaluation*
  - Use a variety of techniques and strategies to assess
    Student performance
    Individual teacher and staff performance
    The achievement of curriculum goals
    The effectiveness of the total instructional program
  - Assess progress toward achieving goals established for students, teachers, the principalship, and the involvement of parents and the community at large
  - Seek and encourage input from a variety of sources to improve the school's program
- *Organization*
  - Comprehend and employ validated principles of effective time management
  - Capitalize on the findings of research and making program decisions

- Develop and implement equitable and effective schedules
- *Fiscal*
  - Understand the school district budget and its specific implications for the school
  - Plan, prepare, justify, and defend the school budget
  - Manage the school within the allocated resources
- *Political*
  - Understand the dynamics of local, state, and national politics
  - Develop plans and strategies for helping to achieve appropriate financial support of education
  - Involve the community's movers and shakers in the development and support of the school's program. (National Association of Elementary School Principals 1986)

During this same period, the work and effectiveness of the principal were spoken of in terms of outcomes—that is, what student learning was supposed to look like, what model teaching was supposed to follow, and what those with a stake in the school were supposed to be like. So less time was spent on the processes of the school and more time was spent on being responsive to the mandates of central administration and of accrediting agencies, to student needs, and to the requirements of shared governance.

Technical and Nontechnical Views. There has been a continuing tension between seeing leadership as a technical skill of management and seeing it as a nontechnical skill of facilitation. The first view sees the principal's role in terms of work, legal ramifications, moral issues, and staff relationships. The second view tends to focus on principals as "sensemakers" (Ackerman, Donaldson, and van der Bogert 1996) who see the school's purpose in a broad context and who are constantly adjusting the focus and work of the school's community. The technical view of leadership emphasizes leadership characteristics and evaluates success based on the tasks performed. The nontechnical view sees principal leadership as a process or a quest, a journey during which all fellow travelers help address challenges as they arise, celebrate beauty as it is experienced, and explore uncharted territory in pursuit of new questions and answers. Whichever view one takes, the goal is maximized opportunities for learning that lead to success for all students.

Pivotal Position. The principal's position as the designated leader in the building is both pivotal and fundamental. It is the principal who sets the tone for the staff and the students. The principal can protect issues of "turf" or top-down authority. This is a kind of power structure in which all employees are effectively subordinate workers attempting to produce top-notch products, namely students. Alternatively, principals can promote support, ownership, and problem solving, and build leadership in others.

Contemporary Thinking and Leadership Building. New Era leadership challenges principals to build teams, to sustain and encourage the informal authority and leadership capacity of others who have a stake in the school. For leadership is becoming less about the leaders themselves and more about collective learning, the collaborative shaping of schooling in general and the shaping of knowledge in particular. Effective principals who nurture the leadership capacity of their constituents are constantly in tune with the process of change in their building. They remain focused on collaboratively-shaped goals, outcomes, and values. Lambert (1998) challenges principals to develop a shared vision based on common beliefs that are examined, evaluated, and constructed communally. She calls on them to harness, focus, and fuel momentum in our society's conversation about schools and learning. In the process, the principal creates a vital environment promoting peer growth by using some of the following strategies:

- Posing questions that hold up assumptions and beliefs for reexamination
- Remaining silent, letting other voices surface
- Promoting dialogue and conversations
- Raising a range of possibilities but avoiding simplistic answers
- Keeping the value agenda on the table, reminding the group that what they have agreed on is important, focusing attention
- Providing space and time for people to struggle with tough issues
- Confronting data, subjecting one's own ideas to the challenge of evidence
- Turning a concern into a question
- Being wrong with grace, candor, and humility
- Being explicit and public about strategies, since the purpose is to model, demonstrate, and teach them to others. (Lambert 1998, 27)

This is all about creating teams of leaders and communities of learners, often defined as a group of learners who share a common focus. In helping to create leaders and learners, the principal has assigned human relationships high priority. Effective principals know their teachers, their students, and their families. They understand impediments to learning success and the things in which kids excel. They know the ways in which their students' families are struggling and how they are celebrating. They function as people-leaders, as developers of leaders, just as they are instructional leaders, as was often observed in the late 1980s and 1990s. They are facilitators, or even democratic leaders.

Democratic Leadership. Sharing authority of the school can be both rewarding and challenging. The thoughtful work of Blase et al. (1995) found that when teachers and principals shared the responsibility of the school, outcomes improved for everyone. They also found that principals are honestly interested in an open dialogue that results in the best practices of teaching and learning. Not all principals or teachers have this type of relationship, nor do all experience the same amount of success, but when they pursued democratic leadership the following themes were evidenced: "trust in teachers' motives, the ability to listen and to communicate openly, and the willingness to risk letting go of their traditional veto power" (Blase et al. 1995, x).

On the other hand, challenges are presented when a principal believes in and implements democratic leadership:

1. *Increased time.* Attempting to arrange substitutes for classes or rearrange teachers' schedules so that they can participate in meetings can be a thorn in the side of an administrator who feels she could otherwise render a decision more expeditiously.
2. *Teachers' ingrained perceptions.* There are teachers who see no immediate or long-range need to move beyond the two covers of the textbook or the four walls of the classroom (a "two-by-four teacher"). Past experiences have also left them suspicious of exactly how much response their opinions or work will generate. Yet democratic principals provide the opportunities and foster an environment for dramatic overall school improvement.
3. *Central office perceptions.* Just as teachers may tend to be skeptical, democratic principals must, in many instances, create the culture at the district level that values shared governance.
4. *Need for deliberate openness.* Changing the ways in which the daily operation of the school has been conducted for many years is difficult both in process and in perception. Old ways are familiar and more comfortable; people are skeptical. The democratic principal must be persistent in listening to all voices and in responding in substantive ways. (Blase et al. 1995)

The various models of leadership discussed here and in chapter 3 are not to be worn like a total wardrobe. Rather, a school and its staff will shape and fashion democratic leadership and shared governance in ways that reflect their basic beliefs and assumptions about ownership. Some schools will directly engage parents in this dialogue. Others will not. Some will solicit the voices of students, while others will not. What is important is not that a model be adopted wholesale, but that elements of democratic leadership begin to be practiced.

Authority Shift. This represents a shift in perspective from one-person, power-over authority, mandating directives to and from subordinates, to a collegial power-with ownership and honest sharing. Dunlap and Goldman (1991) describe the power-over approach as focusing on control, the aligning of subordinates' attitudes and beliefs so that they work with the leader's vision in mind, and manipulating workers' behavior to accomplish that vision. This was the most prevalent type of leadership during the 1980s and 1990s, a period of high accountability. On the other hand, power-with leadership is collegial and values reciprocity, mutuality, the leadership capacity and growth of others, and equality of positional relationships. Anne Conzemius says that effective principals "let go of control, but they don't just let go" (1999, 34). Rather, power-with leadership shares responsibilities. For instance, issues such as building budgets and administrative paperwork for the total school are better left to the principal, while other responsibilities (such as those listed above) may be delegated to faculty.

Power-with, or democratic, leadership is neither easy nor tidy. Because it is based on the interactions of people actively engaged in a struggle to achieve an ideal, collaborative leadership is an ongoing work-in-progress, often difficult, more often messy. Just as students struggle to learn to work together in cooperative groups in the classroom, the school's adults must model democracy in action.

Yet there seem to be conflicting messages sent to the principal. Superintendent Rick DuFour captures this tension when he says that principals have been challenged to

- Celebrate the success of their schools and to perpetuate discontent with the status quo
- Convey urgency regarding the need for school improvement and to demonstrate the patience that sustains improvement efforts over the long haul
- Encourage individual autonomy and to insist on adherence to the school's mission, vision, values, and goals
- Build widespread support for change and to push forward with improvement despite resisters

•• Approach improvement incrementally and to promote the aggressive, comprehensive shake-up necessary to escape the bonds of traditional school cultures. (DuFour 1999, 62)

In light of all these directives, the timely work *Breaking Ranks: Changing an American Institution* (National Association of Secondary School Principals, 1996) challenges principals as instructional leaders to build learning communities in a collaborative culture. It unequivocally states that the past practice of authoritarian leadership is no longer viable in the age of site-based or school-based, rather than district-based, decision making.

DuFour says that it is possible to do all this when attention is paid to the following responsibilities:

1. Lead through shared vision and collective commitments rather than through rules and authority
2. Create collaborative structures that focus on teaching and learning
3. Pose the questions that help the school focus on issues of teaching and learning
4. Provide staff with the training, information, and parameters they need to make good decisions. (DuFour 1999, 63)

He further suggests that once the two basic questions—what do we want the school to look like? And what do we need to do to get there?—have been asked, principals then protect the work and the workers striving to find the answers. Effective principals of collaborative learning communities must provide and sustain the structures necessary for this work. For instance, during the school day, teachers need both individual planning time to prepare for their classes and to respond to family phone calls and responsibilities, as well as common-team planning time during which they meet with other teachers on their teams who share the same students. The work of the teams (to be discussed in chapter 4) must be purposeful, focused, and valued.

All of the teams' work is centered around such critical questions as, What are the students required to know and be able to do? (Many states now have content standards and benchmarks that specifically address this question.) Other questions include, What are the most effective teaching and learning strategies for our population? How do we differentiate our teaching to match the entry points of students' knowledge? How do we translate the school's vision or mission statement into goals, outcomes, and objectives? What knowledge is valued?

How are issues of equity addressed in resources and curricular content? What basic beliefs about learning and learners do we hold? How do those beliefs inform our practice?

And, finally, the effective principal as instructional leader is knowledgeable about the best practices to follow given the learning needs of the students. Based on reading, learning, and attending workshops, the principal in collaboration with the teachers provides focused staff development, directed at the teaching and learning processes and the development of professional relationships with all of the school's constituents.

However, just as many citizens do not exercise their democratic rights and responsibilities in the voting process, there are teachers and schools who abdicate their potential roles beyond the classroom. Sometimes they simply allow other people to do the work. At other times, they look to a charismatic leader for guidance.

Critical Attributes. The trait theory maintains that the effectiveness of a school depends primarily on the personal and professional characteristics of the principal. Although New Era leadership is about the team, not the leader, those schools that have experienced dramatic improvements in student achievement, professional commitment, the learning environment, and public engagement have done so because of an effective building principal. It is worth examining common attributes as they reflect leadership in all arenas of engagement. Table 1.3 is a research-based profile of an effective leader.

To be able to exhibit these traits while making sense of a very ambiguous and complex system such as a school is quite a challenge. Although this is not a checklist for success, it is a snapshot of effective leadership. As we examine this list we see attributes that reflect professional expertise, but many that reflect intrapersonal, interpersonal, and democratic skills.

Most often, teachers cite the basic characteristics of honesty, decency, respect, and communication as indicative of the effective leader. Honest principals appear to be nonmanipulative; have no hidden agendas; tell a teacher the truth about a particular situation; are consistently fair with all teachers; will uphold their word; and hold in confidence private matters (Blase and Anderson 1995).

Blase and Anderson (1995) found that communication, like honesty, was also valued by teachers. Those principals who took the time to engage teachers personally, rather than simply writing memos to them, were found to be more effective. These were principals who were willing to listen to teachers' and students' problems and ideas in an open, nonjudgmental, and encouraging manner. Also, they were principals who

Table 1.3

Profile of an Effective Leader

Critical Attributes	Values	Skills	Strategies
Knowledgeable	Self-disciplined	Analytical	Collaborator
Organized	Celebrates differ-	Provocative	Risk-taker
Honest	ence	Synthesizer	Encourager
Dependable	Mutual respect	Manages crises	Nurturer
Efficient	Trustworthy	Develops cohe-	Motivator
Flexible	Acknowledges	sion	Listener
Creative	success	Works produc-	Evaluator
Imaginative	Respects others	tively	Team builder
Hopeful	Student-centered	Thinks holistically	Communicator
Open-minded	Collegial	Tolerates ambigu-	Implementor
Independent	Community-	ity	Consensus
Trusting	minded	Models expecta-	builder
With a sense of	People-oriented	tions	Mentor
humor	Self-motivated	Confronts dissent	Shares informa-
Focused worker	Goal-directed	and works to re-	tion
Visionary	Idea-based	solve it	Shares authority
Conscientious		Politically astute	Delegates respon-
Approachable and		Advocates for	sibility
open		change	Learner
Insightful		Agent for change	
Self-assured		Functions well in	
Compassionate		loose situations	
Tactful		Advocates for	
Reflective		coalition build-	
Responsible		ing	
Attentive		Technologically	
Enthusiastic		aware	
Concerned and			
caring			

sought teachers' opinions, suggestions, and even decisions. They presented themselves as a safety net of sorts, making "bottom line" or difficult decisions when deemed necessary, but were nonetheless solicitous of participation and decision making by faculty and staff.

They also served as conduits of information, bringing opportunities to the attention of faculty or presenting work at national and state conferences; sharing information from the school board or the central office; sharing timely information about potential grant monies; and apprising faculty of partnerships or service-learning projects. The teaching faculty sees this type of principal as one who cares about each of them to the extent that new resources and opportunities outside of school are provided for their benefit.

Effective principals are informal, meaning they are calm, warm, caring, and can be approached without fear of rebuke or reprisal. They have a friendly disposition that also attests to their confidence in the faculty's decision making. They trust the expertise of the faculty both inside and outside the classroom. Their trust is reciprocated. Teachers express a greater willingness to take risks, to engage in new practices, when they know the principal will support them, and will stand behind them when tensions arise between teacher and student, or between the teacher and the public.

Often teachers are unaware of the buffering that principals do on their behalf. Principals commonly "run interference" for their teachers, handling phone calls or complaints from parents or people in the community who might not understand the context of a given situation or event. Knowing the teacher, knowing their professional integrity in the classroom, the principal serves as an advocate for the teacher, and seldom shares these potentially discouraging exchanges with them. At the same time, the principal acts as an advocate for the child by seeking the most amenable working environment for all concerned.

The Cornerstone of Relationships. In every school district there are occasions when teachers may have differences of opinion with the elected school board or the central office administrators. In these situations, the teacher is the advocate of what is best for the student in the classroom, and the school board or central administrators represent their own political agenda. And although the school board or central administrators may be well-intentioned, the feeling on the part of the teacher is that they lack expertise on curricular, instructional, or particular cultural issues in the school. When principals have been willing to stand with their teachers in such circumstances, both the people involved and others in the school have forged even deeper relationships of trust and shared commitment.

It is this trust that is the linchpin for both shared governance and democratic practice in the school. While barriers erected by past practices are being vaulted, trust builds new structures and processes—team decision making, the work of groups whose decisions are implemented, risk-taking that is both substantive and supported.

As with students at any developmental stage, consistency and dependability are among the most critical attributes. Students learn to count on the presence and fairness of the teacher. So, too, teachers count on the consistent presence and approachability of the principal. Many principals make a habit of being in the lunchroom or in the hallways when students are moving from class to class. This kind of visibility presents a constancy and is necessary in buildings that house between 500 and 3,500 students. Such unstructured situations offer students and faculty opportunities to talk to the principal in less formal ways. In some schools, the faculty and principal eat lunch in the cafeteria with the students. Often, valuable information regarding a student's family situation or daily life experiences—information that could have a direct impact on the work of the classroom and that has no other outlet—is shared.

Performance Characteristics. Hallinger, Leithwood, and Murphy (1993) found that in New Era collaborative problem solving, "appearing calm and confident, demonstrating genuine respect for staff, and exhibiting habits of self-reflection" were critical (120). They also examined expressions of expertise in all venues of leadership. Looking particularly at thinking, reasoning, and learning, the following seven characteristics emerged:

1. *Experts excel mainly in their chosen area.* Because an administrator is excellent in the school district does not mean she will be as effective as a legislator.
2. *Experts see the patterns in the larger picture of their area.* Experts are able to group all of the kinds of information into categories rather than getting bogged down in discrete pieces of information.
3. *Experts are fast.* They are quick both at using skills and at problem solving.
4. *Experts have superior short- and long-term memory.* Experts are able to group, encode, and store large amounts of information from past experiences and more recent events.
5. *Experts see and understand situations in their area in a deeper and richer way than those new to the field.* Effective administrators are able to see the concept that underlies a particular challenge, issue, or problem, rather than only the problem itself. For instance, a new principal may be faced with two angry teachers, but the expert principal will see the perceived unequal allocation of resources that precipitated the issue.
6. *Experts extensively evaluate the problem.* As is often the case in education, the novice principal will quickly move to develop possible solutions to a problem, whereas the expert principal will take much more time to thoroughly analyze the problem before suggesting possible solutions. The novice bases his work on trial and error, while the expert is more goal- or principle-directed.

7. *Experts use self-reflective and self-monitoring skills.* The effective leader will consistently be aware of what he does or does not know and how to access the appropriate information; the novice principal may find himself on unfamiliar ground and not know how to proceed. (Hallinger, Leithwood, and Murphy 1993, 148–149)

In essence, the work of the effective school administrator is governed by self-awareness, practice, relationships, and underlying beliefs.

Effective Leader Practices. Robert Ramsey in *Lead, Follow, or Get Out of the Way* (1999) has adapted Stephen Covey's popular work *The Seven Habits of Highly Effective People* for school administrators. Ramsey and Covey state that a leader must

1. *Be proactive.* When the school administrator is sensitive to the ongoing shift in needs of students, to the growing body of research on teaching and learning, and to the work of the school in general, she can proactively move the school forward from within.
2. *Begin with the end in mind.* Leaders' resistance to "what's currently in vogue" is well-founded. The school's long-range goals and daily learning outcomes must be grounded in practices that will have the most significant and substantive impact.
3. *Put first things first.* Value-based and principle-centered leadership (as discussed in chapter 4) takes precedence over the demands of a management-oriented perspective. When leaders manage time based on a richer set of concepts than school finance, student discipline, or personnel evaluation, all other functions of the role assume a reasonable place.
4. *Think win-win.* No matter what the challenge or the problem, effective school leaders collaboratively seek solutions that will benefit everyone.
5. *Work harder at understanding than at being understood.* The school leader who is most successful in the often messy business of relationships is an aggressive listener. Understanding and proposed solutions are based on a clear perception of the problem and the people who are involved.
6. *Synergize.* Effective leaders know the power in connections and relationships. They are constantly finding ways to bring people both within and outside of the school together, for they know that everyone together is greater than the sum of the individuals involved. Many schools have followed the

middle school movement's lead in moving to interdisciplinary teaming for some of these same reasons.

7. *Sharpening the saw.* Respected and effective leaders know that they must attend to their own growth in all dimensions—spiritually, communally, professionally, personally, physically—in order to offer themselves as healthy, well-rounded people, ready for the demands of the tasks at hand. (Ramsey 1999, 131–132)

Critical Skills. Some of the skills, then, necessary for principal leadership include effective communication, team building, conflict resolution, problem solving, and decision making. Principals must also analyze the effects of school improvement measures upon student learning. In chapter 3 we will expand on some of these skills.

Climate for Leadership Development. There are environmental factors that encourage the kinds of relationships vital to the development of communal leadership. Donaldson (2001, 46) suggests that they are

1. *A common ethical ideal,* or core set of beliefs, assumptions, and principles around which the relationships will be built.
2. *Ease of communication,* both among formal and informal leaders, sufficient enough to judge the integrity of the information and the person.
3. *The work itself depends on coordinated efforts for its success.* The interdependence of all people who are involved proves its worth in the process and the product.
4. *Interactions between people are direct,* as demonstrated in common meeting and planning times, shared space, and shared students.

The core dynamic of leadership is not about the leader, then, but about the people engaged. It is less about the critical attributes examined above than it is about their translation into quality relationships. It is more about conduct by example that affirms the merit of interactions grounded in trust, dignity, worth, and shared development.

Crisis of Leadership. There has been much written in the past seven years about the dwindling number of candidates preparing to assume defined roles of leadership. With all of the responsibilities listed above, the pressures from numerous constituencies, and the explosion of social problems brought to the school (e.g., violence, drugs, weapons, gangs), the exceptional number of vacancies owing to retirement are presently in jeopardy of going unfilled.

Other researchers contend that there is a second type of crisis of leadership in the form of entrenched leadership training that is unresponsive to current needs. Barbara Kellerman set the tone for her book on leadership (1999) by quoting the eloquent Winston Churchill: "We are shaping the world faster than we can change ourselves, and we are applying to the present the habits of the past." She charges that, since business, politics, and education are inextricably intertwined, leadership education in the United States has failed to

1. Focus on character
2. Place attention on cross-sector collaboration
3. Respond in significant ways to diversity
4. Distinguish between nature and nurture, and between predisposition for leadership and for followership
5. Initiate a meaningful dialogue between theoreticians and practitioners
6. Engage followers or build leadership capacity
7. Address in substantive ways the social, political, and economic problems that have proven most persistent and pernicious
8. Offer fundamental ways in which effective leadership may be measured or evaluated (212–213)

New Era leadership must address these issues because they lie at the crux of both research on leadership (often referred to as Leadership Studies) as well as the practice of leadership (often referred to in the literature as Leadership Training and Development).

Conclusion. Where once principals were responsible to the state for implementing policies and mandates, and did so by focusing top-down leadership efforts on visioning, inspiring, motivating, and managing the teaching staff, New Era leadership is more grassroots in that now the public holds the school directly accountable. This shift in leadership challenges principals and public policy makers to open the formerly closed walls of the school to involve a variety of stakeholders in joint ownership and direction of the neighborhood school and in the development of their own leadership capacity.

At the same time, principals must respond to various overlapping constituencies—the state, the local school board, parents, teachers, students, business, and other sectors of the public. The building administrator must be able to see the commonalities across these groups and to scaffold the varied resources with each group's expectations—no easy task. Yet it is the business of being a community, of dispersed or shared governance.

Retired principal Judith Azzara (2001) maintains that developing positive personal and community relationships is intrinsic to the development of a leader's particular style. The sense of family, of belonging and growing, of learning and stretching, of conflict and resolution, of ownership and attendant responsibility lie at the heart of the work of the principal.

SYSTEMS-LEVEL LEADERSHIP

Superintendents

Two hundred years ago, the school superintendent was little more than a clerk. Following the War of 1812, as urban areas expanded, more local communities turned to an executive officer who could operate and manage the burgeoning school populations. School reformers such as Massachusetts' Horace Mann urged larger cities like Boston to create the office of superintendent. The superintendent would administer and coordinate the work of the entire system with the help of the lay citizens who served on school committees, later referred to as school boards. While the local committees supported smaller schools in their wards, Mann and his colleagues advocated the standardization of bureaucratic formulas for superintendents. Mann's approach considered the number of students, teachers, and support staff to be hired for each school. With the formalization process came heightened expectations for both teachers and principals (Sergiovanni et al. 1999).

In many instances communities hired two superintendents, one who addressed district concerns, the other focusing on individual school and curricular matters. However, by 1930 these two positions were consolidated into a single superintendent and the school committee, now school board, was reduced in size and elected by the general populace.

The adoption of scientific methodology and its evolution between 1900 and 1930 "ignored three issues that were to emerge as significant problems for superintendents in the 1950s and 1960s . . . the role of teachers, students of minority and special needs, and the politicizing of education" (Sergiovanni et al. 1999, 214):

1. The superintendent's sense of teachers was little less than contentious in that teachers were viewed as workers who were to comply with the mandates of the principal and follow a single instructional approach for all teachers. Diametrically opposed to this stance, the teachers viewed the students as workers. Teachers saw themselves as skilled

classroom managers, sensitive and adaptive to the needs of their students. Teachers individually produced craft knowledge that could not be mandated by those removed from the classroom.

Further conflict arose over the perceived value of teachers and their skills. Though teachers saw themselves on a par with scholars and other trained professionals, superintendents viewed them as easily replaceable assembly line workers. The important work of supervision and leadership was also gender-biased, being conducted mainly by men, whereas the teaching profession was considered the work of women. This continues to be a prevalent and ubiquitous problem, for although 80 percent of the nation's teachers are female, only 10 percent of superintendents of leading school systems are women. From this clash rose teachers' unions, first in the schools in Chicago. The value of the individual teacher and her craft knowledge continues to be a fork in the river of reciprocal regard, as attested to during yearly teacher contract negotiations. This is often where true colors show, where administrators who say they highly value teachers fail to demonstrate that regard with commensurate salaries. Instead they seem to say, "Pay them less than they are asking because anyone can do their job."

2. Given the prescriptive teaching that Sergiovanni calls formulization of the scientific method—that is, one instructional method scientifically determined to work for all students—all students had to fulfill certain preconditions before they could begin the standardized experience of school. Many students with special needs and many minority students were left out, thereby denied mainstream resources and opportunities, despite the claims of superintendents that all students were treated equally. Yet "equal" does not mean "equitable." Not all students started at the same point. Students with special needs found that the heavy hammer of the scientific method had nailed shut the door to public schools. It was not until passage of the Individuals with Disabilities Education Act, or PL94-142, in 1975 that those doors were again opened to all students.

3. The scientific model argued that research expertise, void of any political bias, should be the determining factor in issues of class size, the closing of schools, teacher hiring, and provision of support staff. Armed with such trusty phrases as "research indicates" or "the experts say," superintendents and their school boards charged anyone who disagreed with ignorance and ill will. Yet the public continued to press for the kind of education for their children that would allow them to compete in the work world.

Today the superintendent is the community's designated protector of its young, the most visible symbol of hope for getting a good education. The role of the superintendent requires vision, commitment, and stability in a societal milieu that is at best unstable and constantly changing. It is a kind of leadership that draws diverse constituencies, environments, and agendas together. It is a political position.

Despite the prominence of the superintendent's role historically, the major reform initiatives of the past twenty years, beginning with the *Nation at Risk* report (1983) and continuing through the report of the Carnegie Task Force on Adolescent Development (1989) and the more recently convened governor's commissions, gave scant attention to the office of the superintendent. Because superintendents were held more directly accountable for reform efforts in the preceding two decades, more control and authority were moved from the schools to the central office. However, with the public and political attention paid to individual school accountability beginning in 1983, that power was slowly returned to the local school site.

External Factors. Barbara Jackson (1995) cites several major environmental factors that have helped shape the role of the superintendent:

1. *Shift in student diversity.* Given changes in immigration laws, many urban city schools have increasing numbers of South and Central American, Caribbean, Asian (including Vietnamese, Japanese, Chinese, Filipino, Korean), and Eastern and Western European students in addition to the large proportion of African Americans. Therefore, striving for a black-white racial balance has given way to multicultural perspectives.

2. *Uncertainty.* Schools have always had to deal with a measure of instability. Most recently, declining federal funds (apart from those for targeted programs) and the changing student and family populations have challenged the political skills of the designated school leader.

3. *An arena of mandates.* Although federal legislation has freed up monies for schools, the funds come with specific mandates and regulations, and are designated for targeted programs. Through testing, licensure, and accreditation, the states have leveraged greater control over curriculum content, graduation requirements, and program planning and evaluation. The state and federal courts have increased their involvement with schools, not only through desegregation laws, but through services for special needs students, and in general school finance.

Internal Factors. Jackson (1995) further cites several key internal changes that have affected the position and the responsibilities of the superintendent:

1. *Unions.* Teachers' associations have changed to become teachers' unions and as such have grown in power and size.

2. *Decentralization.* Authority as well as accountability have moved from the district's central office to the individual school site. This, coupled with the growth of teachers' unions, has reshaped the appearance and role of the superintendent.

3. *Representation.* With the increased number of superintendents of color comes the particular dilemma of representing all the district's children while meeting the expectations of a given constituency that they are seen to reflect.

New Era Perspectives. Beyond the community's commitment to paying taxes for their public schools, the schools themselves were seen to be the province of those with whom they were directly engaged—students, their families, school personnel. Whether by design or by disposition, schools and their designated leaders allowed themselves to become disconnected from the larger community. However, superintendents today realize the following:

1. Links to other service providers in the broader community are necessary to address the needs of their students.

2. Budget cuts at the district and building levels are requiring superintendents to forge collaborative and cooperative bonds with community agencies and social service providers.

3. Although the substantive part of a district's budget is still allocated through state and local revenues, federal initiatives (primarily through the Elementary and Secondary Education Act of 1965, revised in 1994) target specific programs for competitive grants, e.g., foreign language programs, science programs, after-school initiatives. Yet recently there has been a marked increase in monies targeted for community collaboration. Superintendents must be savvy in the ways of community collaboration and entrepreneurship that lead to partnership.

New Era Decentralization. Ambitious reform efforts today (discussed in later chapters) have transferred particular types of authority and decision making to the individual school site. A wide gamut of observers, from researchers and higher education practitioners to families and communities, have argued that when teachers and families exercise more control in their school, improvements in teaching and learning will follow. Figure 1.2 suggests shared governance relationships that affect students and their families.

The major locus of control for the superintendent then becomes the creation and enabling of a systemwide or districtwide organizational structure that maintains its focus on teaching and learning, with clearly defined and measurable academic objectives and outcomes for all students from all schools. Decentralization has the potential to create an imbalance, although it may well be healthy, between schools that aggressively move forward and those with the same opportunities who choose to remain stagnant. The following elements are suggested for an effective decentralization strategy:

Figure 1.2
Decentralized Governance

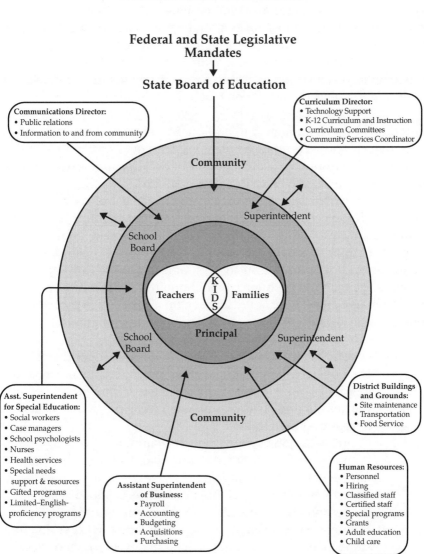

Federal and State Legislative Mandates

↓

State Board of Education

Communications Director:
• Public relations
• Information to and from community

Curriculum Director:
• Technology Support
• K-12 Curriculum and Instruction
• Curriculum Committees
• Community Services Coordinator

Community

Superintendent

School Board

Teachers · KIDS · Families

School Board

Principal

Superintendent

Community

Asst. Superintendent for Special Education:
• Social workers
• Case managers
• School psychologists
• Nurses
• Health services
• Special needs support & resources
• Gifted programs
• Limited–English-proficiency programs

Assistant Superintendent of Business:
• Payroll
• Accounting
• Budgeting
• Acquisitions
• Purchasing

District Buildings and Grounds:
• Site maintenance
• Transportation
• Food Service

Human Resources:
• Personnel
• Hiring
• Classified staff
• Certified staff
• Special programs
• Grants
• Adult education
• Child care

1. *An effective assessment of student achievement.* Schools involved in reform efforts on any level must gather and interpret data as decided by the school community. The assessments must be valued by the educators as part of the reform effort, and the educators must evaluate the effectiveness of their work. This information must be shared with the broader constituency in an ongoing and timely fashion.

2. *An intervention process for nonperforming schools.* In most districts, there will be a school that, for a variety of reasons, does not involve itself or its students and their families in the initiative. The decentralization initiative must have a strategy in place that will allow for intervention in the case of a dysfunctional school.

3. *Building principal leadership.* In nearly all effective school reform initiatives, a common denominator is an effective principal who continues to focus the faculty on teaching and learning.

4. *Flexible budget.* In a decentralized district, the local school has autonomy over its budgetary operation. As the school adopts its reform initiative, develops its strategic plan, implements its programs, and accesses its own resources, it must be able to fiscally support itself through district funds given to the school (DeRoche 1997).

Formal Role Responsibilities. Even in a decentralized district, one of the major tasks of the superintendent is to gather, interpret, and present data in ways that enable the school board to make informed decisions. The superintendent acts as a conduit between the schools and the board, providing information to both and suggesting appropriate responses to perceived problems. In addition to functioning as a district-level manager and school board advisor, the district's designated educational leader commonly has some of the following functions:

1. Organizes and supervises professional and support staff
2. Presents recommendations on employment, dismissal, and buildings and grounds maintenance to the board
3. Carries out and ensures implementation of state-level and board-level mandates
4. Coordinates long-range strategic planning
5. Prepares budget for board approval and administers funds following that approval
6. Coordinates all internal functions of the school district
7. Represents the school district to the community
8. Evaluates curriculum and instruction at school sites and in some instances assists in curriculum development or delegates this responsibility (Lunenburg and Ornstein 1996, 299)

An Example of a Superintendent's Strategic Plan. Given these responsibilities, what does an actual superintendent's strategic plan look like? Dr. Thomas Payzant, noted superintendent of the Boston public schools, presented the Boston School Committee the following goals and objectives:

1. *Student achievement.* All eligible students will take the Stanford

9 achievement tests required by the city and the state. Ninety-nine percent of students enrolled for a minimum of two consecutive years will achieve at levels 2–4 on the multiple-choice achievement tests and on the open-ended assessments in reading and math. The achievement gap will be reduced to the extent that 99 percent of students in each ethnic group and status group (Regular Education, Students with Disabilities, Limited English Proficiency) who have been in attendance for three consecutive years will achieve at levels 2–4 on the multiple-choice achievement tests and on the Massachusetts Comprehensive Assessment System.

2. *Unified student services.* The superintendent will submit a strategic plan including action steps, implementation, and timelines for all students to meet citywide academic standards, graduate from high school, pursue further learning, and contribute to the community. Additionally, he will submit a plan to work with parents and collaborators in the community.

3. *Human resources.* The superintendent will submit a plan for the recruitment of a human resources director with accompanying budget.

4. *Communications and customer service.* The superintendent, in company with the school committee chairperson, will present a plan for fostering clear and timely communication both within and outside the school district. Emphasis will be placed on listening to parental and community concerns and welcoming all community participants.

5. *Professional development.* The superintendent will present a plan for districtwide and school-based professional development, including action steps and implementation strategies that will develop the capacity of all school personnel to meet the goals and objectives for effective teaching and learning.

6. *Mathematics plan.* The superintendent will ensure the district's alignment with all appropriate city, state, and content-area standards and will develop a plan to support student academic improvement for grades K–12 in math (Payzant 2000).

Superintendents are called upon to respond to various overlapping environments and constituencies. Parents/families of students in urban schools may rightfully demand of the superintendent better facilities— schools whose roofs don't leak, schools that don't conduct classes in hallways, schools that have up-to-date textbooks for all students—and better programs, perhaps including appropriate services for special needs students. They may also rightfully demand a reduction in the achievement gap between blacks and whites, desegregation in practice rather than simply in policy, and high expectations and challenges for all students.

Schools in suburbia often challenge the superintendent to improve a school's comparative performance on standardized tests. The superintendent frequently responds by explaining the meaning of the test scores, listening to the concerns of families, and developing a long-range plan while expressing sincere concern and informed understanding.

And in still larger districts, the office of the superintendent includes assistant superintendents, supervisors, directors, heads of subject-area departments, coordinators, and special staff facilitators, as shown in Figure 1.3. For example, the Chicago public schools is the third largest U.S. school system with 45,000 employees, 597 schools, and 431,750 students in the 1999–2000 school year. One layer of Chicago's leadership structure, the office of the deputy chief education officer, alone services programs such as charter schools, ombudsman, parent/community outreach, school partners, special initiatives: small schools, the policy office, and school and community relations, with directors for each program. Another layer, the chief education officer, provides leadership and support for all schools along with the six regional offices that implement the Chicago public schools' policies. The office also acts as a liaison between the community and the school, communicates with all constituencies, and implements mandated policies from another level, the Chicago School Reform Board of Trustees and the chief executive officer.

In contrast, the governance in rural or smaller districts is less complex, as presented in Figure 1.4. The superintendent in these districts is often faced with a nagging tension between the need for a balanced district budget and parents' resistance to the closing of small, neighborhood schools. Effective district-level leadership engages families as they lobby for a neighborhood school, and then seeks to involve them in problem solving that will lead to consensus. There are instances when the superintendent must make the final decision, balancing budgetary concerns with appropriate teaching, learning, and provision of services.

Critical Attributes. Unlike their business counterparts spoken of above, superintendents represent noncompetitive, nonprofit organizations. Their primary focus is students rather than finances. They are political representatives rather than economic processors. And their political prowess at navigating the often dangerous waters of the school board is critical to their success.

Karen Matthews, president of the Savannah–Chatham County school board, wrote the following advertisement for a new superintendent in collaboration with community representatives, faculty, school principals, students, and building leadership teams:

Figure 1.3
Governance Flowchart:
School Districts of More Than 25,000 Students

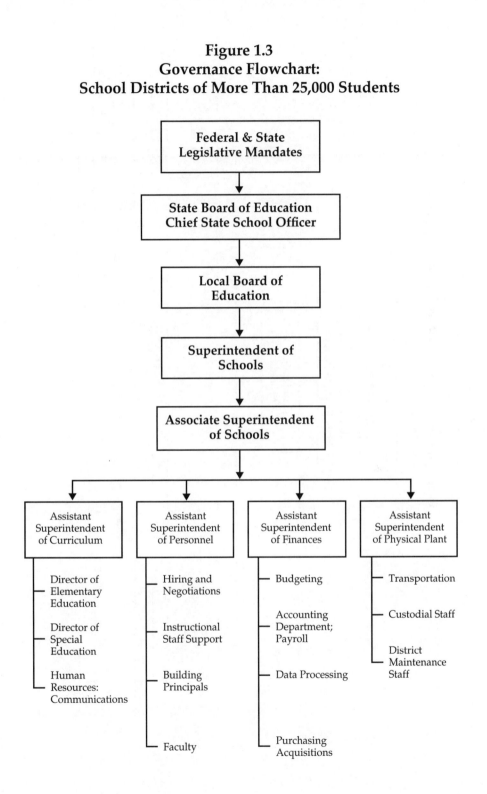

Figure 1.4
Governance Flowchart: School Districts under 5,000 Students

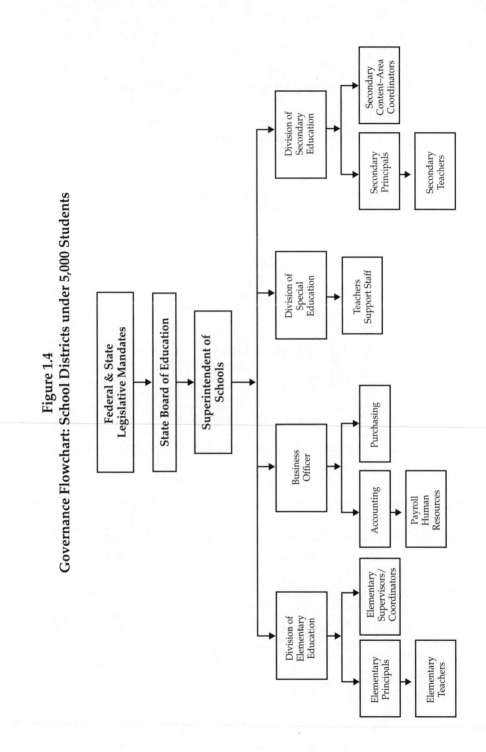

- Experience as a classroom teacher and school principal required
- Experience as a superintendent extremely important but not mandatory
- A master's degree or higher required, but a Ph.D. or Ed.D. degree not required
- Preferably from the Southeast
- Leadership experience in school administration, curriculum, personnel, budgets, total quality management, and site-based management
- Proven success in academics, team-building, and administration. (Devine 1998)

Additionally, Matthews indicated that the large student population of 35,000, the district budget of $200 million, and the large school board of nine members (to whom the superintendent would directly answer) would challenge even the heartiest of educational leaders.

The above examples from very different yet similar school districts point to the general attributes critical to an effective district-level leader:

- Ability to do long-term planning
- Managerial expertise in setting, implementing, and continually focusing all schools on systemwide goals and objectives
- Systems awareness—recognizes the interrelationships within the organization as well as the external factors that affect it
- Emphasis on the affective—value is placed on vision, attitudes, beliefs, motivation, and team building
- Political astuteness—the ability to perceive and sort out conflicting and overlapping constituencies and to communicate with them effectively
- Systems thinking—the ability to consistently and persistently move forward, with continual reforming and reshaping while investing in and developing the leadership capacity of others (Gardner 1988, 143; Gardner 1989, 58)

Conclusion. Even with the local emphasis on decentralization, superintendents will continue to function in bureaucratic ways in response to the state's more centralized mandates and control of resources. This leaves the superintendent with less flexibility in goal setting and funding (Sergiovanni et al. 1999, 222). Moreover, with more site-based management and decision making at the building level, the superintendent must have greater flexibility in dispositional relationships with both the school and the school board. As noted, the superintendent will act more as an aggressive advocate on behalf of the school system as she negotiates partnerships with human service agencies, social and health providers, the business and corporate sectors, and the community at large.

Local School Board

Citizen governance is a hallmark of our nation's democracy. It is embedded in our historical distrust of distant government that is uninformed about and uninvolved in the particulars of the local community. But as schools become more and more complex, as the number of school boards multiplies (currently 15,000, with nearly 100,000 school board members), the ability to maintain standardized or consistent relationships between elected lay people and educational professionals becomes more difficult. Figure 1.5 portrays the overlap of responsibilities and the distinctions between leadership bodies.

Critical Attributes. Yet the country's persistent skepticism of expertise positions the local school board to serve the needs of all the people, to mediate and make accessible the expertise of designated educational leadership. The call for citizen leadership is founded in the very rudiments of civility and common decency—the principles of honesty, trust, patience, caring, openness, confidentiality, and the right to be heard and supported. Loyalty born of a student-centered focus and a belief in the common good allows challenge with conscience, disagreement with respect, and diversity that is celebrated. An effective board member is most often

- Ethical
- Open-minded
- Goal-oriented
- Organized and dependable
- A team player
- A follower and a leader
- A communicator
- Patient both in listening to all aspects of an issue and in seeking possible solutions
- Comfortable with ambiguity
- Accepting of challenge and difference
- Unafraid to stand on the high ground, sometimes alone
- Passionate about students and education

Figure 1.5
New Era Collaborative Structure

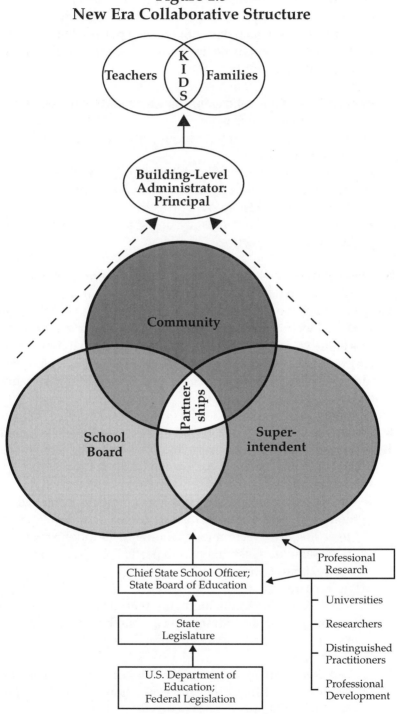

- Committed to the process of citizen governance
- Impartial, willing to embrace an opinion that is well grounded but which does not reflect a personal bias
- Willing to commit extensive time and energy for little immediate personal gratification
- An advocate for students and the district
- Aggressive about establishing partnerships that benefit students
- Comfortable with change
- Informed and consistently seeking growth in their own leadership capacity
- Respectful of others' skills, abilities, and disabilities
- Deliberate in hiring a superintendent and in other district hiring, policy decisions, and programmatic determinations
- Able to see both the long term and short range in determining policy and practices

Many of these attributes are common to superintendents as well as to other educational leaders. Some of the role responsibilities appear similar to those of the designated district leader, too. As with all local governance, leadership roles will reflect the particular values and expectations of the community and the differences within it. However, the commonly held performance distinction between the board and the superintendent is that the board makes policy while the superintendent administers that policy.

To better understand this leadership team's division of labor, the Educational Policies Service of the National School Boards Association provides some of the following examples:

1. Staff personnel
   Board: sets overall policies that affect personnel management—hiring, salaries, dismissals, leaves, staff development
   Superintendent: recommends for board adoption specific salary schedules, assigns staff to particular sites, and oversees general operation
2. Pupil personnel
   Board: determines policies on matters such as truancy, promotion, graduation, admission age, and bus transportation; authorizes support services and services for children with special needs
   Superintendent: recommends policies on student issues such as graduation, promotion, and evaluation; collects data for ongoing evaluation

3. Educational program
   Board: determines general curricular policy given recommendations of superintendent on issues concerning textbooks,
   continuing education, after-school programs, child care programs, and special initiatives; provides resources for schools;
   examines and acts on recommendations based on data collection by the superintendent
   Superintendent: administers instructional and curricular programs; implements testing and evaluation programs determined by the board
4. Physical plant
   Board: determines general operating policies on buildings
   and grounds; determines future building needs and construction sites; selects architects and awards building contracts;
   determines maintenance policy
   Superintendent: examines population flow, school trends, potentially shifting building needs, and reports to the board; supervises the construction of new facilities; makes recommendations to the board on the status of the physical plant,
   general operating procedures, and maintenance needs
5. Finance
   Board: determines general fiscal policy; provides for purchasing and storage; establishes policy for fiscal accounting; reviews annual budget and audit; determines capital outlay;
   considers investments
   Superintendent: recommends policies on fiscal operation; analyzes, determines, and makes recommendations to the
   board concerning long-range fiscal needs; prepares and interprets annual budget; supervises purchasing and budget
   appropriations; examines capital outlay and recommends to
   the board the need for issuing bonds and fundraising
6. Public relations
   Board: determines broad policy on communication with the
   community and the media; represents community's values,
   beliefs, and principles; advocates on behalf of the district to
   all public and private sectors, including legislative (local,
   state, and federal), corporate, and business; establishes partnerships with the district and the community
   Superintendent: recommends policies on information sharing, public engagement, and public relations; represents and
   presents the district's programs, practices, and initiatives to
   the public; functions as the key spokesperson for the entire

district; advocates for the district; seeks partnerships with the business and corporate sectors; builds coalitions with service providers in the community; nurtures healthy relationships among board members, educational staff, and the community (National School Boards Association 1982, 101–102)

Theoretically, school boards manage the community's schools in ways that build public trust and for the good of all children, i.e., they represent the wishes of the people while monitoring the operation of the schools and leading the entire system toward positive outcomes.

Effective Practice. In 1992 the National School Boards Association (NSBA), in an effort to bring about more consistent practices by school boards, adopted after much deliberation a four-part framework for the governance of public education by local school boards. Predicated on the belief that all students can learn and have the right to a rigorous education, the framework embraces the following:

- *Vision.* Developed collaboratively with the community; sees, shapes, implements, and evaluates the community's educational future.
- *Structure.* Supports implementation of the crafted local vision; specifically, hires superintendent; sets program goals, objectives, budgets, and policies; works with community to obtain resources on behalf of all children.
- *Accountability.* Challenges the school board to support student achievement and to respond to and communicate with the community.
- *Advocacy.* Acts on behalf of students and schools in order to protect and nurture the public good. (Shannon 1994, 387–390)

Expanding on these four basic areas, Figure 1.6 offers a model of the workings of an effective school board.

Elaborating on the model, the NSBA describes the effective board as

- Focusing on teaching and learning to the extent that its primary goal is student achievement
- Providing a structure for success in that it provides a management system that not only allows but encourages school personnel, in particular the superintendent, to optimize talents and abilities

Figure 1.6
Functions of an Effective School Board

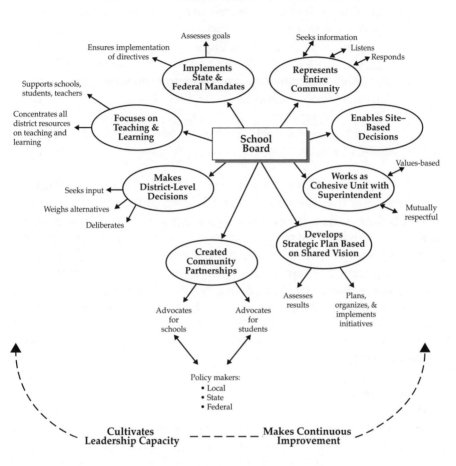

- Developing a vision through collaboration between members of the community and school personnel; ideas are based in research, innovative, and contain high expectations for everyone with a plan of resource support
- Advocating for schools and students in all public arenas (to policy makers at all levels, community taxpayers, and private and corporate sectors)
- Involving the community through cooperative and collaborative support of student learning
- Accounting for results through the establishment, implementation, and evaluation of goals and objectives
- Empowering the staff through more decentralization and site-based decision making

➺ Collaborating with other social, health, and service agencies in the community on behalf of students and families

➺ Fulfilling the policy maker's role through an established system of operation

➺ Committed to continuous improvement in all areas of importance to the school, e.g., changes in state/federal mandates, curricular standards, and benchmarks; best-practice research on effective instructional strategies and learning practices; areas of importance to the district such as legal, ethical, legislative, and fiscal issues (Education Commission of the States 1999)

Role Responsibility. The state gives school boards the authority to broadly ensure that the community's schools are operating appropriately. The board then hires a superintendent to oversee the implementation and management of an effective system. The superintendent and the board address issues that affect the entire district, e.g., segregation/desegregation practices and changes in graduation requirements. The superintendent hires principals who may decide issues such as the kind of discipline program the school will use, how the students' schedules may operate, how parents are to be involved in the school, and what the most effective practices are for that particular school's developmental level.

A former school board member explains the work of the board in the following way:

> My colleagues and I are the members of a five-member board of directors of a $190 million annual corporation. . . . We're responsible for 4,500 employees at 67 different plants. We negotiate annually with four different unions. Our plant managers manage four to five times the number of employees that private sector managers manage. We're responsible for 38,000 units of production on an annual basis, but we have a 13-year production cycle, rarely with any of those products staying within our company for the entire length of time. We have no control over our raw materials. . . .
>
> On the side, we operate the second largest transportation agency in the county. We serve 22,500 meals a day. We operate, if we're lucky, on a 2 to 3 percent fiscal margin. . . . We're required to provide supervision in over 89 languages. (Davis and Greene 1994, 391–392)

Built on the NSBA framework described above, the school board has six primary districtwide responsibilities:

- Guides the district's focus, purpose, changes, structure, goals, and programs
- Filters, supports, and monitors key programs and initiatives
- Selects, supervises, and evaluates work of superintendent
- Oversees disbursement of all district resources
- Serves as a liaison between the community and the school district, actively advocating for the schools, seeking support, building partnerships
- Oversees legal, fiscal, personnel, and program issues; maintains an efficient organizational structure (Smoley 1999, 4–5)

The school board has the political clout and the legitimacy among constituents to broker the kinds of programs and services for the community's children that can focus everyone's efforts on student achievement—academic and social. Yet there are multiple occasions for dissension between the superintendent and the school board, or between the board and the school district, to the extent that superintendents have resigned or board members have walked out of meetings. What are some of the factors that might cause such a valued trust to be placed in jeopardy?

Challenges. The second of the American Association of School Administrators' (AASA) eight "Professional Standards for the Superintendency" (1994) charges the superintendent to develop the kinds of working relationships with the school board that will assist in the formulation of internal and external programs, allow flexible responses to changing state and national mandates and directives, and apply legislative standards to civil and criminal liabilities. This standard is felt by many to be the most difficult to meet. The National School Board Association and the AASA examined the struggle over this standard and observed that the following societal factors impinge on developing positive relationships: the growth in special interest groups, stretched district budgets in light of national and state curriculum mandates, changing student demographics to include a more diverse and poorer population, and an aging population that is more resistant to higher taxes and bond issues (Basom, Young, and Adams 1999).

Most disputes based on these factors center around issues of responsibility and ownership. We need to answer questions such as, What are the respective tasks and responsibilities of each group? Yet there are serious instances in which a board member will be elected based on a narrow interest that is not focused on the achievement of all students. Contentious and divisive relationships develop between the two groups who should be united in their commitment and agenda for the entire district.

However, it is not usually the policies that school boards develop that impede progress, but rather false steps in the process itself. Part of the robustness or health of citizen governance lies in the exercise of disagreement, in diverse opinions as to a particular direction the board should move. But the board must build its capacity to govern while it embraces diversity. Smoley (1999) observes that there are six common ways in which school boards may falter. They may

1. *Make political decisions,* or decisions based on political alliances or agendas rather than on informed beliefs and objective information and assessments
2. *Function without ground rules* defining the respective roles and responsibilities of the superintendent, the board, or the chair of the board; and they have not determined the rules of engagement regarding mutual respect, civility, and trust
3. *Respond to coercion* from particular constituent groups rather than keeping their focus on the best teaching and learning methods for all students
4. *Fail to connect with community* both in sharing information and in soliciting community input
5. *Neglect self-improvement* that keeps them abreast of the best practices and develops their own leadership capacity
6. *Take fragmented actions* rather than continuing to focus on how individual initiatives fit the strategic plan (Smoley 1999, 14)

The greatest single impediment to effective school board functioning and to leadership team (board and superintendent) progress is poor communication. The effective district educational leadership team values the consistent and timely flow of information to all members. When a board sorts through all the data and printed material placed before it, the board only gives attention to the information that addresses the district's goals and objectives, teaching and learning, mission and values, collaborations and curriculum, standards and accountability, and budget and personnel. The board places a premium on cooperation and investment from the community that further the stated goals and shared commitments. And just as it is critical for a board to be open to new information, it must likewise be a conduit of information back to the community. The board's ability to remain focused on critical issues while being responsive to its constituency lies at the heart of healthy leadership and healthy relationships with leaders.

Changing Impediments to Empowerment. The effective board

consistently undertakes four actions that exhibit ethical attitudes about citizen leadership. The board researches, accesses, and uses appropriate information; discusses openly, routinely, and deliberately; weighs and evaluates alternative viewpoints, perspectives, and plans; and consistently works toward consensus through informed compromise (Smoley 1999, 18). The board must be willing to tackle difficult and complex problems and to implement often unpopular decisions such as redrawing the boundary lines of a school district, sending some students to different schools, or closing smaller schools as other neighborhoods grow.

The work of the board is always long range, strategic, and of different consequences to different constituent groups in the community—for one group a decision may be favorable; for another, negative; and for a third, inconsequential. Board members are principled, thoughtful, and always willing to examine the effectiveness of both the board itself and the programs and policies that it implements. Board members often run for office on a platform that maintains that current policy is not working. Newly elected as well as tenured board members likewise scrutinize the effectiveness of their own work and ask the difficult questions, such as

- Is the district moving forward?
- Are all schools providing enriching opportunities that challenge all students?
- How does the district provide both equal and equitable opportunities for all students?
- If board members conclude the district is providing equal and equitable opportunities, what evidence supports that conclusion?
- If board members decide the district is not providing equal and equitable opportunities, what needs to be done?
- What role does the board play in such action?
- How can the board forge new partnerships and coalitions with the community?
- How can the board address the social challenges students and families bring to the school, e.g., poverty, homelessness, disenfranchisement, violence, abuse, fragmented service delivery, and lack of health care?
- How can the board respond to the growing need for services provided at the school site with fewer available resources?
- What is the board's vision for the future of the district and its children?

These are complicated and knotty problems. But the board shoulders its responsibility for devising responses to them as it shares its authority with the superintendent. Together they work with and listen to the entire community.

New Era Leadership and Governance. As decentralization of decision making and authority is becoming more common, school boards are being challenged to redefine themselves, their role in the district, and their representation of the community. "To suggest that reforms are needed in the roles and responsibilities of school boards is not to conspire to remove the public schools from citizen control," Danzberger (1994, 368) argues. But in cascading eras of school reform, it is to call into question the most effective use of all human resources. Boards are seeking new ways of melding services, once available in discontinuous ways through multiple providers, for students and families. The work of the board is now often spoken of in terms of partnerships, collaboration, teams rather than separate units. Many researchers and educational leaders have begun to question the role of the school board as it currently exists.

Phillip Schlechty, president of the Center for Leadership in School Reform in Kentucky, challenges the moral authority of the local school board. In *Schools for the Twenty-First Century* (1990), he maintains,

> Boards of education must create the conditions of invention in school systems, but board members cannot provide leadership to the school district. Rather, board members ensure that such leadership is provided by those they employ to serve the interests of the community and its children . . . Only boards of education, working in consultation with educators, parents, and other community leaders, have the moral and legal authority to assert what kinds of knowledge have social and cultural value within the context of the local school system. (Schlechty 1990, 12)

From a very different direction, Albert Shanker, the former long-time president of the American Federation of Teachers, proposed that school boards operate as corporate boards who meet quarterly to assess general policy decisions, leaving the daily operation of the school district to a management team (Lewis 1994, 356–357). Lewis notes that this same sentiment was expressed in 1992 from a very different quarter, the Twentieth Century Fund of the Danforth Foundation. Some people have criticized school boards' unwillingness or inability to get past the issues of communication and board relationships. They argue that the substantive issues of policy and funding on behalf of the district's children have been neglected.

Multiple studies conducted by the Institute for Educational Leadership (IEL) found that more than 400 school board chairs felt that too little time was spent during school board meetings on substantive issues. "Survey respondents . . . also expressed concern about how the concept of board service is shifting away from trusteeship or leadership and about the growing number of representatives of special interests who serve on boards" (Danzberger 1994, 369). IEL recommended the move to education policy boards that would more clearly focus on the academic achievement of students. Fiscal and management issues would no longer interfere with the more substantive work of the elected leadership.

Similarly, researcher and governance analyst Michael Kirst maintains, "The school board has become more of a reactive force, trying to juggle diverse coalitions that change from issue to issue" (Kirst 1994, 380). When boards of large urban school districts are labeled dysfunctional because they cannot even agree on the length of board meetings or on how members should be seated, and when the tenure of a superintendent in these districts is less than three years, a point could be made for seeking alternative forms of educational leadership.

Typically, New Era efforts at decentralization transfer authority not only from the district office and the superintendent, but from the school board to the school site. The site leadership body then becomes some form of a school council or joint council, composed of students, parents, teachers, community members, and administrators. Among the important tasks of the council is to reflect the needs and characteristics of the individual school while remaining in broad agreement with the goals and objectives of the district.

Conclusion. Though different forms of governance are being examined and exercised, it is safe to assume that the local electorate will remain represented by its local school board in some format. Despite the exclusion of local school boards from discussions about reform, whether on the state or national levels, and despite the growing control state governments and policy makers are exercising over the operation of the local school district, citizen leadership plays a vital role in the education of young people. Through the balance it offers the educational community, through its commitment, resources, vision, and investment, schools are a construct of their community rather than entities set apart. The present operating system of many local boards does not appear to be working as effectively as it could be. The willingness of boards to evolve, to adapt, to develop their own capacity for leadership, will dictate the extent of their health and longevity.

PROFESSIONAL-LEVEL LEADERSHIP

Professional Developers

The health of any organization is directly proportional to its willingness to challenge its capacity for growth. Education is a process that constantly moves from the known to the unknown, a process of change that requires continual renewal and learning. Where once staff development was intended to keep teachers abreast of current research on teaching and learning, now all those with a stake in schools are provided access to workshops, materials, resources, and conferences to sharpen their skills on behalf of students.

Because staff development (usually intended for a group of people) and professional development (for the most part directed at the individual) were usually disjointed and unfocused when it came to the teaching and learning goals of the school, the National Staff Development Council (NSDC) established formal standards for quality and effective staff growth. The standards are designed for three major areas:

- *Context*—the environment in which learning takes place
  - These standards address issues of vitality and sustainability across the life of the school, i.e., that staff development must be ongoing, supported within the structure of the school, valued by the school, and aligned with the strategic plan of the school or district for student outcomes
- *Content*—the new skills and knowledge that will be acquired
  - NSDC has separate standards for each developmental level (elementary, middle, and high school), but in general they all foster the fundamental understanding of appropriate developmental practices, and embrace the concepts of equity, equality, and challenging educational opportunities for all students
  - The standards also instruct schools to write school improvement plans and to provide staff development founded on a robust understanding of their own data collection and interpretation of research
  - Further, NSDC encourages thoughtful family participation in the work of the school through developmentally appropriate experiences
- *Process*—the way in which this new learning takes place
  - The standards address the value of leadership and decision making by those with a stake in schools, and acknowledge that change is a process involving stages rather than a single event (NSDC 1995)

Practical Synthesis. Bruce Joyce and Beverly Showers (1995) have written a rich text on the types of staff development that achieve results in the learning outcomes of students. Essentially, they found that staff development opportunities were most effective when they addressed emerging instructional needs of teachers. As with professional development for other constituents, the more the participants can shape those experiences, the more meaningful they become. And the closer the staff development experiences are tied to the school's learning outcomes, to the needs of the school, to authentic teaching and learning, the more the new learning experiences will be incorporated into the daily work of the school.

What does this look like in practice? During a summer course in Bellevue, Washington, administrators evaluate what children learn and how they learn most effectively by viewing videotaped classroom instruction. Their skill at distinguishing effective from ineffective teaching is honed, as are the ways they may nurture struggling teachers and support expert teachers. In Boston, a network of principals has established text-based discussion groups that focus on a unifying theme (in this case, it was to improve literacy across the school district), examine the research on that theme, and then critique student work that shows growth (U.S. Department of Education 1999).

These examples demonstrate the need for professional development at varied levels of leadership. As will be discussed in chapter 3, when a culture of learning and collaboration is crafted, the school continues to grow and develop. This is a culture or environment in which all groups see themselves as continual learners. Blase and Blase (1998) note that when principals initiate whole-school peer coaching teams, the learning culture is even richer. The use of "critical friends" or peer coaching demonstrates the effectiveness of people within the school addressing their own problems and supporting each other in critical yet cooperative ways.

From Theory to Practice. Previous professional or staff development was disconnected from the ongoing operation of the school and the classroom; it was unfocused and fragmented, and attempted to motivate faculty to implement piecemeal initiatives. New Era staff development charges those who are responsible for providing such experiences to apply their research-based theories to the rigors of instructional practice and student learning in a way that fits the long-term strategic plan the school has implemented. This requires a thorough preassessment of the school's needs, the construction of a deliberate plan focused on student achievement, and systematic, collaborative implementation and evaluation of that plan.

The National Staff Development Council suggests the following ways of assisting groups in their development as collaborative units. It indicates that a leader must be able to

- ❧ Assist groups in learning how to solve problems and communicate
- ❧ Teach groups that both verbal and nonverbal skills are important
- ❧ Understand group structure and processes in order to complete tasks and learn process skills
- ❧ Assist groups in creating and nurturing collaborative cultures within their school (Garmston 1999, 64–65)

Conclusion. Staff development, whether in-service for practicing teachers or preservice for prospective teachers, is usually unsuccessful when it is imposed on the faculty or constituent group; when there is no ownership or opportunity for participation in needs identification; when there is no administrative support for the new learning; and when there is a perceived disconnect between the new learning and the reality of the classroom. This challenges technical assistance providers or staff developers to base their professed expertise on research, and to share this expertise in practical and applicable ways.

Researchers

With increased emphasis on accountability, educational leaders have come to have new respect and regard for research. Test scores are printed in the local newspapers. Real estate agencies sell houses in neighborhoods where schools have earned high marks in student achievement. The public wants to know about the effectiveness of the school. Educational leaders at all levels are now challenged to conduct school-based and district-based research, to interpret that research both locally and on a broader scale, and to implement strategic plans supported by that data and by other best-practice research conducted by universities, professional developers, and independent educational researchers.

Levels of Research. State and federal political leaders look to research to help shape their policies and support their legislation. Local educational leaders look to both research and researchers to translate theory into practice, to validate the selection of particular systemic reform initiatives, and to buttress an argument for the implementation of programs. This coupling of the researcher with the practitioner is healthy for both sides, for the more closely engaged they are, the more problem solving itself is emphasized rather than the implementation of isolated and unsupported projects. What is critical to authentic reform and to growth in schools is the active engagement of practitioners in the process of inquiry. Although chapter 6 presents the more widely used national models of reform, it is not enough to simply use a model as one would don a set of clothes. The lack of ownership this represents has proven to be fatal for initiatives and schools. Rather, the focus should be on cultivating the capacity to solve problems as an important and critical element of leadership.

What are the implications of this researcher-practitioner partnership for research that becomes educational policy? The Policy Forum on Educational Leadership (U.S. Department of Education 1999) argued that the following questions should shape research on educational leadership:

- How effective is the current credentialing system for leaders? Why do some people who are certified for principals' jobs not pursue those jobs?
- To what extent are hiring decisions based on competent performance?
- What are the main characteristics of administrative practice in high-performing school systems? What mechanisms do good leaders use to influence instruction from the system level?
- How do successful districts make the difficult choices necessary to channel more funding into leadership development?
- Which administrative structures work best in large or geographically dispersed districts, where it is harder to sustain collegial relations among principals, teachers, and superintendents?
- How can we develop a broader repertoire of effective strategies, including some less expensive ones, for providing professional development for leaders?
- Which kinds of evidence of student performance (such as test scores, performance-based assessments, and samples of student work) are the best indicators of the quality of instructional leadership? Which are the least telling? (U.S. Department of Education 1999, 19–20)

These are questions that can easily be adapted to any level of leadership development, from the classroom, or practice level, to the policy level.

Conclusion. There are no simple solutions to the complex problems of a school. Too often, past efforts at professional development, or even the use of research and data, have focused on "quick fixes" to immediate problems rather than on research-based, long-term strategic planning. Collaboration that benefits from multiple perspectives is best suited for developing solutions to a school's problems. Often, teachers, who are inundated by the daily interaction with hundreds of young people, and principals, who share similar feelings as they support the work of the entire school, do not see themselves as researchers. However, New Era leadership has launched the kinds of cooperative partnerships with universities, researchers, and staff developers that help all constituent groups gather data, interpret it, and act upon its implications.

POLICY LEVEL

State Level

Governmental power for education has been passed from the federal government to individual states in accordance with the Tenth Amendment to the Constitution. It is the state's responsibility to provide and maintain public schools. A collection of laws and codes set the operational procedure for state public education. The state's jurisdiction includes the following:

- Determining school taxes
- Supporting schools by providing resources and financial assistance through specially designated or categorical funding based on a formula, and through block grants
- Determining state curricular standards and benchmarks—what all children should know and be able to do
- Providing transportation for students
- Providing textbooks and meals free or at a reduced price for students from lower socioeconomic levels
- Setting licensure and certification standards for both classified and certified school staff
- Acknowledging and certifying minimum standards of higher education programs that prepare school personnel
- Establishing minimum salary schedules for school personnel
- Creating minimum requirements for school attendance, including for who must attend and for how long
- Determining graduation requirements

➮ Mandating competency testing for all of the state's students and setting basic criteria for passing

In the 1980s, during the first wave of major school reform follow-ing the *Nation at Risk* report of 1983, Kirst observes, nearly all initiatives came from state legislatures, governors, and the business sector (Kirst 1984). That left all other constituent bodies, such as administrators and teachers' associations and local school boards, to assume a reactive rather than a proactive position. What was particular to this wave of re-form, however, was that it advocated systemic or all-school change, re-form on a broad scale moving from the national to the local level.

Division of Power. The authority the state wields is exercised through distinct offices or branches of power: the governor, the state legislature, and the state courts. Just as the governor acts on the advice of a group of advisors and consultants, the contemporary legislator acts on legislation based on the trusted counsel of a group of policy analysts and budget directors. The state legislature has established state educa-tional agencies (SEAs), which consist of the chief state school officer, the state board of education, and the state department of education.

Governor

The major influence the governor has on state policy lies in the creation of a state education budget. Although this authority is dictated by law, the budget is submitted to the state legislature, which has the power to override the governor's recommendations. The shaping of the budget sparks invested conversation—intense debate among a variety of con-stituent groups who stand to benefit—over which new programs will be funded and which older programs will be continued. In many states, the governor also has access to any accumulated monies that may be added to school allocations.

Political Promises and the Governor's Power. In most cases, it is the governor (with the approval of the legislature) who appoints people to the state board of education, and who can appoint people to state-level educational administrative positions or remove them. In some states, state board members are still elected by popular vote, but in most states the governor appoints either some or a majority of the state board members. And in some instances, the governor may appoint the entire board. In other cases, the governor may also appoint the chief state school officer.

What is consistent in the contemporary political arena is the plank in a candidate's platform, which generally speaks to the improvement of education in the state. What the candidate means by improvement varies dramatically. To some, it means abolishing all schools of education in higher education institutions, based on the erroneous belief that everyone can teach and that no particular preparation is necessary. It may mean increasing both educational allocation and access to these resources, based on beliefs in equity and equality. Governors may propose placing more money in vocational education, in science and math education, or in early childhood programs. Still others may tighten the requirements on teacher and administrative licensure and certification, or may require new standards in preparation programs in higher education. And in still other cases, governors have proposed programs for incentive pay for teachers, career ladders that acknowledge varied levels of teacher expertise and that reward teachers accordingly.

National Education Goals. In 1989 the country's governors took a bold step into uncharted territory and began to jointly craft a strategic plan for the nation's schools. Governor Carroll A. Campbell of South Carolina stated that there were certain beliefs about education that drove the collective process:

- Focus needed to be on achievement
- Participation should be voluntary rather than federally mandated
- Implementation should be directed at the state and local levels rather than nationally
- Information given to parents on student achievement, as understood on the international level, would cause families to be political allies
- Standards and expectations should be raised for all children
- Ownership of the process of education belongs to a broad constituency of stakeholders, both inside and outside the school (Campbell 1995, 77–97)

Once a rough draft was completed, the national goals were sent to the National Governors Association Task Force for preliminary hearings, examination by researchers and educational experts, and further refinement through individual state summits. In 1990 the governors submitted to President George Bush what was to become a six-point National Education Goals initiative. Signed into law on March 31, 1994, under President Bill Clinton, the goals became the Goals 2000: Educate America Act, which provided additional funding and resources for states to implement ambitious and challenging new standards for all children. Goals 2000 required that by the year 2000,

1. All children in America will start school ready to learn.
2. The high school graduation rate will increase to at least 90 percent.
3. American students will leave grades four, eight, and twelve having demonstrated competency in challenging subject matter, including English, mathematics, science, history, and geography; every school in America will ensure that all students learn to use their minds well, so that they will be prepared for responsible citizenship, further learning, and productive employment in our modern economy.
4. The nation's teaching force will have access to programs for the continued improvement of their professional skills, and the opportunity to acquire the knowledge and skills needed to instruct and prepare all American students for the next century.
5. U.S. students will be first in the world in science and mathematics achievement.
6. Every adult American will be literate and possess the knowledge and skills necessary to compete in a global economy and to exercise the rights and responsibilities of citizenship.
7. Every school in America will be free of drugs and violence, and will offer a disciplined environment conducive to learning.
8. Every school will promote partnerships that will increase parental involvement in fostering the social, emotional, and academic growth of children.

The 1998 report from the National Education Goals Panel, "Promising Practices: Progress toward the Goals" (Wurtz 1998), examines each goal and its indicators and lists those high-performing or most improved states that are undertaking exemplary work.

To this point, funding for standards came from the U.S. Department of Education. However, when Congress passed the Educate America Act in 1994 (later amended in 1996), states were encouraged to set their own curricular standards and benchmarks. The creation of the National Education Standards and Improvement Council (NESIC) in conjunction with this initiative offered a way for national policy to support state work in curriculum and instruction. Secretary of Education Richard Riley added to this landmark legislation with the Elementary and Secondary Education Act, and echoed the words of President Clinton when he said, "Goals 2000 is a new way of doing business in America" (Riley 1995, 23). In truth, it is the embodiment of the history of a nation that maintains, at least in theory, that all children have the right to a free, quality public education.

Because there was no mention of how attaining these goals was to be funded by the states, it was up to the governors to develop their own initiatives and strategic plans.

State Legislature

The state legislature has the broad authority to establish, maintain, and enact laws for its public schools. In an interesting 1986 article, then-Governor Bill Clinton, who was the chairman of the National Governors Association Task Force on Leadership and Management, maintained that strong leaders create strong schools. He argued that effective schools are headed by strong leaders and that it is up to local leaders to translate the National Education Goals into local school reform. However, he recommended several long-term ways in which states, particularly the governor or the legislature, could provide leadership and assistance:

1. Begin a dialogue to determine the state's broad goals for education and to identify ways in which schools can achieve those goals.
2. Revise state selection and certification requirements to reflect the skills and knowledge needed by effective principals.
3. Match the content of state-approved educational administration programs to the training needed by effective school principals.
4. Develop a system to evaluate principals effectively and accurately.
5. Provide in-service training to school administrators through, for example, state-sponsored training centers or higher education institutions.
6. Provide incentives and technical assistance to districts to promote school-site management and improvement.
7. Collect statewide information on the process and the outcomes of schooling.
8. Reward principals and schools for performance and effectiveness.
9. Highlight success by documenting and disseminating effective strategies and models.

10. Be patient and remain committed. (Clinton 1986, 208–210)

State legislatures also usually perform specific tasks. They may determine

- ◆ How state boards are to be selected
- ◆ Duties and functions of the state board
- ◆ How the chief state school officer will be chosen
- ◆ Duties and functions of the chief state school officer
- ◆ Functions of the state department of education
- ◆ Types of local and regional school districts
- ◆ How local school boards will be selected
- ◆ What kinds of authority the local school board will exercise
- ◆ State tax formulas and school funding
- ◆ Specific policies such as length of school day, length of school year, what may and may not be taught, compulsory require-ments, and testing and evaluation procedures
- ◆ Funding for vocational technical schools, community col-leges, and adult education
- ◆ Standards for physical plant construction, renovation, and maintenance
- ◆ Support services such as transportation, school breakfasts, school lunches (Lunenburg and Ornstein 1996, 262)

In any of these areas, the legislature's role is to set minimum cri-teria. It is then up to the local board of education to exceed the basic re-quirements. When the legislature does not assume these functions, they are relegated to the state board of education.

State Education Agencies (SEAs)

All states have some formal system of education shaped by the North-west Ordinances of 1785 and 1787, which stipulated that territories that became states must establish a system of public education imple-mented by state agencies. These education agencies are usually led by a state board of education, a chief state school officer, and a state depart-ment of education. As noted, usually the governor appoints the state board, and the state department appoints the chief state school officer or state superintendent of education. The state department is usually comprised of professional educators, people who have previously been teachers, administrators, or school support staff, or who may be educa-tional researchers.

SEAs typically perform three functions:

- Administer and regulate legislated mandates (certification of administrators and teachers, the number of days that school is in session, approval of charter and private schools, accreditation of teacher education programs in universities and colleges, enforcement of physical plant building codes for all educational buildings)
- Provide technical assistance or consultation services through their professional staff to local schools and districts
- Propose new legislation and assist parent, teacher, and administrator associations in changing particular laws (Sergiovanni et al. 1999, 287–288)

State Board of Education

The state board represents another layer of representative governance beyond the local school board. In fourteen states, state board members are elected by the general public. Working closely with the legislature (from whom it draws its power), the state board acts in an advisory capacity to the legislature. Except for Wisconsin, all states have a state board of education.

Board Composition. Although there are usually nine members on the board, the number of members may vary across the country from three to seventeen. The length of service is typically a four- or five-year term. Historically, the composition of the board reflected the dominant class in that board members were usually white men. However, a recent survey indicates that 31 percent of board members are women and 20 percent are minorities, a healthy move in the direction of broader representation (NASBE 1993).

Board Responsibilities. Early state boards were responsible for such things as choosing textbooks, selecting courses of study, determining teacher qualifications, and handling problems that arose in the administration of special institutions. The board also functioned as an emissary of the public schools, promoting the state's work to the general public. And the state board supervised the care of school finances and the maintenance of school property (Council of Chief State School Officers 1983).

Although there is no mention of education per se in the U.S. Constitution, many state constitutions include articles like this one, from the Illinois State Constitution:

Leadership and general supervision over all public education, including adult education and instructional programs in state institutions, except as to institutions of higher education granting baccalaureate degrees, is vested in a State Board of Education. It shall serve as the general planning and coordinating body for all public education, including higher education, and shall advise the Legislature as to the financial requirements in connection therewith. (Article VIII, Section 3)

Each state board exercises many direct supervisory duties in conjunction with local school districts as well as community colleges, and it indirectly coordinates the responsibilities of four-year state colleges and universities. Although board functions vary from state to state, Lunenburg and Ornstein list the following responsibilities as characteristic of most state boards:

- Setting statewide curriculum standards
- Establishing qualifications and appointing personnel to the state department of education
- Setting standards for teacher and administrative certificates
- Establishing standards for accrediting schools
- Managing federal and state funds earmarked for education
- Keeping records and collecting data needed for reporting and evaluating
- Adopting long-range plans for the development and improvement of schools
- Creating advisory bodies as required by law
- Advising the governor or legislature on educational matters
- Appointing the chief state school officer, setting minimum salary schedules for teachers and administrators, and adopting policies for the operation of institutions of higher learning. (Lunenburg and Ornstein 1996, 267)

The board plays another key role in state education. Unlike members of the legislature, who may respond to limited short-term proposals that reflect their political tenure either in a given session or in office, the state board has the opportunity to both influence and implement long-range planning. It also has the option to bring credibility to the proposals of the chief state school officer.

Chief State School Officer (CSSO)

The chief state school officer, who may also be called the state superintendent of schools, the state superintendent of public education, or the state commissioner of education, functions as the head and chief executive of the state department of education. This position has been created for every state by constitutional provision or statute. Historically, this position was elected by the general public, but today the CSSO is usually appointed by the state board of education. He or she is a professional educator whose previous career was in elementary or secondary education as principal of a school, or who served as a local school district superintendent, or was in higher education.

The first appearance of a CSSO was in 1812 under the title of superintendent of common schools (Lunenburg and Ornstein 1996, 267). His duties largely revolved around management and coordination. By 1859, after the popularization of the office by Massachusetts Commissioner of Education Horace Mann, over half of the nation's states had CSSOs.

Today the CSSO may be elected by the general public (which imparts more authority to the office) or appointed by the governor. More frequently, the CSSO is selected to serve by the state board of education. By 1994 there were only three chief state school officers of color and only nine women held that office.

Role Responsibilities. Essentially the CSSO serves as a liaison between professional educators across the state and government policy makers (the governor, legislature, and state board of education). Because the method of selection of the officeholder, and therefore the legal relationships between the CSSO and the state board, vary from state to state, there is no one set of duties assigned to all CSSOs. However, the following appear to be common responsibilities:

- Serving as the chief administrator of the state department of education
- Selecting personnel for the state department of education
- Recommending and administering an educational budget for the state department of education
- Ensuring compliance with state educational laws and regulations
- Explaining and interpreting the state's school laws
- Deciding impartially controversies involving the administration of the schools within the state
- Arranging the studies, committees, and task forces as deemed necessary to identify problems and recommend solutions
- Reporting on the status of education within the state to the governor, legislature, state board of education, and the public
- Recommending improvements in educational legislation and policies to the governor and state legislature

•➡ Working with local school boards and administrators to improve education within the state. (Lunenburg and Ornstein 1996, 268)

State Department of Education

The state department is most often headed by the CSSO and works under the supervision of the state board of education. Since the first decade of the twentieth century, state departments of education (SDEs) have nearly tripled in size and responsibility. Their resources are appropriated through the state legislature. It stands to reason that in larger states that have more school districts, students, and staff, the SDE will be more centralized and larger than in other states. Conversely, in states that have fewer school districts, the authority and responsibilities of the SDE will be more decentralized.

For the most part, people who work in the SDE are career professionals—researchers, statisticians, curriculum specialists, instructional supervisors, and clerical staff. And generally they too have come from the public school sector or colleges of education.

Role Responsibilities. In general, the SDE collects, interprets, and disseminates data on education across the state. In the past forty years, the SDE has expanded its functions to include

•➡ Accrediting schools
•➡ Certifying teachers and administrators
•➡ Apportioning funds
•➡ Overseeing transportation and safety
•➡ Monitoring state rules and regulations
•➡ Monitoring compliance with federally funded initiatives
•➡ Collecting results of research, evaluating programs, and disseminating information (Lunenburg and Ornstein 1996, 268)

Although SDEs are not usually considered the initiators of reform, they are responsible for the implementation of reforms. In 2001, evidence of this was seen in the Comprehensive School Reform Demonstration initiatives. While local schools chose the model of school reform that best suited their needs (see chapter 5), it is the state department of education that monitors the integrity with which these federally allocated grants are implemented. More particularly, if a school chose a particular reform model, the money spent for professional development in the implementation of that model must be consistent with the model's design. SDEs in forty-one states have reorganized their departments to support this kind of responsibility. A recent report by the Council of Chief State School Officers directed SDEs to begin seeing their roles in making reforms from a leader and facilitator's position rather than from a more passive regulating and monitoring stance (Lusi 1997, 2).

Influence for Change. One of the major difficulties SDEs are confronting in the face of this second wave of systemic reform (the first coming in 1983 with the *Nation at Risk* report) is one of proximity. Complex school reform intends to change the learning outcomes for students. This means effecting changes directly in the classroom where teaching and learning occur. But given the physical and organizational distance between the SDE and classroom teachers, the SDE's influence on such changes is questionable.

Recent challenges for SDEs reflect the social and cultural conflicts played out in the larger society. SDEs have had to address such issues as school violence and unrest, desegregation, compensatory programs, education for English-as-a-Second-Language (ESL) students, appropriate services for special needs students, school finance (in some cases fiscal crises), declining enrollments, and shifting enrollments. They have also had to address competency testing for teachers, state testing for students, certification of teachers and principals, supplementary aid to minority groups, home schooling, schools of choice, curriculum development, and administering extended-learning services such as educational opportunities for adults, children of migrant workers, and families.

Conclusion. Despite what may look like insurmountable problems, state education agencies continue to play an active and direct role in policy making and educational leadership. Closer working relationships between the governor, legislature, and state agencies attest to their growing commitments to maintain rigorous academic programs for all students. The National Institute on Educational Governance, Finance, Policymaking, and Management, however, urges policy makers on the state level to implement higher standards of leadership development. Among their recommendations are to

- Authorize full-time 2-year fellowships for senior teachers to pursue national board certification and train for a leadership position through a site-based preparation program
- Involve private sector representatives in planning incentives to reform administrator preparation
- Revise state standards for leadership preparation programs based on the new standards recommended by national professional associations for administrators, and require these programs to collaborate with practitioners

‣ Mandate an external quality review of all leadership preparation programs and eliminate those that are not working

‣ Make the criteria and assessments for principal certification
more relevant to the skills actually needed to do the job, and
align them with new standards for educational leadership
suggested by national professional associations

‣ Encourage local districts to explore different governance
models that promote new definitions of educational leadership. (National Institute on Educational Governance, Finance,
Policymaking, and Management 1999, 23–24)

Complex and controversial issues such as those listed above,
coupled with declining federal funding for public schools, have challenged state departments to critically examine their programs, assess
their development of leadership capacity, and evaluate ways in which
supplementary funding can be obtained.

Federal Level

Since the early days of the American colonies, communities were
charged by legislative bodies to levy taxes and thereby subsidize free
public education for all children. That education, both then and now,
was to be controlled by the public and represent the public good.

Historical Perspective and Legislation. The nineteenth century
saw little involvement by the federal government in educational initiatives apart from two significant events. In 1862 the federal government,
through the Morrill Land Grant Act (see chapter 2), gave 30,000 acres of
federally owned land to each state (a total of six million acres) either to
build colleges on or to sell, with the funds to be used to create colleges
focused on agriculture and engineering. In a reflection of the prevalent
need at the time to rebuild and sustain a war-torn nation, the act established land grant colleges that are still a cornerstone of higher education today. Additionally, in 1867 as noted, the U.S. Congress created
the U.S. Office of Education, which later become the U.S. Department
of Education.

Following World War II, federal involvement increased dramatically, beginning in 1944 with what is commonly known as the GI Bill
(Servicemen's Readjustment Act). Faced with wide-scale national unemployment, the federal government put $15 billion into retraining re-
turning servicemen through free college educations. The precedent was
set. The federal government now showed its concern for the social well-
being of its constituents through this bill and other legislation, such as

the National School Lunch and Milk programs (1946) and the Federal Impacted Areas Aid program (1950).

The landmark U.S. Supreme Court's 1954 decision in *Brown v. Topeka Board of Education,* which declared segregated schools to be unconstitutional, presented more evidence of the federal government's willingness to become directly involved in the education of the nation's children.

Three years later, the federal government was put to another test, this time on the international front. In 1957 the U.S.S.R. launched the first space satellite, *Sputnik,* and with it came the first threat to the nation's defense. In response, the federal government initiated the National Defense Education Act (NDEA), which provided funding for higher education in the areas that would most improve the nation's ability to defend itself. These were deemed to be science, math, and foreign languages. The NDEA funded professional development programs for those teachers who were teaching in lower socioeconomic neighborhoods. It provided student loans and scholarships for hundreds of thousands of baby boomers. And it initiated a wave of guidance, counseling, and vocational-technical programs in public schools. By 1960 the federal government allocated over $240 million annually for this initiative, and by the middle of the decade courses of study eligible for scholarships were expanded to include history, English, reading, and geography (Ornstein 1978).

Other key federal programs and legislation included

- ➡ The Elementary and Secondary Education Act (ESEA) of 1965, which reflected the emphasis on social equity and equality at that time. The Johnson administration's War on Poverty; the attention given to minorities and the disenfranchised; and the ESEA, which earmarked money for education for the disadvantaged, were all part of the federal government's changing leadership role. Today, most of the funds from the ESEA are focused on urban youth who are deemed to be at risk for academic and hence social failure.
- ➡ Title IX, the 1972 Education Amendment to the Civil Rights Act, which prohibited discrimination against women in federally funded educational programs or institutions. Specific guidelines were to provide for equal facilities and opportunities in sports programs in particular and for the hiring of women in general (Lunenburg and Ornstein 1996, 244).
- ➡ Bilingual Education. In 1968 Congress passed this piece of legislation to ensure that an appropriate education be given

to all students. This bill was directed at providing an education in both English and the native language of non-English-speaking families. The bill sparked much debate between conservatives and liberals, including over immigration rights and the responsibilities of a democracy in the face of shifting ethnic dominance.

➤ Public Law 94-192, which focused attention on disabled students' right to an appropriate and free public education. Previously, students with disabilities were often taught in separate institutions removed from the general public. With this act came the "mainstreaming" of disabled students—that is, the placing of students with disabilities with the rest of the school's population.

From Categorical Support to Block Grants. As evidenced here, the federal government's involvement or leadership in education does not usually address the general operation and functions of the public school. Rather, it has focused on specialized or categorical programs— unemployed war veterans, a threat to the national defense, issues of race and poverty, and separation and discrimination, whether by gender, ethnicity, or disability.

However, during the Reagan administration Congress began to shift its focus from targeted programs to general assistance to schools in the form of block grants. These were monies that states and local school districts could use to satisfy very broad needs. And although some categorical programs were preserved (programs for the handicapped, non-English-speaking students, and vocational education), this represented a move away from precise federal dictates in programs and fiscal support to increased state and local control in addressing social and cultural needs of students.

Instead of being based primarily on the needs of the disadvantaged, grants were restructured based on

➤ Basic skill development—reading, writing, mathematics
➤ Special projects—parent involvement, school-to-work programs, and those for gifted and talented students
➤ Staff support—professional development, instructional equipment, assessment of student progress, and desegregation (Lunenburg and Ornstein 1996, 247)

In many ways, this decentralization has helped school districts more easily apply for funding, as paperwork is not as picky or redundant, and the administration of funding at the local level is more realistic. However, opponents of block grants point to the programs that have fallen through the cracks, programs the local level leadership failed to pick up, support, and administer through the writing of such grants. Under block grants, states characteristically distribute money per capita or a given amount for each student at that site. This leaves small rural schools in perhaps a stronger position than a large urban and often poor school district, whose students have broader and deeper needs. For the most part, the larger urban schools use their block grants for reading and language programs and support personnel, while the smaller districts (both rural and suburban) use their funding for new textbooks, computers, and computer software.

The Reagan administration also exercised its federal leadership in education in ways that were uncommon up to that time. As I sat with President Reagan in the White House in the summer of 1983, he talked about his education agenda in terms of dramatically reducing the Department of Education; offering vouchers or tax credits for families to take their children out of public schools and place them in private schools; emphasizing schools of choice and teacher testing as measures of accountability; and returning prayer to the public school classroom. Some of these same issues are once again being discussed today. Yet despite the lack of importance that Reagan placed on the Department of Education and other educational issues, through Reagan's outspoken Secretary of Education William Bennett (1985–88), education became a more visible and viable issue in federal politics.

A Charge to the Nation. But the most dramatic educational initiative of Reagan's administration was the National Commission on Excellence in Education's *Nation at Risk: The Imperative for Education Reform* (NAR) report of 1983. Secretary of Education Terrell Bell created the commission and directed it to present a report to the American people on the quality of education. The report began:

> Our Nation is at risk. Our once unchallenged preeminence in commerce, industry, science, and technological innovation is being overtaken by competitors throughout the world. This report is concerned with only one of the many causes and dimensions of the problem, but it is the one that undergirds American prosperity, security, and civility. We report to the American people that while we can take justifiable pride in what our schools and colleges have historically accomplished and contributed to the United States and the well-being of its people, the educational foundations of our society are presently being eroded by a rising tide of mediocrity that threatens our very future as a Nation

and a people. What was unimaginable a generation ago has begun to occur—others are matching and surpassing our educational attainments. (1)

Not since the Soviet launching of *Sputnik* had a single event had such far-reaching effects on this country's educational agenda. Issues of equity and equality were replaced by a discussion of excellence. The commission advocated more rigorous academics, increased math and science requirements for graduation, and tougher teacher testing to stem the nation's "rising tide of mediocrity," a phrase quoted in lectures, research articles, school board meetings, campaign speeches, and local media. The NAR report ignited a controversy over educational leadership that swept the country.

Although it left reform efforts to the states, federal policy makers could claim educational leadership of unprecedented proportions. Whether their claims were justified or not, there is little doubt that they placed education in the national spotlight, and that they positioned the federal government to play an even more significant leadership role in education.

Federal Agencies. What is arguable, however, is whether the nation has ever formulated or exercised a federal policy in education. Reasons for doubt include the less than systematic development of initiatives, the variety of kinds of educational programs, and the attendant lack of a single center of strategic planning. Yet there are those federal agencies, committees, groups, and councils that, when put together, may form a national policy (Sergiovanni et al. 1999, 278).

United States Department of Education

In its inaugural year of 1867, the U.S. Department of Education had a commissioner, three clerks, and a budget under $20,000. Under President Jimmy Carter, the Department of Education was expanded to its present form, which includes a secretary of education, a deputy secretary, and an undersecretary, along with various secretaries who oversee designated programs such as elementary, secondary, vocational and postsecondary education, and special education and rehabilitative services. And although the department is small in comparative size, with only 5, 000 employees, it has a larger budget than the Energy Department or the Justice Department. Yet it falls far short of the fiscal power of the Department of Defense, and will fall even further behind during the Bush administration (Sergiovanni et al. 1999). Although there are thirteen federal departments and fifteen other agencies that address some aspect of education, the Department of Education receives nearly half of all federally allocated funds, amounting to about $21 billion yearly (Digest of Education Statistics 1989, 371).

Responsibilities. The Department of Education was formed in order to collect and disseminate data in support of public education. The department's primary responsibility is to implement and oversee those educational initiatives passed by Congress. Specifically, the department

- Develops rules and regulations necessary for the implementation of legislation
- Apprises the public of new legislation through notification in the Federal Register
- Initiates congressional legislation
- Provides counsel to legislators on educational issues

Congress

It was not until the Great Depression that the U.S. Congress became a player in the educational leadership arena. During the mid-1930s, Congress passed legislation to strengthen schools and provide services unavailable during this economic trauma. However, Congress's rather passive role was embraced both by states who wanted control over their schools and by professional associations, such as the National School Boards Association, who advocated for local control. Nonetheless, Congress had to "provide a clear mission and sufficient resources so that local administrators and teachers [could link] the schoolhouse to broader national and global priorities" (NSBA 1989, 3).

In the contemporary Congress, funding for education comes primarily through the Education Subcommittee, a part of the powerful and prestigious House Appropriations Committee. There is a distinction made in the legislative process between those bills that are supported and those that are funded. For even if an educational bill passes, it may receive severely reduced funding or no funding at all from the Appropriations Committee.

On many educational bills, it is more likely that a representative or senator will give their support based on their desire to represent their constituency rather than on party politics. For instance, a representative from northern Michigan or southern California may vote to support education for migrant children, while a representative from Florida or Texas may vote to support bilingual education.

A National Charge. The National Institute on Educational Governance, in conjunction with the U.S. Department of Education and the Office of Educational Research and Improvement, challenges federal policy makers to assume roles of educational leadership by doing the following:

- ☞ Create a high-powered national commission on leadership
- ☞ Develop national standards for leadership preparation and certification
- ☞ Support alternative approaches to certification
- ☞ Fund alternative professional development for educational leaders
- ☞ Develop collaboratively a partnership model with school, business, and university people in the preparation of instructional leaders
- ☞ Provide federal funding for the demonstration of effective leadership development
- ☞ Provide grants to states to design model state reforms for the accreditation and certification of leadership development
- ☞ Develop academies to identify and encourage new leaders
- ☞ Support research and dissemination of it
- ☞ Enact legislation to encourage reform of leadership preparation programs
- ☞ Create focus groups to examine what is known about educational leadership and about the ways in which public discussions may be generated (National Institute on Educational Governance, Finance, Policymaking, and Management 1999, 24–25)

Conclusion. During the Reagan and Bush administrations, the country's leadership of programs of equity, particularly for the poor, minorities, the disabled, and women, were replaced with the rhetoric of excellence that yielded leadership to the states. Yet local and state resources were and are insufficient to meet the demands of a high-tech information age and to address mounting social problems. Even as the federal government continues to present the United States as a world economic competitor, it is asked to support a just community based on the common good and to play a supportive yet nonintrusive role in educational leadership. It is being asked to provide the resources and then trust the states and local lay people to use them with the wisest discretion.

SUMMARY

New Era educational leadership is not defined in a given person, in critical skills, or in that person's individual function and responsibilities within the system. Rather, it is the sum of all people who believe in a common good accomplished through quality educational opportunities for every one of the country's children.

Peter Senge, the noted author of *The Dance of Change* (1999), defines leadership as "the capacity of a human community to shape its future, and specifically to sustain the significant processes of change required to do so" (16). During the Industrial Revolution, when people in the United States began to leave their own farms and shops to work for someone else under someone else's rules in the factories, people's capacity to shape their own future (and to believe they controlled their own destiny) seemed to decline. It was not until the mid-1950s, when certain distinctions were made between "blue-collar" and "white-collar" workers, that people had a sense of reassuming influence in the workplace.

The same perspective applies to the participation and leadership of the United States in its schools. New Era distributed leadership collaboratively builds both the capacity and support of people for educational leadership and shared change. It seeks to cultivate, enable, and engage leaders on all policy levels through the development of their knowledge, skills, attitudes, and competence.

These new leaders will be leaders "pulled by the future rather than pushed by the past" (Patterson 1993, 38). If this country is to continue to be a leader in the change race, the creation of and insistence on communities of responsibility, cultures of leader-learners, and communities bound by a shared vision, shared governance, and shared purpose will replace educational systems of bureaucratic management.

New Era educational leadership is understood in relationships, in beliefs, and in the same commitment to larger principles upon which this country was founded. It is a leadership that fuses the notion of the common good with the rights and responsibilities each of us has to each other. It is a leadership of spirit as well as a leadership of mind.

REFERENCES

Ackerman, R., G. Donaldson, and R. van der Bogert. 1996. *Making Sense as a School Leader: Persisting Questions, Creative Opportunities.* San Francisco: Jossey-Bass.

American Association of School Administrators. 1994. *Professional Standards for the Superintendency.* Arlington, VA: American Association of School Administrators.

Azzara, J. R. 2001. "The Heart of School Leadership." *Educational Leadership* 58, no. 4 (January): 62–64.

Basom, M. R., S. Young, and T. Adams. 1999. *Getting Better at Building Superintendent–School Board Relations.* Arlington, VA: Educational Research Service, Summer.

Billig, S. 2000. "Research on K–12 School-Based Service-Learning." *Phi Delta Kappan* 81, no. 9 (May): 660–662.

Blase, J., and G. Anderson. 1995. *The Micropolitics of Educational Leadership: From Control to Empowerment.* New York: Cassell.

Blase, J., and J. Blase. 1998. *Handbook of Instructional Leadership.* Thousand Oaks, CA: Corwin Press.

Blase, J., J. Blase, G. Anderson, and S. Dungan. 1995. *Democratic Principals in Action: Eight Pioneers.* Thousand Oaks, CA: Corwin Press.

Bolman, L., and T. Deal. 1997. *Reframing Organizations: Artistry, Choice, and Leadership.* San Francisco: Jossey-Bass.

Campbell, C. 1995. "The Governors and the National Education Goals." In *National Issues in Education,* ed. J. Jennings, 77–97. Bloomington, IN: Phi Delta Kappa; Washington, DC: Institute for Educational Leadership.

Carnegie Task Force on Adolescent Development. 1989. *Turning Points: Preparing American Youth for the Twenty-First Century.* New York: Carnegie Corporation.

Cavarretta, J. 1998. "Parents Are a School's Best Friend." *Educational Leadership* 55, no. 8 (May): 12–15.

Civic Literacy Project. 2000. *Standardized Test Scores Improve with Service-Learning.* Bloomington, IN: Indiana University.

Clinton, B. 1986. "Who Will Manage the Schools?" *Phi Delta Kappan* 68, no. 4 (November): 208–210.

Combes, E. 1999. "At Issue: Teacher Leadership." *Journal of Staff Development* 20, no. 4 (Fall): 13.

Combs, A., A. Miser, and K. Whitaker. 1999. *On Becoming a School Leader.* Alexandria, VA: Association for Supervision and Curriculum Development.

Conzemius, A. 1999. "Ally in the Office." *Journal of Staff Development* 20, no. 4 (Fall): 34.

Council of Chief State School Officers. 1983. *Educational Governance in the States.* Washington, DC: U.S. Department of Education, February.

Danzberger, J. 1994. "Governing the Nation's Schools: The Case for Restructuring Local School Boards." *Phi Delta Kappan* 75, no. 5 (January): 367–373.

Darling-Hammond, L., and D. Loewenberg Ball. 1997a. *The Right to Learn: A Blueprint for Creating Schools That Work.* San Francisco: Jossey-Bass.

———. 1997b. "Teaching for High Standards: What Policymakers Need to Know and Be Able to Do." Paper prepared for the National Education Goals Panel, Washington, DC, June.

Davies, D. 1996. *Partnerships for Student Success: What We Have Learned about Policies to Increase Student Achievement through School Partnerships with Families and Communities.* Baltimore: Center on Families, Communities, Schools, and Children's Learning, Johns Hopkins University.

Davis, C., and D. Greene. 1994. "Defining the Leadership Role of School Boards in the Twenty-First Century." *Phi Delta Kappan* 75, no. 5 (January): 391–395.

Deci, E. L., and R. M. Ryan. 1985. *Intrinsic Motivation and Self-Determination in Human Behavior.* New York: Plenum Press.

DeRoche, T. 1997. "What's a Superintendent to Do?" *Education Week,* February 26.

Des Marais, J., Y. Yang, and F. Farzanehkia. 2000. "Service-Learning Leadership Development for Youths." *Phi Delta Kappan* 81, no. 9 (May): 680.

Devine, L. 1998. "What We Want for a Superintendent." *Savannah Morning News,* April 16.

Digest of Education Statistics. 1989. Washington, DC: Government Printing Office.

Donaldson, G. 2001. *Cultivating Leadership in Schools: Connecting People, Purpose, and Practice.* New York: Teachers College Press.

DuFour, R. 1999. "Challenging Role: Playing the Part of Principal Stretches One's Talent." *Journal of Staff Development* 20, no. 4 (Fall): 62.

Dunlap, D. M., and P. Goldman. 1991. "Rethinking Power in Schools." *Educational Administration Quarterly* 27, no. 1: 5–29.

Education Commission of the States. 1999. *Effective School Governance Practices: A Look at Today's Practice and Tomorrow's Promise.* Denver, CO: Education Commission of the States; January.

Elmore, R. 1999. "Leadership of Large-Scale Improvement in American Education." Paper presented at the Consortium on Policy and Research in Education, Boston, September 15.

Epstein, J. 1995a. "School and Family Partnerships." Paper presented at the annual meeting of the American Educational Research Association, San Francisco, April 18–21.

———. 1995b. "School/Family/Community Partnerships: Caring for the Children We Share." *Phi Delta Kappan* 77, no. 9 (May): 701–712.

First, P. F., J. L. Curcio, and D. Young. 1994. "State Full-Service Initiatives' New Notions of Policy Development." In *The Politics of Linking School and Social Services,* ed. L. Adler and S. Gardner, 63–74. Washington, DC: Falmer Press.

Gardner, J. 1988. "Leaders and Managers." *NASSP Bulletin* 72: 1–2.

———. 1989. "Leadership: Attributes and Context." *NASSP Bulletin* 73: 58.

Garmston, R. J. 1999. "Better by the Bunch." *Journal of Staff Development* 20, no. 4 (Fall): 64–65.

Gilligan, C. 1982. *In a Different Voice.* Cambridge, MA: Harvard University Press.

Giroux, H. 1993. *Living Dangerously: Multiculturalism and the Politics of Difference.* New York: Peter Lang.

Grace, G. 1995. *School Leadership: Beyond Education Management.* London: Falmer Press.

Guthrie, J. 1990. "The Evolution of Educational Management: Eroding Myths and Emerging Models." In *Educational Leadership and Changing Contexts of Families, Communities, and Schools,* ed. B. Mitchell and L. Cunningham, 210–231. Chicago: University of Chicago Press.

Hallinger, P., K. Leithwood, and J. Murphy, eds. 1993. *Cognitive Perspectives on Educational Leadership.* New York: Teachers College Press.

Hayes, C., P. Grippe, and G. H. Hall. 1999. "Firmly Planted: Building Resource Teacher Program Puts Roots of Professional Development into the School Building." *Journal of Staff Development* 20, no. 4 (Fall): 17–21.

Helgesen, S. 1995. *The Female Advantage: Women's Ways of Leading.* New York: Currency-Doubleday.

Henderson, A., and N. Berla. 1955. *A New Generation of Evidence: The Family Is Critical to Student Achievement.* Washington, DC: Center for Law and Education.

Holzman, M. 1992. "Do We Really Need 'Leadership'?" *Educational Leadership* 49, no. 5 (February): 36–40.

Honig, J., J. Solak, S. Golan, and M. Wagner, eds. 1995. *California's Healthy Start.* Menlo Park, CA: SRI International.

Jackson, B. 1995. *Balancing Act: The Political Role of the Urban School Superintendent.* Washington, DC: Joint Center for Political and Economic Studies.

Joyce, B., and B. Showers. 1995. *Student Achievement through Staff Development.* 2nd ed. New York: Longman.

Kellerman, B. 1999. *Reinventing Leadership: Making the Connection between Politics and Business.* Albany: State University of New York Press.

Kielsmeier, J. 2000. "A Time to Serve, a Time to Learn." *Phi Delta Kappan* 81, no. 9 (May): 652.

Kirst, M. 1984. "The Changing Balance in State and Local Power to Control Education." *Phi Delta Kappan* 66, no. 3 (November): 189–191.

———. 1994. "A Changing Context Means School Board Reform." *Phi Delta Kappan* 75, no. 5 (January): 378–381.

Lambert, L. 1998. *Building Leadership Capacity in Schools.* Alexandria, VA: Association for Supervision and Curriculum Development.

Lewis, A. 1994. "Reinventing Local School Governance." *Phi Delta Kappan* 75, no. 5 (January): 356–357.

Lodico, M. 1999. "You Have to Want to Do This Job." *Journal of Staff Development* 20, no. 4 (Fall): 20.

Lunenburg, F., and A. Ornstein. 1996. *Educational Administration: Concepts and Practices.* Boston: Wadsworth Publishing.

Lusi, S. 1997. *The Role of State Departments of Education in Complex School Reform.* New York: Teachers College Press.

Mitchell, D., and S. Tucker. 1992. "Leadership as a Way of Thinking." *Educational Leadership* 49, no. 5 (February): 30–35.

Moss, G. 1991. "Restructuring Public Schools for Internal Democratic Governance: A Circular Approach." *School Organization* 11, no. 1: 71–85.

National Association of Elementary School Principals. 1986. *Elementary and Middle Schools: Proficiencies for Principals Kindergarten through Eighth Grade.* Alexandria, VA: National Association of Elementary School Principals.

National Association of Secondary School Principals. 1996. *Breaking Ranks: Changing an American Institution.* Reston, VA: National Association of Secondary School Principals.

National Association of State Boards of Education. 1993. *How State Board Members Are Selected.* Alexandria, VA: National Association of State Boards of Education.

National Commission on Excellence in Education. 1983. *A Nation at Risk: The Imperative for Educational Reform.* Washington, DC: U.S. Department of Education, April.

National Congress of Parents and Teachers. 1996. *Parent Plus: A Comprehensive Program for Parent Involvement.* Chicago: National Congress of Parents and Teachers; May.

National Institute on Educational Governance, Finance, Policymaking, and Management. 1999. *Policy Brief: Effective Leaders for Today's Schools: Synthesis of a Policy Forum on Educational Leadership.* Washington, DC: Office of Educational Research and Improvement.

National Parent-Teacher Association. 1998. *National Standards for Parent/ Family Involvement Programs.* Chicago: National Parent-Teacher Association.

National School Boards Association. 1982. *Becoming a Better Board Member.* Washington, DC: National School Boards Association.

———. 1989. *A National Imperative: Educating for the Twenty-First Century.* Washington, DC: National School Boards Association.

National Staff Development Council. 1995. *Standards for Staff Development.* Oxford, OH: National Staff Development Council.

Noddings, N. 1984. *Caring: A Feminine Approach to Ethics and Moral Education.* Berkeley: University of California Press.

Ornstein, A. 1978. *Education and Social Inquiry.* Itasca, IL: Peacock.

Otterbourg, S. 1994. *The Education Today Parent Involvement Handbook.* Boston: Educational Publishing Group.

Patterson, J. L. 1993. *Leadership for Tomorrow's Schools.* Alexandria, VA: Association for Supervision and Curriculum Development.

Payzant, T. 2000. *Focus on Children: Boston Public Schools.* Report presented to the Boston Public School Board, January 12.

Ramsey, R. 1999. *Lead, Follow, or Get Out of the Way: How to Be a More Effective Leader in Today's Schools.* Thousand Oaks, CA: Corwin Press.

Rasmussen, K. 1998. "Making Parent Involvement Meaningful." *Education Update* 40, no. 1 (January): 3.

Riley, R. 1995. "The Goals 2000: Educate America Act. Providing a World-Class Education for Every Child." In *National Issues in Education,* ed. J. Jennings, 74–106. Bloomington, IN: Phi Delta Kappa; Washington, DC: Institute for Educational Leadership.

Schlechty, P. 1990. *Schools for the Twenty-First Century.* San Francisco: Jossey-Bass.

Senge, P. 2000. *Schools That Learn: A Fifth Discipline Fieldbook for Educators, Parents, and Everyone Who Cares about Education.* New York: Doubleday.

Senge, P., A. Kliener, C. Roberts, R. Ross, G. Roth, and B. Smith. 1999. *The Dance of Change: The Challenges of Sustaining Momentum in Learning Organizations.* New York: Doubleday.

Sergiovanni, T. 1992. *Moral Leadership: Getting to the Heart of School Improvement.* San Francisco: Jossey-Bass.

———. 1995. *The Principalship: A Reflective Practice Perspective.* Boston: Allyn and Bacon.

Sergiovanni, T., M. Burlingame, F. Coombs, and P. Thurston. 1999. *Educational Governance and Administration.* Boston: Allyn and Bacon.

Seyfarth, J. 1999. *The Principal: New Leadership for New Challenges.* Upper Saddle River, NJ: Prentice-Hall.

Shannon, T. 1994. "The Changing Local Community School Board: America's Best Hope for the Future of Our Public Schools." *Phi Delta Kappan* 75, no. 5 (January): 387–890.

Smith, S., and P. Piele, eds. 1997. *School Leadership: Handbook for Excellence.* Eugene, OR: Clearinghouse on Educational Management, University of Oregon.

Smoley, E. 1999. *Effective School Boards.* San Francisco: Jossey-Bass.

Titone, C., and K. Maloney. 1999. *Women's Philosophies of Education.* Upper Saddle River, NJ: Merrill, Prentice-Hall.

Turnbull, A., and H. Turnbull. 1995. *Families, Professionals, and Exceptionality: A Special Partnership.* Columbus, OH: Merrill, Prentice-Hall.

Tyack, D., and L. Cuban. 1995. *Tinkering toward Utopia: A Century of Public School Reform.* Cambridge, MA: Harvard University Press.

U.S. Department of Education. 1999. *Effective Leaders for Today's Schools: Synthesis of a Policy Forum on Educational Leadership.* Washington, DC: Education Publications Center; July.

U.S. Senate Select Committee on Equal Educational Opportunity. 1972. "Revitalizing the Role of the School Principal." In *Toward Equal Educational Opportunity,* Senate report no. 92: 305–307.

Williams-Boyd, P. 1996. "A Case Study of a Full-Service School: A Transformational Dialectic of Empowerment, Collaboration, and Communitarianism." Doctoral dissertation, University of Kansas.

Wilson, M. 1993. "The Search for Teacher Leaders." *Educational Leadership* 50, no. 6 (March): 24–27.

Wurtz, E. 1998. *Promising Practices: Progress toward the Goals.* Washington, DC: National Education Goals Panel.

Chapter Two

•◦ Chronology: Shifting Perspectives—Involvement, Ownership, and the Business of Community Building

> Communities of leaders beget communities of learners.
> —Roland Barth (1990)

The evolution of the concept of educational leadership has been shaped in part by its context, a marriage of federal legislation and organizational establishment with the social expectations and cultural forces evidenced in our country's history. As American schooling grew and changed, so too did the role of the principal and the notion of leadership.

EARLY 1800s   During the early history of American schooling, the teacher is solely responsible for teaching and maintenance. However, as schools grow it becomes impossible for one person to attend to all tasks. The "principal-teacher" not only functions in the classroom but acts as the school's overseer (Pierce 1935). The single word "principal" first appears in the Common School Report of Cincinnati (1835) and in Horace Mann's writings in 1835.

The shape of school leadership is essentially political, with local school boards directly supervising the work of the school and the teachers. State and federal departments of education are small and have little power to enforce regulations.

LATE 1800s   With a growing number of students and schools, principals provide the school with site maintenance, personnel supervision, minor administrative discipline, and some teaching. School leaders are expected to embrace and reflect the social and religious values, norms, beliefs, and ideals that the United

LATE   States holds, and are viewed as *"managers of virtue"* (Tyack
1800s,   and Hansot 1982).
cont.

In larger cities, the shape of school leadership and governance becomes bureaucratic, with emphasis placed on the need for professional administrators to operate more uniformly. The "principal-teacher" now reports to a district superintendent (Seyfarth 1999).

1862   *Morrill Land Grant Act* gives land to the states for the construction of agricultural and engineering colleges. The vast majority of these colleges are still in operation today.

1867   Congress establishes the U.S. Office of Education. In 1980, under Public Law 96-88, it becomes a cabinet department known as the U.S. Department of Education.

1897   First meeting of the National Congress of Mothers, who are concerned about education, in Washington, D.C. The following year, their constitution and bylaws are adopted. Organization is now called the National Parent-Teacher Association.

EARLY   Although societal values are still similar to those expected of
1900s   school leaders, these beliefs and norms tend to be less religious than in the previous century, and more business or factory oriented, with emphasis placed on technical management, productivity, and efficiency (Beck and Murphy 1997).

State departments of education, consisting of only two or three people, are established to prepare reports, gather data, and garner public support.

1907   In recognition of the importance of parent-teacher cooperation, the Department of Parent-Teacher Associations is formed in the National Congress of Mothers. It takes a leadership role on such issues as the health, welfare, and education of all school children. By 1983 the National PTA would boast a total of 5,359,521 members.

1916   Establishment of the National Association of Secondary School Principals.

1917 *Smith-Hughes Act* provides grants to states for the support of vocational education. As the United States surges into the age of mass production, schools that had been agriculturally driven begin to reflect the economic need for trained factory workers. Federal legislation through the states provides funding to encourage and prepare young men for a variety of occupations.

Although the perpetual shifting of the school's focus in response to societal needs is mirrored throughout the history of American schooling, this is the first dramatic break with traditional educational preparation. The act was the first annual appropriation by the federal government to public secondary education. By 1994 the annual federal budget for education would total more than $1.1 billion.

During the early 1900s, when there are no compulsory attendance laws, by the age of fourteen, nine out of ten young people drop out of school to either work in the fields or (more frequently today) work in industry. This poses new challenges for school leadership.

1920s National recognition is given to the role of the principal with the establishment of the Department of Elementary School Principals and the Department of Secondary School Principals within the National Education Association. With this comes higher education preparation programs for a profession now distinct from teaching, and a sense of accountability to the public and district management for school effectiveness.

After World War I, the title "principal-teacher" is shortened to "principal," who is seen as the *"values broker,"* the person who is expected to transmit the morals, values, and spiritual truths of a democratic society to students. The principal is viewed as a prestigious public servant (Beck and Murphy 1993).

With the sea of immigrants flowing into the United States, and with the move from the rural farm to the urban factory, child labor laws are enacted that lead to compulsory school attendance. Immigrants need to be "acculturated"—that is, integrated productively into the U.S. economy and society.

1920s,   At this point, although education is free for all children, access
cont.   to it is not equal or equitable. Educational leaders are now
confronted with issues that they still contend with today—issues of race, class, and culture.

1930s   With the emphasis on scientific industrial management, the
principal becomes the *"scientific middle manager,"* a CEO of
sorts, a school executive who directs the process of school as
a business venture. Primary tasks focus on personnel, business administration, district grounds management, and fiscal
issues.

Educational leaders and their new business partners place primary value in the scientific experts—psychologists, superintendents, curriculum designers, and managers—to determine
social, cultural, and economic developments in the United
States's schools (Education Commission of the States 2000).

1940s   During the war years, the principal is once again seen as an
important *"democratic leader"* on the home front, one who is
expected to impart and demonstrate leadership, democratic
values, and the social worth of all people to teachers, students,
and the community. Principals function as group leaders, developers of curriculum, ambassadors to the community, and
colleagues of the superintendent.

1944   *Servicemen's Readjustment Act,* also known as the *GI Bill,* provides free education and retraining for returning veterans.
Threatened by massive unemployment and charged with sustaining an economy without the production of wartime services, the government provides $15 billion to 8 million World
War II veterans through this bill. The bill establishes the federal
government as an active participant in addressing the social
needs of its citizenry through educational leadership.

1946   *National School Lunch and Milk programs* are written not only
to provide food for needy children, but in an effort to help reduce the postwar food surplus and maintain erratic prices.

1949   *Federal Property and Administrative Services Act* (Public Law
81-152) provides for the donation of surplus property to educational institutions.

1950s   As university research on the role of educational leadership ex-
pands, the principal, as a *"theory-guided administrator,"* is expected to objectively apply this scientific knowledge to school
management, to represent the intentions of a body of people—such as administrators, citizens, taxpayers, families, or
teachers—and to efficiently implement policy (Education
Commission of the States 2000).

Educational leadership is now spoken of as being the responsibility of superintendents and school board members as well
as principals (Kyte 1952). Also, there is a great increase in the
number of central administrators. In some large urban school
districts, there are as many as one administrator for every
eighteen teachers (Olson 2000, 29).

1950   *Financial Assistance for Local Educational Agencies Affected by
Federal Activities* (Public Laws 81-815 and 81-874) provides assistance for the construction and operation of schools in federally affected areas.

1954   *Brown v. Board of Education of Topeka* (1954) is a decisive turning point in educational leadership and administration, one
that seamlessly joins the school and the community. Yet some
fifty years after this decision, racial segregation is still as strong
in many school districts as it was in 1954. And efforts to provide both an equal and an equitable education for all young
people still permeate and dominate political agendas, at least
in rhetoric. This U.S. Supreme Court decision is the first attempt at massive institutional reform, and presents schooling
as a guaranteed constitutional right.

A work entitled *Administration and the Teacher* (Yeager 1954)
clearly presents the concept and role of educational leadership
as synonymous with administration.

1958   In response to the Soviet Union's 1957 launch of the small, sil-
ver space satellite *Sputnik,* the United States, for the first time,
fears for its place in the international arena, and it launches its
own *National Defense Education Act* (Public Law 85-864),
which provides assistance to local and state school systems to
improve students' achievement in math, science, and foreign
languages. Likewise, the U.S. Office of Education nearly triples
in size (Olson 2000, 28).

1958,   *Education of Mentally Retarded Children Act* (Public Law 85-
cont.   926) provides federal funds for training teachers of the handicapped.

1960s   During this decade of social revolution, the principal is seen as
a *"bureaucratic executive,"* a member of a well-developed hierarchy, the person responsible for implementing the directives
of the policy makers—the local school board and central administration as well as state-level administrators (Abbott
1969). Together they are considered to be the educational leadership (Campbell et al. 1987).

It is interesting that during this time of social unrest and up-
heaval, little is mentioned in the literature about the responsibility of educational leaders to help tackle the larger, more
complex problems of poverty, desegregation, and disenfranchisement. Rather, emphasis is placed on the less messy issues
of the proper application of scientific principles and bureaucratic processes to the local school.

1964   *Civil Rights Act of 1964* (Public Law 88-352) grants the commissioner of education the authority to provide in-service
training for school districts and higher education institutions
in addressing problems caused by desegregation.

Economic Opportunity Act of 1964 (Public Law 88-452) provides grants for college work-study programs for low-income
students; it establishes community action programs such as
the Job Corps, Head Start, Follow Through, and Upward
Bound; and it authorizes the creation of Volunteers in Service
to America (VISTA).

1965   The *Elementary and Secondary Education Act* (Public Law 89-
10) and the *Higher Education Act* (Public Law 89-329) are both
signed into law, providing grants for school programs and
services for children from low-income families. PL 89-329
strengthens and nearly triples state education agencies and
educational research and training and assists universities in
providing student loans and fellowships. The Higher Education Act establishes a National Teacher Corps and provides
needed support to teacher training programs and equipment.
Title I (now called Chapter I) of PL 89-329 calls for the contin-

ual strengthening of parent participation in compensatory programs.

1966   The *Model Secondary School for the Deaf Act* (Public Law 89-694) assists Gallaudet College in the establishment and operation of a model secondary school for deaf students.

With this proliferation of legislation in the turbulent 1960s, the legislature becomes a major player in educational policy making.

1970s   The principal's role is expanded to include *"humanistic facilitator,"* someone who leads teachers and students, reaches out to and is an integral member of the community (Sergiovanni and Carver 1973), and is expected to cultivate an emotionally supportive environment (Fernandes 2000). There is a move away from the hierarchical leadership model whereby the principal protected the bureaucracy and a move toward becoming an initiator of positive, sustaining, interactive, and robust relationships. Principals are expected to function as liaisons to members of the community, not only informing them of the school's work but involving them in its activities (Beck and Murphy 1993).

The term "leadership" now first appears in connection with schools. Until this time, the "administration" was responsible for the daily operation of the schools. However, with the unexpected emergence of large populations of underserved children and families, the resultant shift in responsibilities of those in authority was reflected in new terminology. Later study would reveal that these terms were not interchangeable or synonymous.

Issues of school finance litigation challenge educational leaders in the 1970s to rethink the practice of giving more money to wealthier schools and less to poor communities. Because children in poor communities routinely have fewer resources, underprepared and undertrained teachers, and impoverished facilities, lawsuits assist in moving some (though little) funding into neighborhoods where the need is the starkest.

1970   The National Congress of Parents and Teachers (NCPT) joins

1970,   with the National Congress of Colored Parents and Teachers to
cont.   serve all children through such programs as the New Action
             Program, Quality Living and Quality Learning for All Ameri-
             cans, Volunteer Programs in the Juvenile Courts, and Every
             Child Needs You.

1972   The *Education Amendments of 1972* (Public Law 92-318) es-
            tablish the Education Division in the U.S. Department of
            Health, Education, and Welfare. In addition to granting aid to
            various advisory bodies, the amendments establish a bureau-
            level Office of Indian Education and prohibit gender bias in
            admission to public institutions.

1975   First Americans are granted increased participation in the im-
            plementation and conduct of their own educational programs
            with the *Indian Self-Determination and Education Assistance
            Act.*

            The decisive *Education for All Handicapped Children Act,* a
            landmark in education legislation, provides a free and appro-
            priate education for all children with disabilities. This act,
            along with Head Start, Economic Opportunity, Elementary
            and Secondary Education, Bilingual Education, and Migrant
            Education, gives categorical monies to local governments that
            are earmarked for teaching basic reading skills and providing
            health services for specific groups of children, such as the poor
            and immigrants. Some form of parent or community involve-
            ment in the allocation of funds (usually in the decision-mak-
            ing process) is required by the legislation.

1978   The *Tribally Controlled Community College Assistance Act*
            (Public Law 95-471) provides federal money for the operation
            and improvement of tribally controlled community colleges
            for First American students.

1978   In an attempt to fight tuition tax-credit legislation, the Na-
            tional Congress of Parents and Teachers helps form the Na-
            tional Coalition to Save Public Education.

1980s   Given the sweeping attention paid to accountability as a result
            of the country's response to the *Nation at Risk* report of 1983,
            the principal is once again seen as the *"instructional leader,"*

one who guides teachers and students in the pursuit of effective learning experiences whose success is measured through student assessment. Principals during this decade are expected to initiate and nurture a "vision" to the entire school community, one that projects future possibility and challenges people's moral imagination (Greenfield 1987).

Near the end of the decade, the vision of educational leadership is spoken of in terms of "transformative power" (Bennis 1984), which refers to the dynamic leadership qualities and power of the principal to persuade followers to share and implement his or her vision. Transformative leaders channel the work and energy of their followers to realize that vision.

In contrast to the blurring of roles between the principal and teachers that took place during the 1800s and early 1900s, a clear distinction is made between teachers and educational leadership—the principal—who is now a leader of teachers rather than a sometime teacher of students, in the late 1980s.

During the early 1980s, the federal government turns away from parent participation requirements (previously seen in legislation of the 1960s and 1970s) in favor of more state and local government control. Throughout the 1980s, such programs as Parents as Tutors (PAT), later called Parents as Teachers, gain support of officials who encourage parents to assume supportive educational roles at home (Shields 1992).

Also during the 1980s, the first graduate programs in educational leadership are forged. However, in their haste to be among the first institutions to offer leadership programs, they offer courses of study that reflect relatively unfocused and disconnected or disparate fields of study. Higher education institutions look to both effective schools and to business literature for their models. Both offer mechanistic or prescriptive checklists for strategy implementation and task effectiveness (Donaldson 2001).

1983   Of the four major reports that lay considerable blame for the decline of the United States's economic strength at the feet of the country's schools, the National Commission on Excellence in Education's *A Nation at Risk: The Imperative for Educational*

1983,   *Reform* (1983) becomes the most frequently cited argument
cont.   for nationwide school reform. This report spurs politicians and
state boards of education to initiate more than a thousand reform efforts during the 1980s. However, interestingly enough,
the flood of other national reports that follow do not speak to
educational leadership as a concept or to the specific roles of
educational leaders, i.e., principals, superintendents. (The
other reports were issued by the Twentieth Century Fund Task
Force on Federal Elementary and Education Policy, the Education Commission of the States, and the Business-Higher Education Task Force on Education for Economic Growth, all in
1983.) This is the first time that U.S. public schools are held accountable for the decline in the United States's international
economic competitiveness. Gone is the discussion of moral or
democratic good both in schools and among leadership. Instead, ideas of productivity and efficiency dominate.

1984   The *Human Services Reauthorization Act* (Public Law 98-558)
recommits funding to Head Start and Follow Through programs, and initiates the National Talented Teachers Fellowship, a federal Merit Scholarship, and Leadership in Educational Administration programs.

1987   With support from the Danforth Foundation, the University
Council for Educational Administration (UCEA), composed of
fifty prominent university-based leadership programs, issues
Leaders for America's Schools. The report suggests criteria for
effective programs that are more meaningful, inclusive, and
field intensive.

1989   As the federal government continues to exercise leadership on
social issues relevant to schools, the *Drug-Free Schools and
Communities Act Amendments* (Public Law 101-226) amend
the *Drug-Free Schools and Communities Act of 1986* to provide
drug abuse education and prevention programs in both elementary and secondary schools.

The National Policy Board for Educational Administration,
along with a previous report by the National Commission on
Excellence in Educational Administration (Griffiths, Stout, and
Forsyth 1987), calls for broad changes in the preparation, evaluation, and licensure of school administrators.

President George Bush and the nation's governors craft a series of educational goals for all children, to be met by all schools by the year 2000—goals that have yet to be attained.

1990– 2000   Rather than being viewed as an instructional leader, the principal becomes the head learner, more particularly the *"collaborative leader."* Principals move from being implementers to initiators, from being conflict managers to risk-takers, from controlling others in a transformative way to empowering others through servant leadership (Lightfoot 1983). This is yet another shift in perspective as the principal and administrative leaders shape their schools to meet not only system and organizational needs but also the needs of a changing social milieu.

The principal is seen by others to assume the roles of cutural leader, professionalized manager, and manager-by-results (Seyfarth 1999).

In general, educational leadership in the 1990s is constructed against the backdrop of the belief in the equal and equitable worth and dignity of all engaged in the educational community. This interrelatedness of constituents positions students, teachers, parents, colleagues, and the local community as partners who thrive in a caring, nurturing, and responsive environment (Barth 1990; Noddings 1988; Bellah et al. 1985).

1990   This sense of equality is evidenced in the *Americans with Disabilities Act* (Public Law 101-336), a landmark in legislation that prohibits discrimination against any person with a disability.

1994   The *Goals 2000: Educate America Act* (Public Law 103-227) creates a new partnership between the federal government and state and local communities through its formalization of national education goals and its allocation of resources for the development of individual state standards and benchmarks and appropriate assessment measures.

Among the programs initiated by the *Improving America's Schools Act* (Public Law 103-382), the federal government launches its largest program for children of disadvantaged families through Title I legislation.

1997   The Clinton-Gore administration reauthorizes the *Individuals with Disabilities Education Act,* which focuses on ensuring access to public schools and ensuring quality education for all students.

1998   Education statistics indicate that during the fiscal year of 1998, the federal government, through the U.S. Department of Education, allots $11.5 billion to school districts, $6 billion to institutions of higher learning, $5.5 billion to college students, and $3.7 billion to state education agencies.

1998–
1999   With funding from the Joyce Foundation, the Education Commission of the States (ECS) initiates the Governing America's Schools initiative, which examines K–12 public education from a collaborative viewpoint—that of policy makers, educators, and the general public.

The ongoing tension between the emphasis placed on the technical aspects of educational leadership and that placed on the nontechnical aspects helps to interpret leadership both historically and practically. Both of these models assist in providing separate paradigms in which to view, interpret, and understand both the theoretical and the practical sides of leadership. Beck and Murphy (1993) characterize the period between 1820 and 1900 as the "era of aristocracy of character," an ideological time during which those people who managed schools were "teachers' teachers." However, with the growth of the scientific movement during the 1950s through the 1970s, the technical aspects of school leadership were emphasized. And like a pendulum came a movement back to focusing on the nontechnical aspects of instructional leadership in the 1980s.

Although it took a century for our social and educational systems to move from an agricultural to an industrial focus, the past two decades have witnessed a rapid and dramatic shift, spurred by technological and scientific advancements, to an information, knowledge-based society (Mulkeen 1994). With this shift came a movement away from the hierarchical, management-oriented, and mechanistic educational leadership model of the bureaucratic school to the communitarian model, which embraces the empowerment of communities of collaborative, loyal, self-motivating professionals (Schlechty 1990; Seyfarth 1999).

Education in our society moved from the one-room schoolhouse to a highly complex bureaucracy, then returned to the smaller, invested community. It moved from top-down leadership to collegial and participatory collaboration. And it moved from a focus on values and ideals to a system of managed efficiency and production, only to return to a model of leadership that seeks to intellectually and morally transform thought into democratic possibility.

REFERENCES

Abbott, M. 1969. "Hierarchical Impediments to Innovation in Educational Orga-
    nizations." In *Organizations and Human Behavior: Focus on Schools*, ed.
    F. D. Carver and T. J. Sergiovanni, 42–51. New York: McGraw-Hill.
Barth, R. 1990. *Improving Schools from Within: Teachers, Parents, and Principals
    Can Make the Difference.* San Francisco: Jossey-Bass.
Beck, L., and J. Murphy. 1993. *Understanding the Principalship: Metaphorical
    Themes, 1920s–1990s.* New York: Teachers College Press.
———. 1997. *Ethics in Educational Leadership Programs: Emerging Models.* Co-
    lumbia, MO: University Council for Educational Administration Press.
Bellah, R., R. Madsen, W. Sullivan, A. Swidler, and S. Tipton. 1985. *Habits of the
    Heart: Individualism and Commitment in American Life.* New York:
    Harper & Row.
Bennis, W. 1984. "Transformative Power and Leadership." In *Leadership and Or-
    ganizational Culture: New Perspectives on Administrative Theory and
    Practice*, ed. T. J. Sergiovanni and J. E. Corbally, 64–71. Urbana: University
    of Illinois Press.
Bredeson, P. 1985. "An Analysis of Metaphorical Perspectives on School Princi-
    pals." *Educational Administration Quarterly* 36, no. 3: 29–59.
Brown v. Board of Education of Topeka, 347 US 483 (1954).
Campbell, R. 1987. *A History of Thought and Practice in Educational Adminis-
    tration.* New York: Teachers College Press.
The Digest of Education Statistics. 1998. Washington, DC: National Center for
    Education Statistics, U.S. Department of Education.
Donaldson, G. A. 2001. *Cultivating Leadership in Schools: Connecting People,
    Purpose, and Practice.* New York: Teachers College Press.
Education Commission of the States. 2000. *The Invisible Hand of Ideology: Per-
    spectives from the History of School Governance.* Denver, CO: Education
    Commission of the States.
Fernandes, P. 2000. "Collaborative Leadership in the New Millennium." Paper
    presented at the national conference of the Association for Supervision
    and Curriculum Development, New Orleans, March 26–29.
Greenfield, W., ed. 1987. *Instructional Leadership: Concepts, Issues, and Contro-
    versies.* Newton, MA: Allyn and Bacon.
Griffiths, D. E. 1959. *Administrative Theory.* New York: Appleton-Century-Crofts.

Griffiths, D., R. Stout, P. Forsyth. 1987. *Leaders for America's Schools: The Reports and Papers of the National Commission on Excellence in Educational Administration.* Washington, DC: Office of Educational Research and Improvement.

Kyte, G. C. 1952. *The Principal at Work.* Boston: Ginn.

Lightfoot, S. L. 1983. *The Good High School: Portraits of Character and Culture.* New York: Basic Books.

Mulkeen, T., N. Cambron-McCabe, B. Anderson. 1994. *Democratic Leadership: The Changing Context of Administrative Preparation.* Westport, CT: Ablex.

National Commission on Excellence in Education. 1983. *A Nation at Risk: The Imperative for Educational Reform.* Washington, DC: Government Printing Office.

Noddings, N. 1988. "An Ethic of Caring and Its Implications for Instructional Arrangements." *American Journal of Education* 12, no. 2 (February): 215–230.

Olson, L. 2000. "Pulling in Many Directions." *Editorial Projects in Education* 19, no. 12: 29.

Pierce, P. R. 1935. *The Origin and Development of the Public School Principalship.* Chicago: University of Chicago Press.

Schlechty, P. 1990. *Schools for the Twenty-First Century.* San Francisco: Jossey-Bass.

Sergiovanni, T., and F. D. Carver. 1973. *The New School Executive: A Theory of Administration.* New York: Dodd, Mead.

Seyfarth, J. 1999. *The Principal: New Leadership for New Challenges.* Upper Saddle River, NJ: Prentice-Hall.

Shields, P. 1992. *Bringing Schools and Communities Together in Preparation for the Twenty-First Century: Implications of the Current Educational Reform Movement for Family and Community Involvement Policies.* Boulder, CO: Education Policy Studies Program, SRI International.

Tyack, D., and E. Hansot. 1982. *Managers of Virtue: Public School Leadership in America, 1920–1980.* New York: Basic Books.

Yeager, W. A. 1954. *Administration and the Teacher.* New York: Harper & Brothers.

Chapter Three

☙ Shifting Styles, Changing Metaphors: The Art of Creating Effective Leadership

There was an earlier time, in the first half of the twentieth century, when leaders, viewed as wiser and more powerful, could manage, control, and direct the work of organizations that were perceived to be less complicated and more uniform or standardized. Yet it was a time when emphasis was placed on dependency rather than on mutuality; on outcomes rather than on ethical and moral conduct; on a stability that breeds sameness rather than on continuous improvement that proves volatile; on the role and the person in the role rather than on authentic leadership (Bhindi and Duignan 1998).

Complex forces have flattened this hierarchical and authoritative management structure into a continuum. As suggested in chapter 1, New Era leadership involves relations among people whose work is actively facilitated to guide and direct educational purposes in general and instructional improvement in particular. We have argued for the collective and collaborative responsibility of public agencies and other stakeholders, all of whom occupy positions on this continuum of educational leadership. And we have examined the ways in which schools present unique challenges to the basic institutional or organizational assumptions of leadership in a democratic society.

Now that the leaders have been identified, this chapter will look more closely at six basic leadership questions:

1. What are the ways in which leaders mobilize people for change?
2. What are some of the various roles leaders may assume?
3. What do leaders do and how do they do it? What may be some of the impediments to this action?
4. What are the critical issues leaders confront?
5. Who is considered to be an effective leader?
6. How may effectiveness be measured?

LEADERSHIP STYLES: MOBILIZING
FOR IMPROVEMENT

The culture of any school reflects the basic beliefs and assumptions held by its educational leaders. A few years ago, I worked closely with two urban schools similar in size and demographics, separated by only a few miles. In school A the principal believed in the self-efficacy of her teachers. She trusted them to make curricular and programmatic decisions regarding students. She saw teachers, students, and parents as leaders, and she interpreted her role as one of facilitating the overall work of the school and its people. She also believed in the power of collective ownership as she reached out to local universities, foundations, and businesses for resources and other support.

The principal of school B was frequently absent and rarely attended workshops or faculty meetings. She remained in her office when at school and attempted to deal with the barrage of disgruntled teachers, disruptive students, and angry parents. She complained that she was overburdened and undersupported, and she saw the principal of school A as a competitor.

It is not difficult to imagine how the environment of each of these schools was so radically different, and how students and teachers flourished in one school but struggled in the other. Schools are communities bound together by shared beliefs and do, in fact, reflect the values consciously held and continuously reexamined by their leaders.

The following questions are provocative ones: What style of educational leadership will promote more effective relationships between teachers and students? How might perceptions of authority affect these relationships? And how might both of these factors influence instructional effectiveness and the democratic growth of the school?

Contingency Theory. Schools are often examined, both historically and analytically, as systems. We have discussed the previously common authoritarian or corporate model that current studies, for the most part, do not support. In the late 1950s researchers turned their focus to the ways in which successful leaders handled difficult situations, and to the characteristics that these leaders had in common (Adamczyk 2000). Researchers felt that if such traits could be identified they could be replicated.

However, by the 1970s, researchers no longer looked for the "best way to organize" under all circumstances, or believed that one style fits all. Instead, they argued that the internal goals, needs, and processes of the school and its members should be considered, point against point, against the external mandates, directives, and pressures the school ex-

Figure 3.1
Contingency Theory of Leadership

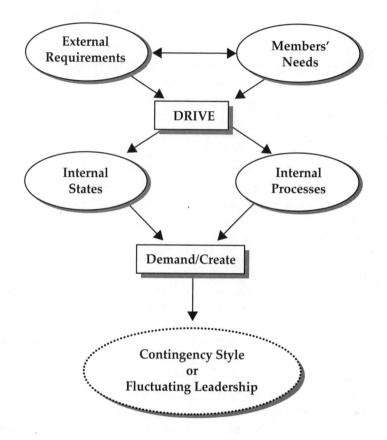

Source: Based on J. E. Roueche, *Shared Vision: Transformational Leadership in American Community Colleges* (Washington, DC: Community College Press, 1989).

perienced. In other words, as represented in Figure 3.1, the appropriate style of leadership was contingent upon the situation (Lorsch and Lawrence 1970).

Upon further examination in the 1980s and 1990s, the contingency theory was felt to be too vacillating, changing erratically from situation to situation. Although goals and even processes may be mutually agreed upon and reasonably communicated, the inconsistent nature of human beings and, even more so, of their interactions meant that the amount of daily attention given to goal accomplishment and growth practices was also inconsistent and unstable. Frequently underestimated was the plurality of interests within a given school, as the goals of the leaders or leader were the only ones addressed. With all of the variables in constant flux, the contingency theory simply added to rather than ameliorated "discontinuous disruptions" in the school's functioning. Therefore, researchers now argue for a continuum of leadership styles, with transactional and transformational leadership represented on opposite ends.

Transactional Leadership. Transactional and transformative leadership styles are frequently compared. Burns (1978) believed that control involved a reciprocal exchange between leader and follower—or, as another author put it, "increased output in return for material incentives" (Gronn 1998, 202). According to this theory, the degree to which followers are engaged is proportional to the reward they receive or the inducement they are offered (rewards and inducements being characteristic of the managerial style of supervisory leadership). In other words, the guiding question is, How can the leader get the followers to become engaged?

All members of schools share common purposes and goals, but with varying degrees of motivation and power. Transactional leadership positions leaders and followers in a distinct hierarchy. They exchange services and resources in the accomplishment of objectives. But because there is an uneven return on investment with regard to the classroom or school, a bargain is negotiated between leaders and followers (Sergiovanni 1991). This bartering system is based on the premise of positive reinforcement. An agreement is fashioned between leaders and followers over the establishment of a goal. Particular objectives will lead to goal attainment, followed by a reward for completion or a lack of reward for noncompletion (Roueche 1989). In other words, the leader offers potential rewards to followers for achievement of the school's objectives.

Leadership in the business world is frequently characterized as transactional because of the extensive use of extrinsic motivators for employees. In the educational realm, transactional leadership is successful only to the extent that all constituents agree on important tasks and goals (Mitchell and Tucker 1992).

Transactional leadership is viewed primarily as a managerial relationship between employers and employees or other constituents who work within an ambiguous, ever-changing, and highly charged decision-making atmosphere. Transactional leaders are, for the most part, managers.

Transformative/Transformational Leadership. Leadership that transforms the culture of the school through aligning the energies, talents, and work of the school with the shared goals of a cohesive team is

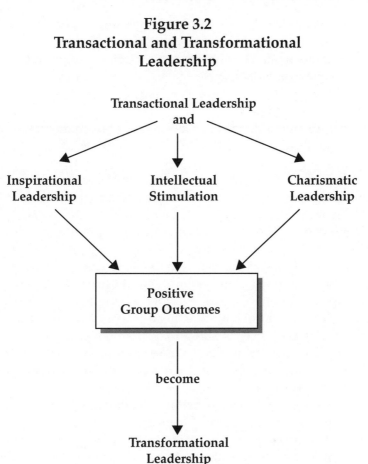

Figure 3.2
Transactional and Transformational
Leadership

called transformational. It involves a reciprocity or mutuality of support and stimulation between designated leaders and followers. As Figure 3.2 illustrates, in many respects transformational leadership is the furthest extension of the transactional leader, for to be transformational the leader must first be transactional. Stated another way, in order to be an effective leader, one must first be an effective manager.

Given the current complicated times, leaders are often called on to construct a vision of the effective school in the future. The term "transformational" first appeared in Burns's seminal study (1978) in which he speaks of the "transforming" leader. Bass (1985) then expanded the notion to apply to the nonacademic arena. Linked to previous studies of leadership charisma that still viewed a leader-follower relationship as one of leader and subordinate, transformational leadership is often expressed by the four i's:

- Inspirational leadership—augmenting constituent motivation through the leader's charisma
- Individualized consideration—tending to the needs of the followers/workers
- Intellectual stimulation—affecting subordinates' thinking and imagination
- Idealized influence—followers' belief in, emulation of, and support of the leader's vision (Gronn 1998, 201)

Leaders are said to be transformational because they incite followers to heights of performance that exceed normal expectations (Avolio and Bass 1988, 33). This type of leader recognizes the needs of the followers, seeks to address those needs, and then attempts to holistically involve the followers in his or her vision. In developing the leadership capacity of multiple stakeholders, the intended result is increased productivity (in both quality and quantity) and greater effort. In this respect, transformational leadership is not the sole province of designated leaders (principals, administrators, head teachers). Rather, the organization sanctions whoever is able to fan the fires of motivation in the stakeholder community, while at the same time demonstrating commitment to individual and group goals and vision through collective action and collective agency.

Burns identifies transformational leadership as the representation of "the transcendence of self-interest by both leader and led" (quoted in Leithwood and Jantzi 2000, 113). This style of leadership has also been described as "the ability of a person to reach the souls of others in a fashion that raises human consciousness, builds meanings and inspires human intent that is the source of power" (Dillard 1995, 560, citing Bennis 1959).

There are at least four facets of a school in which transformational leadership may be exercised and authority influenced:

- Purposes and goals—compelling stated and unstated goals of the school, agreed upon by the school's constituents and worthy of commitment, energy, and shared vision (Reynolds et al. 1996)
- School structure and social networks—nature of the relationships formed among multiple stakeholders; they enable collaboration and facilitate professional growth
- People—coalescing multiple stakeholders' perceived needs, hopes, and visions for the local school; valuing them personally and professionally

➻ Organizational culture—importance of collaboratively shaping common cultural values, norms, and meanings (Leithwood and Jantzi 2000, 114–116)

In working with more than fifty schools, Sagor (1992) discovered that teachers and students in effective schools felt their designated leader (principal) to be a successful leader due to three basic elements of transformational leadership:

➻ A clear and unified focus
➻ A common cultural perspective
➻ A constant push for improvement (13)

Often, as Sagor points out, the key to a successful school may not reside in the wealth of resources, the degree of support, or even the expectations that all constituents work toward. Rather, it may reside in the balance that is struck between supporting the initiative and those directly implementing it and aggressive guidance during the process of change. Schools that are successfully engaged in programmatic, instructional, or even systemic change initiatives all point to principals who are active listeners, visible in the classroom and throughout the school, supportive of teachers who pursue unfamiliar yet sound instructional strategies that may make them feel at risk, and open to discussion from the entire school family. These leaders are able to get constituents to participate in a common agenda; to spur people in various roles to take risks; to champion efficacy and advocacy on behalf of students, families, and the community; to prize the moral value of teaching for the sake of students; and to cause shared beliefs and hopes to be realized through collective action.

Transformational Compared to Transactional Leadership. Unlike transactional leaders and followers, transformative leaders and followers move beyond basic needs to higher-order needs and focus on intrinsic and moral motives rather than on extrinsic motivation. Transformative leaders "are more concerned about gaining overall cooperation and energetic participation from organization members than they are in getting particular tasks performed" (Mitchell and Tucker 1992, 32). Figure 3.3 compares these two leadership styles.

Transformative leadership is focused more on the energetic participation and willing cooperation of the followers than on the performance of tasks (Mitchell and Tucker 1992, 32). Therefore, positive group outcomes become a focal point. Through transformative leadership, both the leaders and followers elevate each other to higher levels of mo-

Figure 3.3
Leader-Follower Relationship

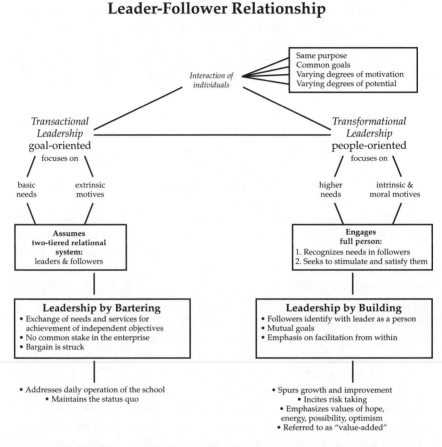

Sources: B. M. Bass, *Leadership and Performance beyond Basics* (New York: Free Press, 1985), *Handbook on Leadership* (New York: Free Press, 1990); T. Sergiovanni, *The Principalship: A Reflective Practice Perspective*, 2nd ed. (Needham Heights, MA: Allyn and Bacon, 1991); J. E. Roueche, *Shared Vision: Transformational Leadership in American Community Colleges* (Washington, DC: Community College Press, 1989).

tivation and morality (Burns 1978, 20). Sergiovanni (1995, 118) distinguishes between two stages of transformative leadership: one that is concerned with moral questions such as responsibility and righteousness (duty, obligation, the moral good, justice), and another that is concerned with the higher-order psychological needs of self-actualization, autonomy, and esteem.

According to Bennis (1989), the transformative leader is characterized by

- Vision—which is communicated to the followers and compels their needed action
- Communication and alignments—communication of the vision to the extent that it engages multiple stakeholders
- Persistence, consistency, and focus—capacity to maintain and navigate the school's focus and direction
- Empowerment—capacity to energize the followers and the holistic environment, and channel their abilities into accomplishing the vision
- Organizational learning—capacity to develop the processes, procedures, group values, and resources involved in the school's ongoing assessment of its performance as compared to its stated goals and objectives

And to create this type of learning environment through collective action, the transformative leader creates growth from within the organization through attention to completeness, workability, communicability, and simplicity. This type of growth is maximized through a sense of hope and possibility, optimism, and energy. Designated transformational leaders, whether in the classroom, school, or the greater community, model the kinds of behaviors and ideologies they value, and expect their school to emulate and initiate them (Carr 1997).

So while transactional leadership is, in essence, based on the leader's control of the "exchange of services" (such as with teachers, parents, or students) for varied rewards (e.g., recognition, salary, merit pay, release time, particular freedoms, increased access, or intrinsic rewards), transformative leadership focuses its authority on facilitation. A school that has transactional leadership has a working environment built on the economic, political, and psychological incentives offered for the completion of assigned tasks (Mitchell and Tucker 1992, 31). Simply put, the person or people who have authority over the incentives have control of the organization.

Transactional practices are, for the most part, necessary for the daily operation and business of the school (i.e., for maintaining the status quo). But they do not spur growth or improvement (Bass 1985; Sergiovanni 1990). Some would argue that transactional leadership assists people in discovering what needs to be done in order to reach designated goals, and that it may even stimulate motivation and confidence (Leithwood 1992, 9). Leaders and followers who work in a framework of transactional leadership exchange services and fulfill needs to accomplish independent objectives, for there is a dispositional and unequal relationship of power between leader and led. Consequently, bargains are often struck between them. This situation differs from transforma-tive leadership in which all stakeholders share a commitment to and ownership of higher-level goals.

For these reasons, transactional leadership is often referred to as "leadership by bartering," while transformative leadership is "leader-ship by building." Leadership by bonding represents an even higher level of transformative leadership (referred to below as facilitative lead-ership). It reaches a new summit of human behavior and ethical aspira-tion that binds both leaders and followers together.

Interestingly, transactional leadership has been referred to as "masculine leadership," for it emphasizes authority based on title, posi-tion, or office, and it uses structural power to reward people or withhold resources. Transformational leadership has been characterized as "fem-inine," for it shapes personal power based on interrelationships, charisma, and a work ethic that establishes and enables other relation-ships in the school (Wilson 1993, 25). To take the feminine concept a step further, Seney suggests that this kind of leadership will

- Reject top-down authority
- Acknowledge connectedness and responsibility
- Encourage people to work in teams and share leadership
- Advocate the development of networks and other support groups
- Value and develop intuitive thinking
- Recognize the importance of authentic conversation. (Seney 2000, 3)

It is transformational leadership that encourages the type of risk taking necessary for growth, improvement, and change. For this reason, transformational leadership is often referred to as "value added" (Avolio and Bass 1988). Also, because the total school environment is viewed as a culture, it brings with it a richness of understanding, a depth of exami-nation, and a sense of behavior that sustains particular values, traditions, and norms (rather than behavior that responds to given mandates). It of-fers the opportunities for leadership and action discussed in chapter 1.

A school with a healthy culture is described as one

- Where staff share a sense of purpose and have an un-bounded sense of commitment and an unlimited work ethic
- Where basic assumptions are collegiality, improvement, and hard work
- Where cultural traditions celebrate student accomplish-

ment, teacher risk taking and creativity, and active family
engagement
- Where the informal network of role models shapes a social
web of information and support
- Where health, happiness, humor, and success are the norm
(Peterson and Deal 1998, 29)

This culture is one of mutuality, shared concern, and care for the
educational success and the socioemotional well-being of all of the
school's students, staff, and constituents. The creation and maintenance of this type of culture is best developed through transformational
leadership, for it does not seek "power over," but "power with." It emphasizes ownership and the enthusiastic participation of all constituents rather than compliance and task completion. It is the shared
power spoken of in chapter 1.

In this cultural context, students are leaders as they challenge
themselves, each other, and their teachers. Parents are leaders as they
share in the school's governance, become directly involved in the work
of the classroom, and buttress the overall beliefs and values held by the
school. Teachers are leaders as they persistently model and speak to the
norms and traditions of the school. Principals are leaders as they communicate the mores of the school to the larger community. And outside
stakeholders are leaders as they share their own commitments and resources and participate in the life of the school in consonance with the
school's cultural ideologies.

More specifically, these different leaders help create the school's
culture by

- Communicating core values
- Honoring and acknowledging the purpose, work, and workers of the school
- Observing and supporting the school's fundamental
values
- Articulating the message and mission of the school to other
constituents
- Celebrating the accomplishments of students, staff, administration, and other stakeholders
- Protecting the school's focus on students, their success, and
their learning (Peterson and Deal 1998, 30)

This is a type of power that does not manipulate or prod, but that
enables others to empower themselves. "If leaders are working in cul-

tural settings where goals are unclear or organizational members do not agree about them, effective leadership (transformational leadership) requires an approach that transforms the feelings, attitudes, and beliefs of their followers" (Mitchell and Tucker 1992, 32).

Transformational leadership is centered around people, for it is as much about the edification of the individual and the group, and belief and trust in people, as it is about growth and achievement. Transactional leadership, on the other hand, is focused on task completion and leveraging enticements to spur accomplishment.

To compare and contrast these two leadership styles, Mitchell and Tucker (1992) examined the superintendency (see Table 3.1).

There are four elements that shape authority and school control: supervision, administration, management, and leadership. In the respective cultures created by each style, these constructs look a bit different. In schools that are stable and consistent in the support they receive (they are often but not always located in middle- and upper-class neighborhoods) and in the environment that is created, supervision and administration prevail. Mitchell and Tucker (1992) succinctly compared these four elements as follows:

Supervision. In such schools, teachers who think about the relationships they establish with students and parents in transactional or reward-based ways tend to place more importance on supervision when considering their own role in the school. Supervisors and principals who hold authority tend to assess any problems in the school in terms of people's inability or unwillingness to support the school's goals. Further, they believe that if a school is not effective, it is because teachers are not following sound, standardized instructional practices. This thinking is also characterized by basic assumptions that

- Teachers are laborers.
- Curriculum directors are experts in task identification.
- Principals are managers and overseers of plan execution.
- Students should achieve mastery levels on course content.
- Supervisors believe in an instrumentalist approach to school effectiveness, including
    - more rigorous mandates;
    - a longer school day and school year;
    - the importance of outside mandates (reflected in "Goals 2000," Carnegie reports, and *A Nation at Risk,* as examined in chapter 1);
    - an emphasis on teachers working harder.

Table 3.1

Transactional versus Transformational Leadership
in the Superintendency

Transactional Leadership	Transformational Leadership
Seeks indirect control through attention to structure	Controls through attention to staff skills and beliefs
Instrumentalist concentration on	Cultural concentration on
2 Defining job functions	2 Creating and sustaining norms
2 Developing district policies	2 Clarifying value assumptions
2 Stabilizing district programs	
2 Standardizing district practices	
School improvement follows organizational and operational improvement	School improvement follows mutually recognized and agreed upon professional best practice, its goals, and the ways they are to be achieved
Emphasis on hierarchical relationships	Emphasis on mutuality and facilitation

Source: Adapted from D. E. Mitchell and S. Tucker, "Leadership as a Way of Thinking,"
Educational Leadership 49, no. 5 (February 1992): 31.

Administration. Teachers who believe that school effectiveness lies not in programmatic implementation but in attitudinal relationships with students tend to reflect the administrative view of school operation. Further, they believe that

2 Their control over and access to incentives is meager.
2 School goals are understood and supported by the entire constituency.
2 Supervisors should give more autonomy to teachers.
2 Improvement comes with professional teacher expertise in assessing the learning profiles of students, their strengths and weaknesses, and their modes of thinking and processing.
2 Teaching and learning are personal and individual enterprises—incentives and mandates are interruptive and extraneous.
2 Curriculum experts support teacher expertise and mediate students' learning difficulties.
2 Administrators coordinate and support the work of the staff.
2 Transformational relationships are expressed by the emphasis placed on staff development, power of communication, and daily interactions.

However, in unstable schools (often but not always located in lower socioeconomic rural and inner-city neighborhoods) that do not enjoy ongoing support, equitable resources, or public confidence, aggressive leadership and management are more dominant. When members of the school and the extended school family lack motivation and investment, emphasis is placed on leadership and administration. These functions help shape common goals, structure incentives, and provide opportunities for the construction of transforming relationships that reshape the work and activity of the school.

Management. In ineffective schools that lack community support, often the notion of change becomes more important than running and assessing already established programs. Characteristics of this type of school are:

- Managers rely on transactional relationships.
- Teacher effectiveness is a direct result of craft skill.
- Task definition takes precedence over interrelationships.
- Effective programs are research-based and instrumentalist (carefully planned).
- There is an emphasis on teachers working smarter—stress on ongoing school and classroom assessment, staff development, and staff performance assessment.

Leadership. Focus is placed on leadership in relatively unsupported schools that believe that effective performance is a product of transforming the beliefs, attitudes, and possibilities of students, parents, and teachers. In addition, leaders believe that

- Organizational support depends on changes in attitude and performance.
- The knowledge base and incentive system are not fully developed or understood by constituents.
- Transformational processes place emphasis on reconceptualizing and recommitting constituents to organizational goals rather than on preexisting programs.
- Effective teachers are creative artists rather than skilled craftspeople.
- Teachers are experts.
- Teacher expertise is valuable only to the extent that it is integrated into a holistic school plan of identified goals, objectives, and collective action.
- School improvement must reflect the needs, values, and be-

liefs of students, parents, members of the community, and teachers.

•➤ School effectiveness is a product of commitment rather than competence (transformational).

•➤ School improvement will result from teacher competence that is directed at new program goals. (Mitchell and Tucker 1992, 33–35)

Charismatic behavior is one of the most significant characteristics of a transformational leader. At all levels, within and outside the school, followers of charismatic leaders describe their leaders as someone who inspires and motivates others in the organization, evokes loyalty in the membership, commands respect, and has a vision for the mission of the school that exceeds expectations but not reach. The environment that these leaders create is one of modeled success, enthusiasm, energy, and possibility, all driven by moral imperatives.

Different leadership styles challenge schools to change basic assumptions and beliefs; adopt new program goals and objectives; improve teachers' craft skills; embrace teachers' expertise; value interrelationships; and work smarter, harder, and longer. Individual schools must assess their own cultural and professional beliefs and values and find their own variations of each style. For it is undoubtedly the combination of heroic or charismatic leadership, supportive administration, dynamic management, and delineated supervision that will bring a school the kind of reform or change that will nurture the development of moral, responsible, and educated citizens.

Summary. It is unsound to attempt to identify one particular leadership style with characteristics that will inspire more minority or family participation in the school, or increased involvement from the extended school family. And one model or even set of models will not prove effective or practical in all situations.

Nevertheless, it is valuable to be aware of the leadership style or styles used in a school district or a particular school, because it informs stakeholders of points of access, ways of understanding conflicting agendas, how influence is leveraged, what is valued, and methods of accomplishing given goals and objectives. Moreover, understanding leadership styles allows one to construct a framework through which a school may be assessed, improved, or even systemically changed. In many ways, understanding leadership styles provides a kind of blueprint or even a genetic webbing that yields worthwhile information about the business, interpersonal makeup, and authority of a given school and of its stakeholders, information invaluable to the designated leaders as well.

By examining leadership styles, we can get an initial contextual or layered look at the culture of the school. This is important because it is the organizational culture and commonly held values that are critical to school reform or change. In other words, looking at the school's culture allows leaders and constituent members to gain varied levels of thoughtful admittance to and an introductory understanding of the complex interworkings of the local school.

And more basically, examining leadership styles provides the initial tools to begin to grapple with the questions of why one school is successful and another is not; why one school may openly embrace multiple stakeholders and another may remain a seemingly closed system; why one school's environment may feel communal and another's competitive; and why one school may enjoy continuing health and growth and another may remain stagnant and ineffective.

ROLES LEADERS ASSUME

Because potential leaders in schools come from a rich and varied field of multiple stakeholders, there are many contrasting metaphors that attempt to portray the roles and attitudes that leaders may assume. Leadership has been described in terms of a set of "role behaviors performed by individuals in the context of a group" (Seyfarth 1999, 76). These roles often include leaders as manager, decision maker, problem solver, instructional leader, change agent, steward, cultural and organizational leader, moral and ethical leader, democratic leader, and facilitator. And although much of the literature and research looks only at the principal or other designated leaders in the school, the following notions are also applicable to the community of leaders particular to shared governance or New Era leadership.

TECHNICAL LEADERSHIP

Leader as Manager

Essentially, educational management is about getting things done. Typically principals have been held responsible for the management of resources such as money, facilities, equipment, people, and time, and for the programmatic order and operation of the school. However, with dispersed leadership, many of these responsibilities are shared. Nonetheless, it remains management of limited resources in an arena of ambiguous and constantly changing information, constituencies, and expectations.

Management style. Management by results rather than by supervision represents another shift in how school leaders work and are viewed and assessed (Schlecthty 1990). Students' results on applied test measures help shape the instructional objectives of the staff. The leader as manager responds with a structure and programmatic design that will increase both quality and equity of student performance.

Those who support this type of management and leadership style advocate that schools place emphasis on the technical aspects or strengths of the school that impel student success and remediate areas of school design or instructional implementation that serve as impediments to this same success. This view maintains that the school should not see itself as a social service institution, providing a variety of services to students and families, but should focus on successfully educating all students (Seyfarth 1999).

According to some, the leaders-as-managers concept reduces leadership to a checklist of operational school functions that, if in place, will bring academic success to students. They argue that leadership is much more than a modified list of things to do or ways to do them, and cannot be so simply analyzed and "fixed." In the leaders-as-managers concept, leadership becomes a part of management.

Although there has been much discussion about the differences between these two concepts, Kotter (1988) offers a fairly straightforward distinction in that he sees strategic development as the focal point of leadership for change, and daily problem solving as the pivotal point in management. And Michael Fullan (1991), an expert in change theory in schools, sees leadership as the discussion of mission, direction, and inspiration, whereas management "involves designing and carrying out plans, getting things done, working effectively with people" (158). Law and Glover (2000, 14) offer a thoughtful comparison between leadership and management, summarized in Table 3.2.

Whatever the distinctions between these two concepts, and whatever the overlapping understandings and attitudes, the skills necessary for an effective leader in contemporary schools are predicated upon the leader being first an effective manager.

Effective Management Profile. While there is no one list of characteristics or qualities in a leader that will ensure effectiveness, a large-scale study found the following characteristics to be held by leaders at all levels in decentralized school districts, not only in the United States but in Norway, England, and Sweden (Slenning 2000). According to this study, these are the necessary attitudes and skills for New Era management leadership.

Table 3.2
Leadership and Management Differences

Management	Leadership
"Building and maintaining an organizational structure" (Schein 1985)	"Building and maintaining an organizational culture" (Schein 1985)
"Path-following" (Hodgson 1987)	"Path-finding" (Hodgson 1987)
"Doing things right" (Bennis and Nanus 1985)	"Doing the right thing" (Bennis and Nanus 1985)
"The manager maintains [and] relies on control" (Bennis 1989)	"The leader develops [and] inspires trust" (Bennis 1989)
"A preoccupation with the here-and-now of goal attainment" (Bryman 1986)	"Focused on the creation of a vision about a desired future state" (Bryman 1986)
"Managers maintain a low level of emotional involvement" (Zaleznik 1977)	"Leaders have empathy with other people and give attention to what events and actions mean" (Zaleznik 1977)
"Designing and carrying out plans, getting things done, working effectively with people" (Louis and Miles 1992)	"Establishing a mission [and] giving a sense of direction" (Louis and Miles 1992)
"Being taught by the organization" (Hodgson 1987)	"Learning from the organization" (Hodgson 1987)

Sources: W. Bennis, *On Becoming a Leader* (London: Hutchinson, 1989); W. Bennis and V. Nanus, *Leaders* (New York: Harper and Row, 1985); A. Bryman, *Leadership and Organizations* (London: Routledge and Kegan Paul, 1986); P. Hodgson, "Managers Can Be Taught, But Leaders Have to Learn," *ICT*, November/December 1987; K. S. Louis and M. B. Miles, *Improving the Urban High School: What Works and Why* (London: Cassell, 1992); E. H. Schein, *Organizational Culture and Leadership* (San Francisco: Jossey-Bass, 1985); A. Zaleznik, "Managers and Leaders: Are They Different?" *Harvard Business Review*, May/June 1977: 67–78.

Leadership Characteristics:

2 People-centered, with a focus on understanding human behavior
2 Self-confident and secure with no personal agenda
2 Identified as a colleague but also has earned the title of leader
2 Goal-oriented, self-motivated, creative
2 Able to make quick yet thoughtful decisions in a quickly changing and ambiguous environment

Interpersonal Characteristics:

- ◆ Motivates and focuses individuals and groups both within and outside of school
- ◆ Deals effectively with conflict, ambiguity, criticism, frustration, and disappointment
- ◆ Helps focus multiple stakeholders and their perspectives on a strategic plan

Educational Characteristics:

- ◆ Exercises pedagogic insight, although does not have to be a teacher
- ◆ Demonstrates a keen interest in both the larger culture of society and the culture of the school, through interpersonal relationships and theoretical insights
- ◆ Has a broad knowledge of management skills in both the educational and corporate arenas

Advocacy Characteristics:

- ◆ Communicates and promotes the work of the school to outside stakeholders and to the school family
- ◆ Creates a shared sense of purpose and the values, vision, mission, and goals of the school
- ◆ Assumes responsibility when appropriate, and incites others to maximum commitment and performance
- ◆ Translates mandates and directives into the school's goals
- ◆ Facilitates compromise between conflicting agendas, stakeholders, agencies, unions, and personnel

Systems Characteristics:

- ◆ Demonstrates a balance between attention to detail and sensible attention to administrative and economic issues
- ◆ Continues to stay current with new technology and its effective implementation at the building level
- ◆ Responds to both perceived and stated staff development needs
- ◆ Utilizes best-practice techniques of quality control
- ◆ Shares economic controller responsibilities (staff management and facilitation, financial control, evaluation of data)

•• Remains open to and initiates change

In a general account of effective leader-managers, Brighouse (1986) suggested there were three basic groups:

•• *Perceptive professional developers* who enabled their staff to engage collegially in planning and implementation
•• *System maintainers* who approached management in a more mechanistic and inflexible way
•• *Inadequate, security-conscious* others whose inconsistent approaches to management reflected their willingness to bend to the predominant pressures of the moment

Other researchers have looked at the ways in which leaders approach their roles, and at their responsibilities and the characteristics that result from their different perspectives. Likert (1967) examined dispersed-power management and posed four possible leadership approaches:

•• *Exploitative and authoritarian*—contributing to postincorporation staffing problems in higher education institutions
•• *Benevolent and authoritarian*—often seen in independent schools and historic grammar schools
•• *Consultative*—characteristic in high schools with subject-area, departmental emphasis that value both individual and group positions
•• *Participative*—the traditional focus of elementary schools that emphasize the group (Law and Glover 2000, 22)

Typical responses to these approaches do not support one style or the other, but often reflect a combination of them along with the leader's own personal attitude. Also, the contingency theory of leadership supports those leader-managers who maintain that the appropriate management style varies in accord with the situation.

Feminine Management. Caldwell and Spinks (1992) suggest that women who are more people-centered and tend to work toward consensual ends tend to be more effective educational managers. On the other hand, Hall's research (1996) found female teachers to be more resistant to managerial positions because they tend to exhibit a deeper concern for the school as an institution, and for learners and their development (Law and Glover, 31).

What is most significant in the discussion of leader-manager styles is not the adoption of a particular approach, but rather the recognition of which framework is being employed as it either impedes or supports change and growth in the school. Further, of greater importance than the style or styles at work is the use of management strategies that address and affect people, systems, resources, and outcomes.

Tasks of Leader-Managers

Given these characteristics, styles, and approaches, we could then ask one of the chapter's formative questions: What do these leader-managers do? We have indicated that they must first accomplish the identified goals and then manage the overall functioning of the institution. Law and Glover (2000) add that managers

- *Plan.* They develop policy through problem analysis, goal setting, and decision making.
- *Organize.* They select activities and get respective personnel to meet objectives.
- *Coordinate.* They motivate staff to reach goals and objectives.
- *Control.* They measure performance standards against strategic plans.
- *Maximize.* They maximize individual performance for collective success.

Managing the Budget. Leader-managers, most often principals, are held directly responsible for the management of the school's finances. There are two commonly used budgeting processes: incremental budgeting and zero-based budgeting. Incremental budgeting retains the bulk of a school's budget from year to year while adding or subtracting funds from various accounts, given fluctuations in enrollment or inflation. Although this is the most frequently utilized process, zero-based budgeting is used in some settings. In this process, each program is carefully examined and a decision is then made to continue the program, expand it, or terminate it.

In incremental budgeting, formulas that consider the number and diversity of students attending the school are used to allocate funds and human resources, such as the number of faculty and support staff (guidance counselors, custodians, nursing and clerical staff, and paraprofessionals), at each school. The school faculty and staff then submit budget requests and set priorities for funding, including for

- The purchase of computers and software, art supplies, and musical equipment

- Professional development, which will include both training and instructional materials used in staff development (workshops, seminars) to train teachers
- Performance area renovations (theater lighting and sound equipment, curtains for a stage, new auditorium seating), auditoriums, stages, and performance areas
- New equipment such as cameras, videotape machines, and televisions
- The purchase of classroom instructional materials such as science laboratory supplies, math calculators, and the Accelerated Math computer program; literature and reading materials such as the Accelerated Reader, multicultural books, and reading programs like Michigan's Real Reading in the Middle
- Building new playground equipment or renovating the building
- Support of after-school or Saturday programs for students and families

New Era decentralized control of the school, or school-based decision making, requires school personnel to share in the management of these fiscal issues. This requires training in interpreting budget accounts, preparing budget proposals, fairly and collaboratively submitting budget estimates, and implementing and monitoring the allocated funds. Yet while these tasks of shared management are indeed substantive, Wohlstetter and van Kirk (1995) suggest that for shared governance to be most effective, school leader-managers must be granted more autonomy and authority to

- Shift school personnel—vary the number of full- and part-time faculty, support staff, and paraprofessionals—depending on shared priorities.
- Control funding for substitute teachers and utilities, and move these funds to other accounts.
- Control the purchasing of materials, supplies, and equipment. Rather than having all accounts circulated through the district office, individual schools could purchase directly from the lowest bidder.
- Carry over unused expenditures from one fiscal year to another. It is characteristic for a school's unspent funds to be returned to the district, which penalizes a school that has carefully monitored its resources (Seyfarth 1999, 325).

Managing Time. Effective time management offers students and faculty the flexibility to teach and learn in an environment free of the artificial restrictions of course divisions, classes, and fifty-minute time slots. When class schedules are constructed, the developmental needs of students and the rigorous activities of each class must be the prime concerns. In middle schools across the country, interdisciplinary teams of teachers who share the same group of students plan the day-to-day, nonbell schedule using flexible 90-minute to 120-minute blocks of time. The team determines how each chunk of time is to be used and by whom, given the projects, activities, or learning experiences in which the students will be engaged. For instance, on Monday the science teacher may ask for the entire 90-minute chunk to prepare science fair experiments. The 120-minute chunk may be divided equally by the language arts and social studies teachers who are team teaching a unit on the Holocaust. The students participate in encore classes or electives and in core explore class, which offers the students remediation, exploration, and acceleration during the remainder of the day.

On Tuesday the 90-minute chunk may be broken up, with the science teacher using the first 30 minutes to complete the previous day's work, and the math teacher using the remaining 60 minutes. The 120-minute chunk may be again combined or divided by the language arts and social studies teachers. On Wednesday the math teacher may be engaged in a unit on angles and may have the students outside measuring shadows, the football field, the school building, and playground equipment. The math teacher may therefore need the 120-minute chunk. And on other occasions students may be preparing for an all-school play, a musical performance, or a community art exhibit. In all of these instances, the decisions about the management of time are collaboratively made by the teaching team as they respond to the needs of the students.

Some high schools have moved to a block schedule that approximates the chunk schedule above by manipulating the use of time on alternating days. Elementary teachers who are the primary teacher for a given class exercise great freedom of time management, and they enjoy the flexibility of teaching subjects and topics as they fit the flow of the class.

Adair (1983) synthesizes the list of effective leader-manager characteristics and points out that managers should

- Set direction and move the organization forward through a clarified and shared strategic plan
- Inspire constituents by offering new ideas, articulating shared beliefs, and energizing all stakeholders

- Build and support collaborative teams as the natural implementation of management techniques
- Model expected behavior, work ethic, and attitude
- Win constituent participation and loyalty

Theories of educational or educative management (Duignan and MacPherson 1992) hold that in the accomplishment of these tasks, effective leaders communicate enthusiasm, creativity, and vigor, rather than merely managing an operation efficiently (Bell and Harrison 1995). It is a kind of manager-leadership that supports others who are collaboratively and actively engaged in the work of the school. It is a kind of manager-leadership that blends "school leadership as manifest moral energy, and school management as social control" (Grace 1995, 30). It is a kind of manager-leadership that facilitates, listens, communicates, organizes, and collectively accomplishes tasks.

It is a management of systems as well as a management of people. The challenge is complex, for both types of management tend to demonstrate qualities of predictability and unpredictability, stability and flux, all within a creatively changing yet ambiguous and volatile environment. And the management of both systems and people requires a flexible, free, thoughtful, yet spontaneous person on the one hand, and a person who follows given role expectations on the other.

Bell and Harrison (1995, 136) support this perspective of leaders as managers who perform multiple tasks. They contend that these leaders manage

- Policy—in developing and presenting the school's aims and goals and in supporting and nurturing a collegial environment
- Learning—in assessing, designing, and implementing effective student learning
- Resources—in securing resources and monitoring and controlling their use
- People—in hiring staff, developing individual and team talents, and fostering positive and productive relationships among all stakeholders

Interestingly, Law and Glover (2000) maintain that the style of leadership and its attendant tasks are dependent on the competence and commitment of the followers. Table 3.3 shows their cause-and-effect approach to the contingency theory.

Transactional leadership, often characterized as getting things

Table 3.3

Follower Attitudes and Skills and Leadership Approaches

Follower Demonstrates	Resulting Leadership Style and Tasks
Low competence	Directing
High commitment	Structure, control, supervise
Some competence	Coaching
Low commitment	Direct, support
High competence	Supporting
Variable commitment	Praise, listen, facilitate
High competence	Delegating
High commitment	Give responsibility for daily decision making

Source: S. Law and D. Glover, *Educational Leadership and Learning* (Philadelphia: Open University Press, 2000), 24.

done, and transformational leadership, or inspiring others to work, are both reflected in management leadership. While transactional focuses on the management of structure, organization, and task completion, transformational engages the followers in direct relationship to meeting their basic professional needs.

However, although they are spoken of as distinct styles, the reality of the classroom shows that management leadership uses a combination of these styles to deal with the tasks at hand. Blake and Mouton (1978) examined their mutual influence in the classroom and suggested four management positions:

- 2 *Impoverished management*—little concern for tasks and people
- 2 *Authority-compliance management*—high concern for tasks, low concern for people
- 2 *Middle-of-the-road management*—concern for both tasks and people is moderate
- 2 *"Country club" management*—low task concern, high people concern
- 2 *Team management*—high concern for both outcomes and people (Law and Glover 2000, 28)

Although their approach to management is somewhat dated, it is a more holistic or team approach to school operation and change than simply asking a leader to choose between one style or another.

Managing Assessment. Management leadership has also been

characterized as professionalized when designated leaders (e.g., principals, lead teachers) recognize the expertise of followers (e.g., teachers,
students, parents) and both expect and enable them to make important
decisions about the school's teaching and learning when those decisions are based on students' needs, expertise, and learning outcomes
(Guthrie 1990). Managers are responsible for assessing the success and
effectiveness of faculty and staff as they make these sorts of decisions. In
order for evaluations to be occasions for learning and growth, as well as
authentic reflections of an individual's contributions to realizing the
goals of the classroom and the school, a recent study suggested, the assessment mechanisms should

- Be outcome oriented and performance-based
- Reflect the school's mission, aims, and values
- Occur systematically in a clear and mutually agreed upon
  fashion
- Mirror agreed upon standards of excellence and quality
- Be measurable, observable, achievable, and time related
- Lead to staff development that is rigorously tied to the
  school's goals and student learning
- Lead to high teaching and learning standards (Law and
  Glover 2000, 199)

As discussed in chapter 1, although there are similarities between
the business and educational worlds, industrial management is ineffective in schools for a variety of reasons. While business managers are held
accountable only to their superiors, designated school leaders are accountable to a variety of stakeholders from whom they must seek involvement, support, and investment (Seyfarth 1999). Moreover, industrial managers' tasks are oriented around tangible results, while school
leader-managers are engaged in the intangibles of cognitive growth, affective development, moral responsibility, and development of democratic participation.

With this distinction in mind, and acknowledging the complex
interrelationship between manager-leaders and followers, Tannenbaum
and Schmidt (1973) suggested a continuum of leadership styles (Figure
3.4), which, moving from left to right, range from group-centered leadership to manager-centered leadership. The manager's roles varied in
accord with the manager's use of authority and the freedom exercised by
the followers.

There are some managerial decisions that are solely the province
of the principal or designated school leader. There are others that need

Figure 3.4
Continuum of Manager-Leadership Relationship

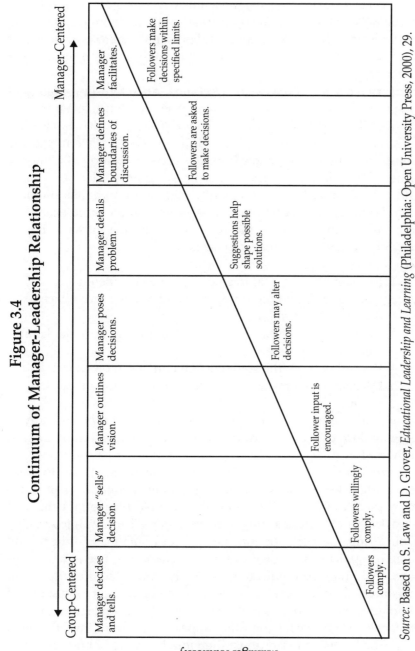

Source: Based on S. Law and D. Glover, *Educational Leadership and Learning* (Philadelphia: Open University Press, 2000), 29.

to be made by the entire team, staff, or stakeholder group in order to maximize success. However, the most effective managers are those who combine collegial follower freedom (that is, the freedom of those who follow to exercise their professional and personal expertise in ways that support each other and the institution or school) with appropriate levels of managerial authority.

Taxonomy of Management Decisions. An interesting argument has been made for a taxonomy of managerial decisions, given the decentralized decision making and shared governance of New Era leadership. Strain et al. (1998) contend that if the improved student learning outcomes that are said to follow from the decentralization of authority become a reality, it will be because shared governance is less a managerial ploy than an authentic means of enabling autonomous problem solving. Strain et al. suggest that management style can be examined apart from who, in fact, makes the decisions. They offer the following hierarchy or taxonomy of managerial decisions:

1. Decisions about what business is to be considered
2. Decisions about how to organize and operate the service delivery of the school
3. Decisions about the types of labor to use and how that labor will be compensated
4. Decisions about the students and families to be served
5. Decisions about what categories of funding to pursue (151)

It is apparent that managerial decisions are complex and overlapping, and that they are most effective when made autonomously at the school site.

Managing People. Yet the above taxonomy misses the most basic and important level of management—the management of people, including oneself and others. We have maintained throughout this text that teaching and leading are about relationships. Through encouraging and nurturing the participation, talents, and abilities of others, and through recognizing one's own strengths, weaknesses, needs, and motivations, the school continues to grow. Such growth requires the use of management skills for developing positive interactions among staff and stakeholders. It also requires identifying, examining, and strengthening those facets of the organization that appear resistant or impervious to change. The leader-manager must therefore be aware of both the environmental forces (the school culture and environment) and the individual dynamics (personality, skills, ethics, attitudes) that are at play. The motivation of students, faculty, staff, and stakeholders in general and of

Table 3.4

People Management Comparison

	Systems-Led	Human Relations–Led
Organization	Market-driven	People-led and values-driven
In-service	Training for select staff	Training for all staff
Assessment	Control, performance review	Professional development
Staff	Human resources: means to an end	Resourceful humans: ends in themselves
Hiring	People to fit organization	People to develop organization
Organizational focus	Technically driven— strategic plan and common goals	Emphasis on excellence of diverse goals
Ethos	Compliance and control	Collegial consensus and common commitment
Compelling ethic	Cost-effectiveness	Effective learning

Source: Adapted from S. Law and D. Glover, *Educational Leadership and Learning* (Philadelphia: Open University Press, 2000), 190.

teachers in particular is fundamental to student growth and improved student outcomes.

Law and Glover (2000) offer a thoughtful comparison between two approaches to people management, summarized in Table 3.4.

One of the challenges the leader-manager confronts is the motivation of followers. Those managers who are charged with motivating teachers recognize that teachers may be compelled to act because of

2 Students' needs for growth and learning
2 Passion for the subject area
2 The opportunity to contribute to a larger enterprise
2 The belief that they can "make a difference" in students' lives
2 The inspiration of others
2 Interest and encouragement, with minimal opportunity or desire for praise or recognition (adapted from Dean 1995)

On the other hand, teachers may well become resistant and unwilling to participate in change when, according to Day, Johnston, and Whitaker (1990), they

2 Are told they "have to"

- Are put in a vulnerable position
- Sense activities and required tasks are not thoughtful, planned, or educationally sound
- Feel manipulated to achieve the leader-manager's self-serving ends
- Anticipate the amount of work required will be largely disproportional to any improvement in student outcomes
- Perceive themselves as being "out of the loop" or outside the group that has responsibility for the required task
- View the leader-manager as the "expert," and their own expertise and craft knowledge is ignored
- Experience pressure or support from colleagues to withdraw participation (adapted from Law and Glover 2000)

Herzberg (1979) suggested the following practices, which are frequently used in human resource management in education:

- Increase accountability—designated lower-level managers such as department chairs, team leaders, or curriculum coordinators should submit reports
- Remove controls—allow designated leaders to plan without excessive paperwork
- Create and support site-appropriate teams and leaders
- Provide immediate feedback
- Introduce new opportunities and tasks to engage potential leaders

Managing Curricular Decisions. Manager-leaders must function in the overlapping arenas of staying up-to-date on the most effective best practice, matching that practice with the culture of the school, assessing its implementation as well as the implements, and engaging multiple stakeholders at various stages in the process. The priorities that instructional strategies and learning methodologies are given reflect the values, morals, and shared beliefs of the school culture. The manager's responsibility in coordinating and focusing the school's teaching and learning on these curricular choices is no small task.

Thrown into that mix is the leader-manager's attention to available resources, appropriate staff assignments, school classroom availability, budgetary considerations, required state and local curricular standards and benchmarks, and the internal politics of teams or departments. Because of the complexity of these issues, managing the curriculum is often less comprehensive and coherent than might be hoped.

Therefore, changes and growth take place in fits and starts rather than in a sustained manner. Likewise, the leader's ability to "manage" the school's teaching and learning is less coordinated than might be desired, and its impact is less profound than the individual teacher's relationship with the students in the classroom.

Managing Interrelationships. Leader-managers effectively marry the need for cooperation with the exercise of control. Students who sense a more caring and cooperative interpersonal school atmosphere tend to feel a greater kinship with the school and individual teachers, and frequently experience more success at school. Yet while some schools lean more heavily toward control and others toward cooperation, orderliness and engagement must both be present in schools if authentic learning is to take place.

As leader-managers attempt to effectively manage the behavior and conduct of students, they engage the family in many of the ways previously discussed. However, they do not, for the most part, facilitate their direct involvement and active participation as shared governance partners. Rather, they value the family's support of the school's work with their children and trust that the family will encourage the kind of student behavior and attitude that will lead to positive educational outcomes. Managers tend to hold cooperative relationships in higher regard than collaborative ones.

Managing Conduct and Behavior. It is not surprising that the prevailing concern of families who send their children to the nation's public schools is that the school be safe. Five years ago, families expressed concern over the lack of discipline in schools and the prevalence of drugs and gangs. In today's world of shootings and bomb threats in schools, leader-managers must not only create a sense of safety for students and families, they must assure that schools will be a safe haven in a world that is anything but.

Schoolwide and districtwide discipline plans, management plans, codes of conduct, and student responsibility training tend to be more successful when they are forged and implemented jointly. When a variety of leaders in and outside the classroom express shared goals, hopes, and intentions, as well as shared fears, frustrations, and anxieties, the school culture belongs to everyone, its safety collaboratively constructed.

However, just as the dynamic for change is most dramatically resonant with the relationship between the student and the teacher within the classroom, so too is the ultimate success of the management of student conduct. Teachers must build their relationships with students upon the belief that their sense of what students can accomplish while in school is more positively persuasive or influential and has a greater impact on students' lives than does the environment beyond the school. This belief calls some school personnel's belief systems into question, for they can no longer blame the social ills of the neighborhood, the lack of family support, or the vagaries of fate for the lack of student success. Rather, teachers must sincerely believe that they have the power to "make a difference" in the lives of all of their students, and then must maximize the time they have with them.

In addition to supporting and nurturing this habit of mind in the teaching faculty, leader-managers must have plans in place that can effectively be put into action in times of crisis. No matter how small or large a school is, or whether it's urban, suburban, or rural, the threats of teen suicide, violence, confrontations, abuse, racial or class tensions, and the loss of family or friends loom large in the lives of students. Schoolwide crisis management plans that can be initiated quickly and efficiently proactively prepare the entire school family for critical times of conflict and tragedy. The technical manager-leader is charged with establishing and maintaining a community that is orderly and stable, and in times of severe strife this duty is particularly conspicuous.

Leader-Manager Impediments. Leader-managers value people, diversity, and effective learning. Yet because individual professional development is largely influenced by the quality and depth of ongoing self-reflective practice, which leads to changes in behavior, managers, by virtue of their role and function, often experience paralyzing predicaments born of conflicting realities. Even when presented with evidence to the contrary, leader-managers rigidly adhere to their sense of "self" and situation. Bell and Harrison (1995) point out that leaders who are managers

> may depend for their confidence on the belief that they are functioning well. There is some possibility that managers have the greatest difficulty in learning and in developing through learning, for this reason. Any recognition that their competence is less than adequate leads to the dilemma of a mismatch between the "ideal" and "real." The "self" has means of guarding our theories-in-use from such threats. (131)

And in order to guard these theories, managers frequently ignore areas of weakness, suppress information that would suggest ineffectiveness due to micromanagement, and aggressively remove elements that would threaten performance. They also frequently act in ways that are self-fulfilling prophecies, and when challenged to make substantive changes they instead address only peripheral issues (Bell and Harrison 1995).

Learning for managers then becomes a perilous business, one fraught with stress and potential conflict with followers who desire to continue to grow and change. They fear that the system and the organization will fail, and even more are beset with the disquieting suspicion that engaging in new activities will mean a loss of power because their personal skills may no longer be needed.

Leader as Problem Solver

Another role of a technical leader that brings management skills and human relationship skills together is the educational leader as a problem solver. Wagner (1993) cites research by Kepner and Tregoe (1965) that is considered to be seminal in the rational management approach to problem solving. Kepner and Tregoe identified five principles of problem solving:

- Problems based in the discrepancy between the actual performance and the expected performance are identified.
- Problems based in the deviation from expected standards are defined—e.g., a school increasingly scored above grade level on state proficiency tests for three consecutive years and fell below grade level during the fourth year.
- Clarity in description of the problem must occur before solutions can be posed—i.e., what is happening, where does it occur, and to what extent?
- Potential cause of the problem may be found by comparing situations in which the problem does and does not occur.
- Problems that result from some unwanted change are identified. (Wagner 1993, 90–91)

Although this scientific managerial approach to problem solving is potentially a clean process, rarely does the human being follow such tidy and rational patterns. Rather, manager problem solvers are naturally influenced by their own professional and personal values, beliefs, and prior experiences, which affect both judgment and reasoning. This interplay is seen in what some researchers hold are biases that affect the gathering and processing of information and the posing of solutions.

On the other hand, Leithwood and Stager (1986) found that many highly effective designated leaders used a collaborative and reflective style of problem solving. Characteristically they used a structured problem-solving model that extended beyond simple group engagement. Rather, use of the model enabled problem solving by multiple stakeholders to emerge, leading to wiser solutions than one designated leader would be able to suggest and manage.

Leithwood and Stager further pointed out that these problem solvers embraced new challenges as opportunities, recognizing that the potential for failure was worth the risk. They saw the process of problem solving as a deliberate and conscious one in which new challenges were linked to past problems. This kind of familiarity, recognizing the connection between new challenges and past problems, gave the effective leaders a clarity that those who saw problems as discrete and nonrepetitive occurrences did not enjoy.

Experts and Novices. Leithwood, Steinbach, and Raun (1995) found that when compared with less successful or nonexpert problem solvers (in this case, school principals), experts

- ➥ Had in place a structured plan and procedure for group problem solving
- ➥ Offered the group pertinent information (e.g., background and introduction to the problem), which led to a more effective solution
- ➥ Verified the group's assumptions and interpretations of the problem
- ➥ Drew a larger informational picture for the group by making connections between the given problem and a larger issue
- ➥ Took a personal stand on the problem, but not to the extent that it intimidated people or swayed the group's decision
- ➥ Were open to other opinions and willing to change positions
- ➥ Facilitated collaborative problem solving through "synthesizing, summarizing, and clarifying" the problem; balanced a focus on the task with the opportunity for open discussion; provided for follow-up
- ➥ Took more time initially to analyze and pose a rational reconstruction of the problem
- ➥ Undertook more rigorous problem analysis and solution evaluation (59–60, 83)

There are other substantive distinctions between novice and expert problem solvers. While the novice tends to focus on the immediacy of the problem, on its appearance and superficial aspects, the expert scrutinizes the underpinnings of the problem and its underlying sources or motives and is able to separate critical data from irrelevant information. The expert is also able to set the problem in a context that leads to a focus on solutions, while the novice tends to see the problem in isolation.

Experts attack problems with what Leithwood, Steinbach, and Raun (1995) call forward thinking, whereby the hypothesis arises from information within the problem. The novice, on the other hand, works backward by posing a hypothesis and then seeking data within the problem to support it. The expert relies on the ongoing development of situational, procedural, knowledge-based, and craft-oriented skills, finding opportunities for flexible growth and problem solving (Hallinger, Leithwood, and Murphy 1993).

Values That Guide Problem Solving. It has been suggested that problem solving and decision making have been given more attention than problem finding, problem shaping, and attempts to make sense of the complex interrelationships within the group. Still less attention has been given to the values that drive the decisions that have to be made, by whom they are made, and to what end. While ethics and values will be examined in greater depth in the next chapter, it is worthwhile here to briefly investigate those values that propel leaders to solve problems in particular ways.

Leithwood, Begley, and Cousins (1992) have grouped values into four conceptual categories. The first category is based on what are assumed to be universally shared basic human needs upon which values are based. They include freedom, happiness, knowledge, survival, a sense of helping others, fulfillment, and respect for others. The values based on these needs frame people's understandings of functional problems: for example, there is a need for personnel to supervise after-school sports, but the decision to volunteer for such activity is left to the staff (freedom). There is a need to set schoolwide goals and objectives, but they must be set in such a way that all staff experience good will and ownership (happiness). There is a desire to seek out all available information regarding a given situation in order to make an informed decision (knowledge).

The second category of values, general moral values, includes courage, justice, responsibility, and attentiveness to a problem's existence. These values may be evidenced in such situations as when a school is faced with a bomb threat. A problem-solving leader may be guided by the belief that a student or students will have the courage to step forward and either take responsibility for the bomb threat or share valuable information necessary for maintaining the health of the entire school (that is, they will display courage). Likewise, when staff development money becomes available for the attendance of workshops or conferences, the designated leader (principal, team leader) may make sure that everyone has an equal opportunity to attend (that is, the leader will exhibit fairness).

The third category, professional values, like general moral values, become standards of conduct, ethical judgments of the performance of individual or collective action. Professional values are those values that guide work in the workplace and address the consequences of actions for students and others. For instance, in a discussion among staff, people may express concern that students are not offered enough responsibility for their own learning, or that kids do not have enough opportunities to interact with each other in constructive educational ways, or even that after removing the bells that begin and end classes kids are not responsibly moving between classes as efficiently as they could be. And in the particular responsibilities of the educator's role, the principal or district administrator may challenge a teacher who refuses to abide by a district directive due to a conflict of values.

And because of the social nature of education, and because humans define themselves in relationship to each other, the fourth category, social and political values, includes values that embrace sharing, participating, assisting others, and the kind of loyalty and commitment that shared governance speaks of in terms of teams (Hallinger, Leithwood, and Murphy 1993). All of these values shape people's interpretation of their own experiences when faced with problems, no matter how simple or complex. And rather than formal training, it is experience and depth of personal and professional interpretative reflection—reflection on professional practice and interaction that interprets experience in the service of improved practice—that usually breathe life into problem solving.

Effective expert leaders contend that they have come to value most the power of collaborative problem solving, not only because of its shared ownership, but more importantly because the solutions reached are better ones (Leithwood and Steinbach 1990). This example of the importance placed on participation also speaks to the overlapping of the categories discussed above. Although the categories of values can be somewhat ambiguous, what is clear is that when stakeholders either within or outside of the school identify the assumptions and values held by the problem-solver leader, they will gain a deeper and richer understanding of the process and the solution.

Leader as Decision Maker

In the rational management approach to leadership, decision making follows problem solving. Kerchner (1993) contends that there are three dimensions to decision making in schools:

•• External and internal decisions—schools respond more dynamically to external decisions, such as desegregation orders, federal initiatives on education of the handicapped, state mandates on content standards and benchmarks, and family migratory patterns, than they do to internal strategic planning.
•• Discrete and incremental decisions—discrete decisions are made by individuals who hold authority based on the concentration of power.
•• Individual and group decisions—moving decisions in either direction is best facilitated by managerial leadership, for at any given time the process may change based on the shifting strategic decisions made by the individuals who are involved or affected by the decisions.

On a simpler level, the process of decision making for educational leaders moves from the examination of what is wrong to what the options are in solving the problem, to the determination of which choice is best, and finally to putting the choice into action. Conventional wisdom holds that effective leader decision makers know what is going on at the school site, collectively know the right things to do, and collaboratively make them happen.

Issues of Control. Given the above three dimensions of decision making, how do educational leaders justify or legitimize the decisions that are made, particularly in the New Era of shared governance? Ortiz and Ogawa (2000) speak of two types of control that site-based decision makers may use to do this: bureaucratic control and use of social capital.

Bureaucratic control places emphasis on what we have called the rational aspects of the decision-making process. Decisions are based on objective fact or on the values we have examined. For example, a school district may objectively redraw boundary lines to balance the student population at all of its schools. However, whether the new redistricting represents equitable situations for low-income or minority students may well rest on the values the school board holds and its courage to make sometimes difficult and unpopular decisions.

A site-based example of objective fact may find the school required by the state to conduct direct instruction with students for a given number of minutes per day. However, objective fact has little to do with how literature, for example, should be taught during that time and more to do with values.

Social capital, on the other hand, draws on the human elements of social interaction and consensus found in people networks. As the designated leader's tasks on site become ever more complex, decision makers tend to move from rationality to the kind of social networking that involves multiple stakeholders in a variety of roles, dispositional relationships, and supportive interpersonal ties. Social capital is particularly central to shared governance as power and authority are shifted from a single designated leader to a community of leaders.

Effective principals and teacher-leaders reach out to the community, the business sector, universities, philanthropic groups, and families in an effort to draw them in and draw valuable resources from them. Ortiz and Ogawa (2000, 491) contend that this type of decision making yields success on many levels: first for the designated leader, then for the school and its community, and then in reconciling the pressures for accountability in the face of responsibility for tasks and mandates that fluctuate according to the needs of society.

In this consensus-building atmosphere of open discussion, compromise, empowerment, team building, and shared decision making, there are practices that offer more success for followers when responsibility and authority are delegated. Table 3.5 shows some of these practices.

In the combustible yet wonderfully invigorating atmosphere of the school, leaders must make decisions daily based on fact and values, shifting back and forth between these bases with a fluidity and flexibility that must be supportive of staff, thoughtful, student-centered, and at times courageous—a challenge in the calmest of environments.

Issues of Planning. Strategic planning is a widely used concept. It challenges decision makers and planners to examine the school, its culture and organization, and to identify those trends that would have a significant bearing on the school's accomplishment of its mission (Seyfarth 1999, 53). Strategic planning is necessary to the extent that schools and school districts must respond to external mandates as well as compete with a variety of institutions and agencies for limited resources. If schools are to survive, much less thrive, strategic planning must assist them in anticipating and adapting to changing demands.

A frequently used strategic model that is usually implemented at the district level, with input from the building site, includes five basic steps:

- Development of district mission statement
- Critical examination of school and district trends
- Development of long-range goals
- Identification of strategies and action plans that will implement the strategies
- Identification and assessment of outcomes (Seyfarth 1999, 54)

Table 3.5
Shared Authority and Responsibility

Successful Support	Detrimental Behavior
Delegate accomplishable tasks	Put follower in no-win situation, delegate only "dirty work"
Define specifically tasks and expectations	Delegate tasks without delegating commensurate authority
Offer needed support and resources	Intrude in the work of the delegate
Be available to answer questions	Dictate specifically how delegated task is to be accomplished
Provide feedback	Regain control of a task unless in dire straits
Champion success	

Source: R. D. Ramsey, *Lead, Follow, or Get Out of the Way: How to Be a More Effective Leader in Today's Schools* (Thousand Oaks, CA: Corwin Press, 1999), 52.

More specifically, the mission statement of a district is a shared vision of purposes and goals, and to be effective it must take into account the input of multiple stakeholders.

A critical trend analysis attempts to gather data and other information on the school's capability to provide quality educational programs and services for all of its students. Teams of action researchers (consisting of parents, students, teachers, administrators, and community stakeholders) collect such information as demographic data, test scores, numbers of students in various programs, numbers of students with particular exceptionalities, and data on family mobility, truancy, class disruptions and inappropriate behavior, dropouts, and the number of students going on to the next level of education.

On the district level, pupil-teacher ratios are examined along with cost of maintenance of buildings, district services and resources available to students, use of technology, and districtwide initiatives for either systemic reform or programmatic focus (such as on school-to-work programs or academic service learning). Likewise, state and federal mandates are examined in light of the school's response to population fluctuations, values held by the community, the community's perception of the quality of its schools, and charges given by the school board or business community.

All of this data is then synthesized to project demands that will be placed on the school and that will influence its ability to respond effectively. Given that change is an inevitability in schools, long-range goals attempt to anticipate these demands and prepare schools to respond to them in thoughtful and respectful ways. Action plans are then developed to implement these goals. For instance, a school may recognize that neither the higher nor the lower readiness students are being challenged in the heterogeneous classroom, so the school plans for the implementation of differentiated instruction by offering intensive three-day workshops and then rewriting instructional practices and methodologies during the summer months. Or perhaps a middle school begins to keep data on the number of young people who enter seventh grade and are immediately referred to the counselor for behavior that teachers feel may place the students at risk of dropping out early. These students are followed until their sixteenth birthdays, and the number of students who drop out relative to the number who had been identified as being at risk compel the school to plan for an alternative middle school that would reach kids before they dropped out.

Common long-range goals include a reduction in the pupil-teacher ratio; an increase in the number of young people attending higher education; a decline in the number of truancies, class disruptions, and violent acts; an increase in the number of students employed following high school; improvement in buildings and grounds; an increase in the use of technology; and strengthened lines of communication between school and community.

Finally, the implementation of goals and objectives must be assessed, reshaped, and reassessed in a cyclical fashion. In particular, administrators, faculty, parents, and students must sense the kind of support from each other necessary for open critique and dialogue that will promote authentic change. The examination of the district's actions in support of the long-range goals becomes both telling and critical.

Issues of Power. Leadership, as we have posed it, is a social act that attempts to encourage followers to move in consort with leaders toward a dynamic, powerful, and exciting yet sustainable goal. It involves an exercise of power, in this case within the school or school district. Based on the work of Handy (1993), Law and Glover (2000) identified five kinds of organizational power:

- Resource power—also called reward power, for followers believe leaders will reward them with resources
- Physical power—also called coercive power, for followers believe leaders may punish them for noncompliance
- Position power—also called legitimate power, for followers believe leaders have the right to exercise their positional power
- Expert power—arises from followers' beliefs that leaders have expertise and special abilities that are valued

➡ Personal power—also known as charisma or person power, because followers are drawn to follow leaders who display a personal dynamism that is worthy of emulation (33)

The discussion of power is important because it gives people with a stake in schools valuable information about the ways leaders and followers interact and how resources are accessed within the school or school district. And although it is often difficult to distinguish between the above categories, since both leadership and the exercise of power are subjective, it is nonetheless worthwhile to examine the use of authority, as that exercise is an avenue for more successful stakeholder participation in the school.

As decision makers, leaders are given the authority and power of their position to make final decisions. They exercise their power to engage followers in a variety of formal and informal ways. They are expected to make timely, wise, and effective decisions. Seldom do they receive commendation for this critical part of their responsibilities. Yet there appears to be little hesitation in criticizing them when these decisions are either felt to be too prolonged or are deemed ineffective. Nonetheless, people step forward, often from the teaching staff, to assume roles as conscientious, hard-working, forward-thinking visionaries who challenge their colleagues—now followers—to join them in the quest for a better school for their students.

Issues of Time. This discussion would be incomplete without acknowledging the reality of the school day. Whether as managers or instructional leaders, designated leaders (principals, team leaders, student leaders, parents, community stakeholders) are constrained by the very real challenge of finding a common time in the school day for conferences, discussions, and expressions of support. Teachers are in the classroom with students; principals are usually tending to problems in the office, observing teachers, or monitoring the school facility; parents are often working or at home with younger children.

Those relationships that are the very underpinnings of effective schools are often established in a hurried, happenstance, and frenetic fashion, e.g., having a common planning period or lunch duty together, or seeing each other in the parking lot before school or even at the local grocery store after school. Just below the surface, the rational, neatly ordered management of a school consists of a series of stolen moments, hurried notes placed in teachers' mailboxes, and phone calls that just happened to catch a parent at home.

Thoughtful conversation becomes conversation of immediacy, focused on what is most important in the moment. The very structure of the school day mitigates against establishing the collegiality that is critical to the health and growth of the school. Unless the school and its designated leaders build into the schedule the kind of time necessary for the development of robust professional relationships, collaborative engagement, and discourse that speaks of teaching and learning, progress will be piecemeal, sporadic, and isolated.

Summary. The technical and more top-down type of leadership brings with it some promise of efficiency, orderliness, and predictability, and therefore of attention to the kind of clean operational atmosphere that will logically bring about improved student outcomes (Lashway 1996). But what is lost in this style of thinking is attention to the creative and innovative spirit that drives commitment, change, and sustained growth. What is ignored is the complex reality of the school, which is anything but predictable, orderly, or neat. From such a myopic perspective, constituents other than the designated leader are reduced to cogs in a wheel, each having a specific place in the organization, knowing that place, and remaining in that role, sensing, too, that their contribution to the school can easily be replaced. In many ways, this restrictive environment is a "dumbing down" both of the profession and the school's presence in the community.

NONTECHNICAL EDUCATIONAL LEADERSHIP

Leader as Instructional Leader

By the mid-1980s, the role of the designated leader in the school had shifted from leader as manager to leader as instructional expert. At that time the principal was viewed as the school's instructional or curriculum expert who could and would mediate effective classroom teaching and learning. She was responsible for coordinating, focusing, and aligning the school's curriculum; setting and assessing goals for teachers and students; and closely following the work of the classroom, the effectiveness of teaching, and the academic achievement of students. In many ways, the principal both coordinated and controlled the school's curriculum as she concentrated everyone's efforts on student learning.

In the 1990s, as schools moved to shared governance and site-based decision making, they also began to evolve into communities of learners where teaching was a collective rather than an individual experience. Leadership for instruction became the process of the community—teachers, students, administrators, and families who participated in peer coaching, study teams, mentoring, action research, professional development, and critical reflective practice. The National Forum on Educational Leadership (1999) indicated that the most important task of an effective leader is to provide instructional leadership. This is the task for which most designated leaders are least equipped.

The term "nested learning communities" refers to a school as a learning community, led by its principal as instructional leader, a school that continues to learn about the teaching and learning process and that enjoys continued progress in student outcomes. Coming out of the High Performance Learning Communities project (Fink and Resnick 2001), the concept refers to Russian nesting dolls, each independent and separate yet resembling the other, shaped by the other, and within the other, one no more important than the other.

States such as Florida have begun to mandate that the principal or designated leader emphasize instruction, in the belief that leaders have both an indirect and direct impact on the success of the instruction of students. They can facilitate learning in the school and influence the culture through their beliefs, attitudes, and actions. New interest has been focused on staff development for principals and teachers; on classroom supervision and assessment; on curriculum alignment with national, state, and local standards; on school scheduling and teacher teaming; on family involvement; and on the use of technology.

In reviewing the current instructional leadership literature, Blase and Blase (1999) found four general areas of discussion: prescriptive instructional models, the indirect effects of principal-teacher evaluative conferences, the direct effects of designated leaders on classroom instruction, and the direct and indirect impact of the principal's attitude and work on student outcomes.

Models of Instructional Leadership. Glickman (1985) conceptualized the primary tasks of the instructional leader as staff development, curriculum development, direct assistance to teachers, group development, and action research. Some commonly asked questions about the development and assessment of curriculum are

- What should all students know and be able to do?
- Where in the curriculum do they learn this knowledge and these skills?
- How will we know when students have both learned the content and acquired the skills?
- What can stakeholders do to spur student learning?
- What additional training or academic preparation will teachers need to accomplish these goals? (Seyfarth 1999, 169)

Other researchers define instructional leadership as an eclectic merging of instructional supervision, curriculum development, and staff development (Smith and Andrews 1989). And to these lists Pajak (1989) adds motivating the staff for change, planning, and organizing as key elements.

More contemporary models of instructional leadership include collaborative, cooperative, developmental, transformational, transactional, democratic, and facilitative approaches. Evident in these models are beliefs in nonhierarchical relationships, shared authority and responsibility, growth in a supportive environment, and communities of learners who work together for consensual goals. These models acknowledge the rich and complex contextual environment of the school and place teachers, teaching, and the facilitation of teachers' professional thinking about instruction as the primary focus and concern of the instructional leader.

Despite the variety of models and the stimulating discussion about them, instructional leadership is often perceived by teachers as exercised by the principal who intrusively observes, assesses, and judges the work done in the classroom. Recently, in a midwestern urban district, a principal new to the school and the district wanted to be seen and to function as an instructional leader, so he began to visit each teacher's classroom, taking notes and asking for weekly lesson plans. The faculty felt this was an infringement of their professional rights, a breach of trust, and took the situation to their union. As a result, the principal was no longer allowed to come into the classroom except at formal, predetermined evaluation times. Clearly, trust had not been established between the principal and the teachers, nor had it been a hallmark of the school, as it struggled through four administrations in the past twelve years. Instructional leadership is as much about relationships as it is about curricular issues.

A study of district superintendents as instructional leaders who had an effect on student learning revealed certain mechanisms that were consistently used:

- Direct supervision by observation
- Resource distribution to smaller groups (departments, schools, centers)
- Input control through the standardization of district plans and procedures
- Output control through the evaluation of performance and outcomes
- Determination and internalization of dispositions, i.e., shared norms, values, and attitudes

➡ Environmental shaping of expectations and behaviors (Wirt 1990, 72)

There are examples of superintendents who carry out their role as instructional leader to the district through their hiring of personnel and selection of textbooks, even to the extent of observing both the principal and the classroom teachers. Yet more frequently the superintendent is required to function as a political spokesperson, mediator, and representative of the school district. It is this person who can effectively mediate between the various agendas of constituents, transforming their values, hopes, intentions, and resources into educational services for students. This is the very nature of facilitative leadership, for it translates politics into educational power.

Leadership Effects on Instruction and Learning. Though research is by no means substantive, there is evidence that certain designated leader behaviors affect teaching and learning. Among them are

➡ Shaping and communicating school goals
➡ Supervising and evaluating instructional practices
➡ Coordinating the school's curriculum
➡ Following and evaluating progress on student achievement
➡ Protecting instructional time as well as shielding instructors from distractions
➡ Sustaining high visibility
➡ Providing substantive professional development
➡ Providing incentives for teaching and learning (Blase and Blase 1999, 353)

And more recently, instructional leadership has been linked to concepts such as transformational and participative leadership, as well as to shared governance and site-based decision making, all of which have had a direct effect on instruction and learning. Of greatest consequence for effectiveness in the classroom is the designated leader's enabling support and encouragement of professional development. This coupled with an emphasis on the community of learners engaged in collegial inquiry and reflection has taken the place of distrustful, top-down relationships with supervisors (Blase and Blase 1994).

Smith and Andrews (1989, 23–48) examine instructional leadership from the principal's perspective and maintain that the instructional leader

➡ Provides resources necessary for achieving the school's academic goals (observable signs of effectiveness: teaching assignments match certification; common planning time for teacher teams; sufficient supplies are available throughout the school year; staff analyzes data to assess student curricular needs and develops the needed materials; written records indicate how staff have been involved in budget decisions; systematic staff meetings are facilitated by instructional leader as well as by staff; provision is made for all staff to attend workshops, conferences, retreats, and to share new knowledge)

- ➻ Holds that curricular knowledge and skills are necessary for teacher growth and improvement (observable signs of effectiveness: school discussion centers around instructional issues; classroom observations and postobservation conferences are systematic and mutually planned; teachers engage in peer observation and feedback)
- ➻ Communicates well in all settings (observable signs of effectiveness: written procedures in place for decision making that indicate the people who are involved and responsible, and the outcomes expected; staff meetings well organized and thoughtfully reflecting school objectives, concerns, activities, and collegial participation; school goals and vision publicized; written recognition of student, family, and staff successes; all staff able to describe the evaluation system and the expectations)
- ➻ Serves as a visionary ambassador or spokesperson on behalf of the school (observable signs of effectiveness: leader is in classrooms, hallways, lunchroom; interactions with students, staff, families, and community stakeholders)

Contrast this view with Blase and Blase's (1999, 370–371) rich study of the perceptions of over 800 teachers of effective instructional leaders. Teachers believed that effective designated leaders

- ➻ Use a broad-based approach
- ➻ Create a culture of individual and common reflection, growth, and critical examination that prepares people for substantive change and improvement
- ➻ Embrace challenges brought about by this change
- ➻ Believe that change is a journey of learning and risk taking
- ➻ Demonstrate respect for their teachers' abilities, skills, and knowledge
- ➻ Communicate openly and frequently with teachers about instruction

- Create trusting, nonthreatening, mutually respectful relationships with all stakeholders
- Sustain a collaborative community-of-learners environment
- Value and support peer interaction
- Provide support, through various resources, for change and innovation
- Prize and promote basic human values of care, trust, collaboration, collegiality, growth, and respect

Blase and Blase (2000, 133–137) offered a two-pronged model of instructional leadership. They contended that effective leaders talked with teachers to promote reflection, and that they valued and provided opportunities for professional growth. They found that effective instructional leaders nurtured teachers' critical reflection on teaching and learning by

- Offering suggestions rather than criticizing—encouraging risk taking, innovation, teacher choice, and professional development; acknowledging teacher strengths; sustaining focus on instructional improvement
- Providing feedback in a positive, timely, and problem-solving fashion—classroom observations were specific, student-centered, and teacher-supportive, and they expressed care and concern and nurtured growth and creativity
- Modeling the expected behaviors—during faculty meetings, parent meetings, and classroom instruction, instructional leaders modeled positive interactions
- Using the inquiry approach, they solicited suggestions and professional input
- Praising accomplishments and efforts in concrete and specific ways
- Promoting professional growth—encouraging attendance and presentations at conferences and workshops, developing peer coaches, supporting the redesign of programs, stressing the ongoing study of teaching and learning, and implementing action research to help shape redesign and problem solving

Effective instructional leadership is embedded in the culture of the school as it joins collaboration, collegiality, inquiry, peer support, and reflective conversation into a circular promotion driving professional dialogue. In order for that kind of professional dialogue to take place during the busy school day, designated leaders must provide times when staff and stakeholders may converse and plan. They must provide the human and natural resources necessary to create and implement innovation and substantive redesign. And they must model the school's ongoing conversation about kids' learning and growth, about stakeholders' professional health and well-being, and about the fundamental principles of respect, trust, honesty, caring, compassion, and enlightenment (Blase and Blase 2000).

Summary. Instructional leaders help to shape and create schools where students continue to learn because the staff and stakeholders continue to learn. Often the principal is considered to be the instructional leader, but with distributed leadership this role is shared with a variety of constituents. Glickman (1991) goes so far as to say that the principal is not the instructional leader but rather a coordinator of teachers who are instructional leaders.

Fink and Resnick (2001) observed in working with principals and others who serve as instructional leaders that their emphasis is on leadership rather than content expertise. Instructional leaders must know enough about pedagogical practice, content-specific knowledge, and critical curriculum issues to understand what it is they are observing, but their primary focus is on determining ways they can provide instructional assistance or professional development for their teachers.

Most important, instructional leaders are fundamentally responsible for establishing, nurturing, and sustaining the culture of learning indicative of a genuine community of learners. This habit of mind is represented at every point on the distributed leadership continuum discussed in chapter 1. Fink, a superintendent in New York City schools, maintains, "If central administrators hold principals accountable for providing instructional leadership for their teachers, they have to be prepared to provide the same kind of leadership for their principals" (Fink and Resnick 2001, 606).

Though there is wide variation in the abilities of designated leaders to motivate, encourage, and manage people, and to create and develop social networks in schools, the one persistent characteristic of the vast majority of effective principals and other designated leaders is their ability to create a sense of community and to put shared beliefs and values into practice in the classroom (Lockwood 1996).

Leaders as Facilitators

Just as educational leaders in the 1990s were charged to be instructional leaders, today they are challenged to be facilitators who build teams, consensus, networks, and partnerships, and who lead from the center of the school—the classroom. It would be daunting, perhaps even discouraging, for a leader who had just begun to develop expertise and comfort with one perspective of engagement in the school to be told that that mode was no longer viable. However, it would require less a shift in the leader's framework of operation than a shift in his perception, thinking, and interacting.

As discussed, management leadership tends to disregard the complex interactions in a highly creative and intelligent community. Transformational leadership, on the other hand, has the potential to inspire and motivate people, and to embrace and value the needs, norms, and shared beliefs of the school family. Yet in some cases it, too, falls short, to the extent that the culture of the school may well be invigorating, exciting, and creative, but the goals and objectives for student learning may not be met.

Conley and Goldman (1994) describe facilitative leadership as the kind of educational leadership that, like transformative leadership, enlists stakeholders in problem solving. But unlike transformative leadership, which tends to retain vestiges of hierarchical problem solving, facilitative strategies present the leader as someone who works with those people responsible for making informed decisions. In conventional terms, the leader is not the sage on the stage, but the guide on the side. The facilitative leader emphasizes the school's collective ability to assess its current performance, solve problems, implement its decisions, and evaluate its subsequent performance.

Blase et al. (1995) note that when a designated leader uses facilitative strategies, the leader engages in practices like

- •• Creating a change-oriented culture in which teachers and other stakeholders develop their leadership skills in pursuit of shared beliefs, much in the ways spoken of in chapter 1
- •• Creating social and communication networks
- •• Building teams and promoting team or collective thinking
- •• Providing support, feedback, coordination, and conflict management
- •• Providing necessary resources, both human and material
- •• Practicing collaborative and cooperative interactions
- •• Modeling the school's mission, values, and goals
- •• Creating and sustaining a democratic workplace that exemplifies and practices the highest ideals

- ◆ Encouraging the expression of different opinions from stakeholders
- ◆ Negotiating informally

Nancy Mohr (1997) expanded on the facilitative strategies listed above in her adaptation of the Standards for Staff Development and Facilitation. The standards maintain that staff development improves all students' learning when adults are organized into learning communities, when skilled school and district leadership guide continual instructional improvement, and when resources support adult learning and collaboration:

- ◆ Communication—instructs groups in how to effectively communicate; asks probing, open-ended questions; listens more than talks; creates safe and open environment for honest discussion
- ◆ Group norms—shares personal norms and values to initiate group construction of common principles and values
- ◆ Community building—realizes that knowing and trusting set the stage for dynamic learning; builds, supports, and nurtures a safe community where the unease created by change becomes commonplace
- ◆ Participation—maximizes all participants' involvement
- ◆ Agenda design—solicits group input for setting programs in which learning is collegial, experiential, research-based, and sustained
- ◆ Pacing—flexibly keeps group moving forward
- ◆ Clear goals—determines goals that are information-based in terms of knowledge, skills, and attitudes
- ◆ Information and feedback—teaches members how to offer and solicit feedback
- ◆ Repertoire—uses a variety of strategies, materials, and structures
- ◆ Transparency—explains the "why" of group agenda and decisions
- ◆ Teaching—understands facilitation in terms of teaching; is responsible to the group that is responsible for achieving the school's goals
- ◆ Reflection—uses frequent self-examination as a model for stakeholders so that they see themselves as learners (1–2)

Facilitative leadership is the exercise of power through teachers, parents, students, and other stakeholders. Facilitative leaders use their authority to support the mutuality of linear, that is, nonhierarchical, power, a power shared by constituents in a free-flowing reciprocal relationship. For example, teachers and students exercise their talents and abilities in the classroom and thrive on the independence to exercise both the art and the craft of their professional knowledge. Students do not learn because the state education department has instituted new content standards, but rather because teachers facilitate a classroom environment built on the respect of, and belief in, each individual student and his or her learning needs. Principals create an environment in which this professionalism is valued. The principal affects the student indirectly through supporting teachers in the classroom. The effectiveness of both principals and teachers is measured by students' affective and cognitive development.

The same can be said of the local school board and central administration, both of which value the work of the principal and other designated school leaders to the extent that they support the school's environment of professionalism, integrity, and trust. The family is valued in the facilitative culture, for its members possess the kind of knowledge, commitment, and concerns that are essential to improving learning outcomes for children.

Dunlap and Goldman (1990) draw attention to a critical aspect of facilitative leadership: "Facilitation occurs within the existing structure, meaning that whoever normally has legal authority to ratify decisions continues to do so. Unlike delegation, where administrators unilaterally assign tasks to subordinates, in a facilitative environment, anyone can initiate a task and recruit anyone else to participate" (cited in Lashway 1995, 1).

Bolman and Deal (1997) have identified four "frames" for examining organizational leadership, any one or two of which may be used by a designated leader:

- Structural frame—how leaders design schools to fit goals, tasks, and outcomes within the culture
- Human resource frame—how managers' assumptions about stakeholder needs can spur higher commitment or resistance to proposed changes
- Political frame—how the school is viewed as a political ecosystem in which stakeholders pursue their own interests
- Symbolic frame—how the culture (shared beliefs, norms, values, rituals, and rites) shapes the organization through expression rather than through the product

However, in facilitative environments, all four of these frames may exist simultaneously. For instance, a designated leader who is facilitating more family involvement in the decision-making processes of the school needs to be aware of the anxiety the family may feel about coming back to a school in which they may not have enjoyed success as a student. The facilitative leader must also be aware of the possible anxiety felt by teachers who may have had little success in engaging parents (human resource frame). In addition, the leader must be aware of the concern felt, on the one hand, by parents who believe that they have a "right" to participate in the school, and the concern felt, on the other hand, by teachers who perceive that their expertise in the classroom is threatened (political frame). The designated leader then situates the relationship—understanding both viewpoints and creating a comfortable environment for the work of both groups by shaping the structure and relational atmosphere—and prepares both groups for effective work using the concepts of shared values and shared concerns (symbolic frame). The designated leader then assesses the work of both groups in meeting the school's goals and outcomes (structural frame).

Impediments to Facilitation. It could well be anticipated from examining these strategies that initially this kind of leadership may produce even more ambiguity than is already present in the school. However, as the staff and constituent stakeholders become more comfortable with their roles and with the shift in responsibility and accountability, their rekindled enthusiasm and commitment frequently are more sustainable and authentic.

Moreover, given the blurring of who will be held accountable, facilitative leadership has been referred to as the control or management of tensions. Whereas in more formal hierarchical systems the principal was directly accountable for all school decisions and held all of the power and authority, with facilitative leadership a chorus of people participate in decision making and are held accountable. Teachers, parents, and community stakeholders who previously may have been protected from some of the more egregious situations in the school now have ownership both of the controversy and its solution.

The principal, as the key designated leader of the school, must also confront the unpredictability of the timing of necessary decisions. For instance, a Title I elementary school shows consistently low scores on state-mandated science, reading, math, and language arts tests. The principal has assembled a multidimensional team of people with a stake in the school to examine the problem and pose a timely solution. The team decides that the pivotal problem, evident in all low performance areas, is poor reading skills. The team writes in their school improvement plan, which is sent to the district and state as required, that they will adopt an all-school reading program by the end of the first semester and pilot the program the second semester, with an eye to full-school adoption the following year. The team examines several reading systems, but by the middle of January still has not found a suitable fit. They have yet to examine one more recommended program or contact a representative of it. With only one week left in the first semester and time slipping away, the principal must decide whether to make the contact herself and schedule a time to bring the program representative to the team, or let the team (which is not scheduled to meet for another month) take ownership of the failure to meet the timeline. Clearly, a unilateral decision would prove expeditious, but when people are committed to shared ownership, efficiency and expeditiousness may well take a backseat to engaging people in that process.

Not all schools are ready for this type of culture; nor are schools that practice facilitative leadership able to carry out this process all of the time. The business of change is more fundamentally targeted at changing people than changing programs. The business of change is about process rather than immediate full-scale initiation.

Leaders as Stewards, or Transcendent Leadership

There are those people who take the facilitative and transformational positions even further and advocate a leadership that practices authentic partnership, empowerment of others, and emphasis on values and moral beliefs. These are leaders who are stewards. As a reaction to the moral injustices that "followers" often suffer at the hands of authoritarian, self-centered managers bent on expedient and efficient behavior at all costs, stewardship seeks to reclaim the ethical and spiritual soul of leadership. It is a kind of leadership guided by authenticity, intentionality, spirituality, and sensibility. Bhindi and Duignan (1998) describe these qualities:

- •• Authenticity—the discovery of the authentic self through meaningful relationships with the school's core values and beliefs; based on personal integrity, credibility, and trust
- •• Intentionality—a visionary leadership that draws its perceptions and directions from the honored intentions of the school stakeholders who have committed their senses of self and of moral purpose to the school's vision
- •• Spirituality—the rekindling of the spiritual in each person and a recommitment to the collective purpose of relationships;

not a sectarian view of the self, but a deeply abiding sense of meaning and purpose drawn from their commitment to and relationship with the greater good
- Sensibility—the quickening of senses to the diversity of feelings, needs, perceptions, backgrounds, cultures, and aspirations of others (53–59)

As stewards, leaders are not given authority but earn it through the authenticity of their actions and relationships with other members of the school family. In turn, they enable others to empower themselves. This is a transcendent leadership whose energy is focused on moral integrity and moral reasoning in the service of what is right, good, and just on behalf of young people (Terry 1993). Together these values shape a unified vision that crystallizes the purpose and mission of the school. It positions each person as an intrinsically valuable part of an organization committed to an enduring and interconnected sense of purpose that exceeds the individual.

Through stewardship, a multidimensional group of stakeholders is transformed into a community that believes in the higher principles of civic justice and passionate caring for the entire school family. Together their sense of a common vision and moral obligation situate them as those who serve, those who care, and those who protect the school and its mission (Ornstein and Behar-Horenstein 1999). It is leadership by the spirit of civic good rather than leadership by technique. It is leadership that seeks to empower rather than leadership that seeks to control, to conform, or to maintain the status quo. It is leadership of the New Era rather than leadership of the twentieth century.

Democratic Leadership. Facilitative and stewardship approaches to leadership appear to be the most consistent with site-based, decentralized governance. Many of the same strategies and characteristics indicative of these forms of leadership are also reflective of democratic leadership, which is often referred to as empowering leadership. Trust, encouragement of creativity and risk taking, authentic caring, honesty, and collegiality are witnessed in all three leadership models. However, where facilitative leadership draws on personal interrelationships in the service of stimulating motivation and increasing productivity, democratic leadership has its roots in the emancipatory tradition spoken of so eloquently by Paulo Freire (1972), and has as its goals democracy and social justice (Foster 1986).

Blase and Anderson (1995) examine the behavior of leaders who use the facilitative style of leadership and those who use the democratic style, and they draw a rich comparison between the two. While facilitative leadership provides the kind of support that fosters teacher autonomy and professionalism, democratic leadership fosters the kind of environment in which the voices of all stakeholders are subject to critique and thoughtful consideration (what Freire refers to as an emancipatory dialectic). Where facilitative leadership focuses on the mutual adoption of change initiatives, democratic leadership focuses on the careful examination of the processes and products in terms of equity and justice. And where facilitative leadership works collaboratively to implement reform, democratic leadership attends to the continual loop of dialogue and action that shapes a just and equitable environment for all stakeholders.

In the ongoing work of the school, these two leadership styles are often used in combination. We would expect the facilitative leader at some point to base the work of the school or the course of reflective dialogue on justice and caring, just as we would expect democratic leaders to attend to the mandates of restructuring on the district, local, and state levels. "The difference is whether reforms equally benefit all constituencies," as Blase and Anderson (1995, 133) write.

In reality, most of the nation's schools have yet to recognize the powerful potential for good that parents and students—when seen as leaders or equal stakeholders—could bring to school reform. Because many states now mandate parent involvement, schools today look more frequently for "programs" that would engage parents, but in very limited ways. Democratic leadership holds that students and the family have a social right to participate in decision making, the shaping of goals and outcomes, and programs and processes in schools. Schools and families are joined in a mutual enterprise: the hopes they have for student success. Few schools would deny this, but the same schools have not yet embraced family participation beyond formalized PTAs or Parent Councils, which on the secondary level allow the exercise of little to no authority, or simply involve sending letters home informing the family of the important business of the school.

Impediments to Democratic Leadership. School boards and central office administration affect democratic leadership of the school in the sense that they can encourage and nurture stakeholders' participation in decisions, limit hierarchical mandates, and value, encourage, and support risk taking (Blase et al. 1995). They can also have the best intentions in encouraging site-based governance but do so in a top-down managerial fashion, hurting trust. For instance, a school board and central administration have encouraged a particular school to move to shared governance. However, when it comes time for science teachers and families to make textbook selections, a very thoughtful and rigorous professional process, they are told that the district has already entered into a contract with a book company (one the teachers and families did not choose) that will sell the school textbooks at a discount if the school purchases both science and language arts books. The decision is made by the central office. Teachers and families who sat on this committee for the past year and whose choice was ignored have reason for distrust.

As in facilitative leadership, issues of accountability and timeliness challenge democratic leadership to make decisions without being able to quickly assemble the necessary constituent groups for discussion. A turnover in superintendents threatens the support for shared governance a school may enjoy from a current superintendent or school board. And the very real constraints of mandated state content standards and benchmarks have threatened the use of professional time, given the emphasis they place on test-taking skills rather than democratic teaching, learning, and distributed responsibility.

And finally, less than honorable motives on the part of designated leaders are impediments to the kind of social justice to which democratic leadership speaks. To move to shared decision making so that all contentious and unpopular decisions can be relegated to someone else does not represent the tenets of this style of leadership. Democratic leadership is a power-with tradition that is seen consistently in the process as well as the product.

Summary of Leadership Roles. Whichever style of leadership used (transactional, transformative, transcendent, facilitative, or democratic) or role assumed (manager, decision maker, problem solver, instructional leader, or facilitator), it is important that the values and shared beliefs of the school are reflected and represented in the leadership, and built upon and held up as constant beacons. As stakeholders view the work of the school, and as they attempt to gain access to their local schools, either on behalf of their children or because they want to democratically participate in schools, the recognition of how power and authority are used is critical. Designated leaders must be aware of their own leadership styles, roles, and values before they can engage others in the risky business of change.

As schools seek to improve the academic and social outcomes for students through either holistic school reform initiatives or programmatic or instructional changes, they must be aware of how they currently operate, for the basis of all change must be an active, deliberate acknowledgment of shared norms, beliefs, and values. This foundation must be frequently revisited throughout the process. Only then can thoughtful, stepwise progress be substantive and successful. Strategic decisions about what is valued, what is needed both in the current school year and the long term, what is consonant with the culture of the community, what reflects the talents and abilities of the faculty, the students, and the family, and what reflects best practice—all must be weighed and balanced.

Effective New Era leadership speaks in terms of ownership, of flexibility, of responsiveness to the needs of the school family, and of facilitation and empowerment. It is a multidimensional shared governance that honors all constituent stakeholders in the service of increased opportunities and outcomes for all students.

WHAT ARE THE CRITICAL ISSUES
EDUCATIONAL LEADERS CONFRONT?

Educational leaders in the New Era are faced with a rising tide of challenges that reflect the angry times in which we live. Schools are confronted with kids who carry the adult trappings of a world bent on its own destruction, including disinterest, disaffection, and denial. Some of the issues leaders will face could be grouped into cultural challenges, student challenges that are socially mediated, and professional challenges (see Table 3.6).

Few, if any, of these challenges or issues exist in isolation. Rather, they provoke other challenges for the student, the family, the classroom, and the school. How we unravel the agenda or hidden curriculum that lies just beneath the explicit curriculum will perhaps determine whether these issues are seen as problems or as opportunities for change and growth. Likewise, it will determine whether students will be taught from a deficit perspective (what is wrong and therefore what needs to be "fixed") or from a positive vantage point (capitalizing on strengths and resilience).

Shifting Canvas. The changing demographics of the twenty-first century will pose challenges to the educational system on several levels. Hodgkinson (2000–2001, 8) notes that 65 percent of this country's growth in the next twenty years will be in minority populations who have higher fertility rates than do the currently dominant Anglo-Americans. The differences presented by different values and cultural norms will challenge the essentially white, middle-class institution of school. Educational leaders will be faced with a dominant non-English-speaking population, which will cause the school to provide different programs, new instructional strategies, and culturally appropriate instructional materials.

Hodgkinson further points out that although most poor children

Table 3.6
Challenges to New Era Leadership

Cultural Challenges	Student Challenges	Professional Challenges
Racism	School violence	Resistance to change
Classism	Gangs	Absence of effective leaders
Sexism	Child abuse	Unengaged parents
Violence	Adolescent depression	Shifting demographics
Diversity	HIV-AIDS	Conflicting politics
Inequity	Learning disorders	Vouchers and home schooling
Poverty	Poverty	Poverty
Ageism	Truancy	Lack of functionally supportive
	Homelessness	families
	Eating disorders	Divided school board
	Substance abuse	Difficulty of building culture of
	Dropouts	learning communities
	Inclusion programs	Paper blizzard
	Cheating	Lack of coordinated curriculum
	Latchkey kids	Lack of human resources
	Suicide	Failure to pass bond issues
	Crime (theft)	Aggressive unions
	Grade inflation	Difficulty of reconciling mandates
	Problems in social	with values and beliefs
	promotion and retention	Problems in leading, facilitating,
	Litigation	guiding, and supporting change
	Growing culture of	Book controversies
	disrespect and disruption	Personality conflicts
	Apathy	Repetition of fads
		Uncoordinated services

are Anglos, blacks and Hispanics have a higher percentage of children in poverty. They present to schools different kinds of layered problems that must be dealt with before teaching and learning can even be approached. Many states put these kids through remedial instruction in their early years, mandating preschool programs for children in poverty in an attempt to equalize their chances for success from the outset.

A staggering 20 percent of U.S. children fall into this poverty category. Many of these students have their educational opportunities threatened by discontinuity born of transience. With transience comes low academic achievement, disruptive social behavior due to lack of community connectedness, and low graduation rates from high school and post–high school training or study. How do schools respond to half of their student body changing in midyear? In the standards age and the era of reform, Tirozzi (2001) asks, "Do reform efforts take into consideration the pronounced effects of a constantly changing student body?"

At the same time, both teachers and the country's general population are aging. Will these baby boomers continue to support their local schools after their children and grandchildren have left the school systems? And what about the dearth of qualified teachers to fill retiree's classrooms and of principals to fill the front office?

Equity. Taking into account all of the above factors as well as some that follow, the single most challenging issue educational leaders will face in the New Era is the issue of equity. The irony of this issue (which is tied to the issue of poverty) lies in the fact that it is the one critical issue the country has the capability and potential to solve, but chooses not to.

In an interview in November 2000, Leah Meyer Austin, program officer for the W. K. Kellogg Foundation's Middle Start Initiative (which is geared toward working with middle-grade schools in high-poverty areas, first in Michigan and now across the country), wisely and passionately observed, "Will we ever come to terms with the fact that we must educate all children?" Speaking of the ideology that chooses to ignore this question, she continues, "Will we ever understand that some kids need more resources than other kids?" Children are not variants of the same model. Rather, they come to school with diverse and often disparate experiences that frequently do not prepare them for the learning environment but instead put them at risk from the outset. Austin contends that the discussion about resources should not be centered around how the "pie" is cut up, but rather on the fact that the pie needs to be bigger on behalf of all children. Put colloquially, the playing field needs to be leveled so that all children have both equitable and equal opportunities. Austin shares the perceptions of Jonathan Kozol, a longtime outspoken and articulate voice for the poor and the disadvantaged in our country, who writes, "Equal funding for unequal needs is not equality" (1991, 54). Educational leaders at all levels will be faced with growing needs in a sea of shrinking resources. They will be challenged to effectively access and use human, financial, and informational resources in creative and respectful ways.

Other critical issues leaders will confront in the New Era include

- ➥ The creative establishment of partnerships and collaborative and cooperative endeavors. Because of the competition for limited funds, coupled with the complexity of the needs that children bring to the school, educational leaders will be called upon to forge various associations with social and human service agencies, community and business organizations, and corporate and philanthropic foundations. The school will be challenged to see and then present itself in the community as a hub of services for students and their families, a model referred to as "full-service schools." The services may include health and dental care, social services, crisis intervention, family counseling, and providing connections to other community services.

•• The creation of a culture of high-achieving learning communities where all adult stakeholders and all students are engaged in active, relevant, meaningful, creative, culturally responsive, and challenging teaching and learning as a habit of mind; where higher-order thinking skills are cultivated in all students; where teachers use authentic assessments and differentiate their instruction within heterogeneous groups; and where academic service-learning projects that tie the classroom curriculum to active community engagement become the standards of performance. Educational leaders will be called upon to create teaching teams that share a collective vision and purpose, that strive for higher-order learning, and that focus on collective goals and objectives tied to student outcomes that drive the hands-on teaching and learning, where depth of understanding is as valued as breadth of knowledge.

•• The initiation, management, and ongoing assessment of change. As examined in chapter 5, educational leaders must be able to flexibly and thoughtfully respond to the fast-paced developments in technology and in the production of new knowledge. They must lead the kind of change that is shaped by substantive, informed, collective, and visionary ideas that yield improved outcomes and opportunities for students and families. And in doing so leaders must have the kinds of skills that help discriminate between fad and fundamentally sound practices, between healthy chaos and destructive resistance, between unfocused activity and authentic learning, and between what is and what can be.

•• The construction and protection of a safe learning environment that is not hampered by the violence and anger that surround the school grounds and that have come to characterize the social fabric of the new millennium. Leaders will be called upon to be proficient in resolving conflict of all kinds.

-» The understanding that a balance needs to be struck between students' cognitive development (or what they know and are able to do) and their social responsibility and values or affective development. The latter is often left out of the current standards-based reform conversation.

-» The re-engagement of families and community constituents in the active business of the school. As students' needs are ever more complex, the family's expertise regarding their children and the community's direct involvement in the school are critical to the success of each student.

-» The involvement of a teaching population that reflects the diversity of its student body. In a profession that has traditionally been Eurocentric, both the teaching and the administrative staff, as well as their instructional practice, will be challenged to be culturally astute in addition to being culturally representative. However, despite efforts to entice minorities into the teaching field, the profession remains disproportionately Anglo-Saxon.

-» The growing threats of litigation and issues surrounding rights and protection under the law. Such areas as appropriate curricular or reading materials, religious observances in the school or on the school grounds, equal access to all school activities, drug testing, freedom of speech, zero-tolerance policies, and issues of violence in schools are all being discussed more prominently at the turn of the century.

WHAT IS CONSIDERED TO BE EFFECTIVE, AND HOW IS EFFECTIVENESS MEASURED?

We have examined the specific tasks of leaders as they assume the roles of manager, problem solver, decision maker, facilitator, and instructional leader. Yet there are functions of leadership that are common to all of these leadership stances:

-» Affirm and articulate the values of the school or school district

-» Set goals and objectives for the educational outcomes of all students

•• Create and sustain trust with all stakeholders
•• Motivate all stakeholders to share a common vision and mission for the school that supports teaching and learning and all who participate in it
•• Solve problems through team consensus and collaborative action
•• Represent the school to all constituent groups, families, the school board, the central administration, the community at large, health and human service agencies, accrediting agencies, teachers unions and professional organizations, and state boards of education
•• Manage a stable environment that maximizes the human interactions between teachers and students in the service of educational and social outcomes for all students and their families (Gardner 1990)

Effectiveness in Leadership and the Business of Lists. Is it possible to agree on what effective leadership should be? The vast majority of researchers contend that all leadership only indirectly affects learning outcomes for students. And the farther removed from the classroom a leader is, the less direct the effect on learning. Yet we have presented above ways in which leaders, as far removed from the classroom as the state department of education, state boards of education, the U.S. Department of Education, and state and national legislatures, have influenced the teaching and learning that go on in the classroom.

Ramsey (1999) offers some very practical field-based observations of how effective and successful leaders use their school day. He maintains that leaders

•• Spend the majority of their time doing what they do best
•• Handle routine matters such as mail, phone calls, personal contacts, and e-mail
•• Perform the three basic functions of planning, directing, and controlling (based on motivating, goal setting, assessing, monitoring, training, supporting)
•• Focus on what they need to do that no one else can do
•• Give back to the community
•• Balance their professional and personal lives
•• Protect a time for quiet reflection or meditation (82, 83)

He also challenges designated leaders at the building and district level to

•➤ Delegate tasks to involve more people
•➤ Focus on their priorities
•➤ Follow through and follow up
•➤ Know their own "biological clock" and maximize the "optimal time frame," that is, the time when one is physically keenest and able to best accomplish the most work
•➤ Expect and plan to be spontaneous
•➤ Know what their weaker areas are, and ask others to help them in those areas
•➤ Pace themselves
•➤ Mentally prepare for the events of each day
•➤ Be organized
•➤ Address problems as they arise without putting them off until later
•➤ "Don't give every task the same effort; just give every task the effort it deserves"
•➤ Protect their planning time (81, 82)

Given that every text and every researcher offers a different checklist of attributes possessed and practices followed that will lead to success, we will refer to one more reference that offers somewhat different ideas. Hoyle, English, and Steffy's work entitled *Skills for Successful Twenty-First Century School Leaders* (1998) synthesizes research on effective leaders. It discusses the skills, knowledge, and dispositions that are considered by the following organizations and their respective publications as standards of best practices for educational leadership:

•➤ Interstate School Leaders Licensure Consortium (ISLLC)— for elementary and secondary principals
•➤ American Association of School Administrators (AASA)— *Professional Standards for the Superintendency* (1993); *Guidelines for the Preparation of School Administrators* (1982)
•➤ National Council for the Accreditation of Teacher Education (NCATE)—*Curriculum Guidelines for School Administrators* (1993)
•➤ National Association of Secondary School Principals (NASSP) — *Performance-Based Preparation of Principals* (1985)
•➤ National Association of Elementary School Principals (NAESP)—*Principals for the Twenty-First Century* (1990)
•➤ American Association of Colleges for Teacher Education (AACTE)—*School Leadership: A Preface to Action* (1988)

➡ National Policy Board for Educational Administration
(NPBEA)—*Principals for Our Changing Schools* (1993)

Hoyle, English, and Steffy examine the skills of visionary leadership, policy making and governance, communication and community relations, organizational management, curriculum planning and development, instructional management, staff evaluation and personnel management, staff development, educational research, and evaluation and planning, as well as the values and ethics of leadership. They construct inventories, checklists, and bibliographies of relevant resources, and provide readings and activities for each of the standards listed.

Effective Leadership Attributes. In addition to the specific leadership roles and styles discussed above, Moss and Johansen (1991) have synthesized the research on the concept of leadership and its attendant tasks as follows:

➡ Inspire shared vision—focus shared values and set goals and objectives based on high ethical standards
➡ Foster collaboration, ownership, and a sense of valued team and individual contributions—establish unity
➡ Exercise power to enable others—nurture strengths in team planning and change management
➡ Model the behavior of a collegial community (3)

The accomplishment of these guiding tasks depends more on the person than the method of engagement. A leader's underlying assumptions, beliefs, values, and rules of interpersonal behavior either impede or empower a relationship in the service of school change and growth.

In advancing this argument, Moss and Johansen have compiled a list of thirty-seven attributes common to successful leaders, attributes that they maintain can be learned and exercised. They include such personal attributes as dependability, reliability, persistence, insightfulness, energy, enthusiasm, personal integrity, respect for and sensitivity to others, and the ability to motivate followers with an optimistic vision. Their leadership inventory, which they call the Leader Attributes Inventory (LAI), includes skills such as planning, delegating, organizing, team building, assigning and accepting accountability, tolerating frustration and ambiguity, and utilizing management skills that address conflict, time, stress, problem solving, and decision making (8–9).

The underlying assumption of their inventory draws on the strong correlation between the exercise of these attributes and effectiveness as an educational leader. However, they do pose questions about the initial results of their inventory. For instance, they ask if there are different stages of leadership development that are not factored into their inventory and, if so, to what extent these have a cumulative effect on both the organization and other traits. They also ask if there are some characteristics or skills that are prerequisites for the development of other attributes. Most importantly, they ask how these attributes can be cultivated in the field. And they ask what circumstances, mentor relationships, support systems, and ongoing growth experiences sustain a novice leader's or potential leader's resolve and aspirations for leadership roles.

McEwan (1998) has developed a checklist of thirty behaviors characteristic of effective educational leadership. She offers the following seven practices as steps toward becoming an effective instructional leader:

- •• Support of the staff
- •• Establishment of instructional goals
- •• Creation of a learning culture
- •• Communication of the school's vision and mission
- •• Development of teachers as leaders
- •• Establishment of high expectations
- •• Maintenance of positive attitudes toward all stakeholders (13)

Even though she has constructed this list for building administrators, it could easily apply to other constituents. Her checklist of behaviors for teacher leadership could apply to distributed leadership as well. A teacher-leader

- •• Mentors, coaches, and collaborates with new staff
- •• Brings continual learning perspectives and ideas to the school and the classroom
- •• Hones presentation skills for sharing new knowledge with others
- •• Focuses on increased student learning
- •• Engages in creative problem solving
- •• Takes open risks
- •• Shares information and new ideas (101)

Samuel Krug (1990) adds one more measure of the development of effective school leadership in the service of creating effective schools. He contends that among the variety of models for successful schools,

Blaine and Merrifield's (1986, 9) best explains students' achievement in terms of changes in abilities, temperament, motivation, and situation, each of which mediates or affects the others. For example, changes in instructional abilities of teachers will affect students' learning outcomes, which, in turn, affect motivation.

Further, he asserts that most research aimed at understanding why schools are successful provides lists of practices and personal characteristics of designated leaders, rather than focusing on leadership behaviors. Hallinger and Murphy (1985, 11) have developed a measurement tool that they call the Principal Instructional Management Scale (PIMS). It examines leadership behaviors such as framing and communicating the school's mission and goals, coordinating the curriculum, monitoring student progress, maintaining visibility, providing incentives for effective teaching and learning, and promoting professional development.

Both of these lists, although somewhat useful, tend to relegate particular compartmentalized tasks from a rather narrow viewpoint, confining people to given defined roles. However, McEwan does argue for the importance of developing and nurturing a collegial atmosphere that would be conducive to fostering the more integrated shared leadership indicative of the New Era.

Ramsey (1999, 23–131) characterizes successful leadership as being

- Decisive in decision making
- Creative in thinking about all aspects of the school
- Logical in problem solving—recognizes what is wrong, identifies the choices, chooses the best possible solution, converts the choice into action
- Planned—purposeful action moves one from mundane school management to visionary leadership
- Visionary—positive, goal-driven, challenging, doable, organized, focused on goals and on motivating members to accomplish goals; unifies stakeholders through shared goals and mutually agreed upon priorities, values, beliefs, assumptions, and outcomes; assesses necessary resources
- Strategically planned—SMART:
  S   specific, well defined
  M   measurable to the extent that it assesses progress
  A   action oriented
  R   realistic—challenging but accomplishable
  T   time oriented

•• Hopeful and encouraging—relentless in its support of staff and student teaching, learning, and achievement
•• Enjoyable—professional fulfillment comes from the position, which supports and challenges others
•• Visualizes change
•• Visible—engaged at the building level, the district level, the school board, and the community level
•• Politically astute about the overlapping politics of varied constituencies
•• Divergent in thinking—open to all possible solutions
•• Positive in thinking

Whatever the agreed upon characteristics of effective leadership, the role of the designated building leader, the principal, will shift in the New Era. There is a movement from thinking of leadership as management to thinking of leadership as facilitation. John Kotter of the Harvard Business School maintains that "successful transformation is 70–90 percent leadership and only 10–30 percent management" (1996, 26). New Era principals and other educational leaders will be scrutinized for their ability to initiate and sustain change, to engage groups of people in innovative curricular and diversified instructional strategies, and to create, support, and nurture the kind of environment that provokes risk taking in the service of improved student outcomes.

Barriers to Effectiveness. Impediments to the kind of educational leadership discussed here tend to come from external as well as internal deficiencies. When there is a lack of support, either perceived or actual, from other designated leaders, the added frustrations of working in a complex environment, coupled with the natural or anticipated challenges, become overwhelming. For instance, if a principal is attempting to engage and develop the capacity of teachers, parents, and students as leaders in a district in which the central administration, the school board, or the community does not value shared governance, the lack of support, the adversity, and difficulties in relationships would make it easy for a building principal to revert to managerial, top-down decision making. Likewise, if parents strongly desire to participate in the business and governance of the school but are not encouraged to move beyond sponsoring fund-raising projects or assisting with field trips, they will be less likely to be involved at any level.

An even larger barrier to the effectiveness of educational leadership is our country's historical conduct of putting more resources into remediation than into prevention. One need only look at the funding put into prisons as compared to the resources put into education to starkly see this choice. Again we can ask, What is valued? Prisons are air-conditioned but many schools are not. Those schools that are air-conditioned tend to air-condition the principal's office and the library, leaving many students in lower socioeconomic neighborhoods in over 100-degree classrooms in the early fall or late spring. Where are the country's priorities? And where are those champions for young people who will stand up like Jonathan Kozol and say, "Elements of childhood that bear no possible connection to the world of enterprise and profit get no honor in the pedagogic world right now, nor in the economic universe to which it seems increasingly subservient" (2000, 135). He passionately observes that children "come to understand the processes by which a texture of entitlement is stitched together for some children while it is denied to others" (2000, 100).

Are designated leaders being prepared to become purveyors of hope and possibility for all children? Even though institutions of higher learning have been carefully reshaping their leadership programs in light of the apparent shortfall in the number of people prepared to fill the many positions held by current designated leaders who will retire in the next four years, there is little selection and counseling of potential leaders in the field where they are immersed in the struggles of students and families. Despite the theoretical preparation offered at the master's or doctoral levels, frequently those people who assume formal leadership roles in schools and districts have few skills or little practical training in a "real world" leadership situation. Though there are some internships that place those studying for leadership roles in a mentored field situation, there is little consistency across institutions or program areas.

McEwan (1998) maintains that the biggest impediment to effective educational and instructional leadership is a lack of vision, will, and courage. Effective leadership requires having the kind of courage that allows one to take risks, to thrive on complexity and ambiguity, to enable others to empower themselves, to be willing to work long and hard for little extrinsic reward but with a wealth of intrinsic satisfaction born of the successes students experience.

Effectiveness in Schools. The predominant characterization of a good school, even up to the 1960s, was a "tight ship" free from disruptions, one that was orderly, calm, and quiet, with a principal who was firm and discipline oriented. Today perhaps the most valid indication of leadership effectiveness and good schools is student outcomes—social, developmental, and cognitive. We have entered the age of accountability. Yet with the rush and flurry of the standards movement and the proliferation of high-stakes state tests, we are left to question what kind of performance is valued. What kind of learning really matters in the business of comparative test scores by school and by school district? And what about the dynamic social and developmental outcomes that are so important to the healthy growth of students?

Betts (1997) contends that in light of single-measure assessments (for example, state exams, the Scholastic Assessment Test, or the National Assessment of Educational Progress), what is measured is what is watched. He points out that these assessments lack accountability effectiveness for the following reasons:

- Reports are not disseminated frequently enough or in a timely enough fashion to be useful for school improvement.
- Data are neither accessible nor timely for local accountability.
- Neither achievement scores nor financial reports reflect any thoughtful integration with classroom, school, or local initiatives.
- Data disproportionately stress financial measures, such as cost per student or pupil-teacher ratios, or the number of computers per student in the school.
- Current conventional reports do not address the question suggested above: "Are we measuring the right things?"
- The stakeholder community—staff, administrators, family, community members—have little, if any, opportunity for input into the communication and accountability processes. (70)

Betts suggests that a balanced approach to examining effective accountability should tie strategic planning to more appropriate measures. Also, technology-based tools should help stakeholders understand the relationship between the daily work of the classroom and student outcomes. By focusing on a designated set of significant measures, stakeholders on a variety of levels—from the classroom and the community to state departments of education—can more appropriately measure how strategic improvement efforts influence student outcomes.

Bolman and Deal (1997) examine the effectiveness of the leader through another approach—by analyzing the effectiveness of the school as an organization. They suggest four frames of analysis:

- Structure—does the structure reflect the expectations and beliefs of all stakeholders?
- People—are the needs of the school appropriately matched with the talents and needs of the people involved in it?
- Politics—is the leader keenly aware of political influences

internal and external to the school, and the political force
she or he could represent on behalf of the school in the
community?

- Symbols—do representative symbols reflect and interpret
the school's foundational assumptions and beliefs?

They contend that when a leader examines what the school,
neighborhood, and culture value, how meaning is constructed, how
people are engaged or regarded, and how the school builds and acts
upon expectations, the leader or leaders will be effective. The success of
that leadership is contextually dependent; in other words, the ways in
which leaders may be effective in a given school depend in large measure on the school's academic, cultural, structural, and social environment (Griffith 1999).

The pursuit of excellence has been the banner behind which varied constituent groups—the business sector, legislators, private foundations, community organizations and individuals, school personnel, and
the family—have rallied. It is excellence that advocates quality and instructional autonomy, and that first and foremost values the interests of
young people who are viewed holistically. When we rush to measure effectiveness in terms of a single norm-referenced performance score, we
must ask what we have ignored about the growth of young citizens that
will ready them to step into their contributive roles in a democracy.
Should we then turn to what have often been called the "correlates" of
the measures of effective schools, namely, strong instructional leadership, high performance expectations of all students, and academic goals
(Leithwood, Steinbach, and Raun 1995)? Do we measure progress toward the goals, or the evidence of thoughtful school improvement plans
and intended outcomes for students? How can we measure or compare
a middle school that has raised the basic reading scores of all its students from a third-grade level to a fifth-grade level in a year, to another
middle school just ten miles down the road that has challenged all of its
staff to incorporate higher-order thinking skills into their on-grade-level
seventh-grade reading scores?

We come away from these questions with the definition of an in-
structionally effective district that Peterson, Murphy, and Hallinger
(1987, 216) offer: "one in which there were high overall levels of achievement across subject areas, growth in achievement over time, and consistency in achievement across all subpopulations of students." Mortimer (1991, 9) suggests a broader definition of an effective school: "one
in which pupils progress further than might be expected from consideration of its intake." Most effective schools are defined in terms of student

test scores in math and reading. Yet most people in conventional conversation suggest good schools are something far more than the results of the restrictive, quantifiable paper-and-pencil test. Families send their children to the neighborhood school and taxpayers support that school with broader and deeper hopes than for high test scores. Absent in the above definitions is attention to the growth of the student as a person.

In New York City, leadership effectiveness is measured by students' growth and performance in terms of school goals and objectives (Lashway 1999). In Bellevue, Washington, on the other hand, the effectiveness of the designated building leader is assessed against the breadth and depth of teacher growth. The Bellevue model represents the spirit of mutuality and the building of people's capacities, for as designated leaders are held accountable for the leadership performance of the staff whom they evaluate, they are also responsible for nurturing the capacity for leadership in these same people.

Scheerens (1992) poses six questions that attempt to frame discussion of the evaluation of an effective school:

- From whose perspective is "effectiveness" being judged?
- What areas of activity within an organization determine effectiveness?
- At which level of the organization is effectiveness to be judged?
- Within what time span is effectiveness to be judged?
- What data are to be used for assessment?
- What standards or measures are to be used for effectiveness judgment? (Quoted in Law and Glover 2000, 7–9)

Brighouse and Tomlinson (1991) and Sammons, Hillman, and Mortimore (1995) argue for a positive culture of support, one of high expectations with a focus on teaching and learning, a culture of leadership, of family involvement, of student ownership of rights and responsibilities. They argue for a learning community that is focused, structured yet flexible, continuously learning in a collegial and collaborative fashion.

Lashway (1997–1998, 2) suggests the following work by researchers on leadership assessment:

- Frederick Wendel, Allan Schmidt, and James Loch, "Measurements of Personality and Leadership: Some Relationships" (1992), which takes a conceptual approach to leadership testing.

↦ Richard Hughes, Robert Ginnett, and Gordon Curphy,
"Assessing Leadership and Measuring Its Effects," in *Leadership: Enhancing the Lessons of Experience* (1993), which
looks at some techniques used to measure leadership traits
and their effects.

↦ Kenneth Leithwood, Paul Begley, and Bradley Cousins, "Performance Appraisal and Selection of School Leaders: Selection Processes and Measurement Issues," in *Developing Expert Leadership for Future Schools* (1992), which compares
the ways schools assess leadership.

↦ Richard Santeusanio, "Using Multi-raters in Superintendent
Evaluation," in *The School Administrator,* which describes
his own feedback system and offers suggestions for the use
of multirater feedback.

Lashway further provides a guidebook of sorts for the selection,
assessment, and ongoing development of school leadership with his
work *Measuring Leadership: A Guide to Assessment for Development of
School Executives* (1999). The text examines the selection of school leaders as they match the goals of the school or district; suggests appropriate district- or building-level assessments; and describes in greater detail a variety of assessment instruments.

The thoughtful Roland Barth (1990), founder and director of
Harvard University's Principals' Center, opposes this list-mania and
disagrees with those outside of the school who assume that, by simply
and clearly enumerating characteristics, directives, mandates, and role
attributions, "good" schools will naturally follow. He contends that
such an approach denies that a school is able or willing to help improve itself. The approach maintains that student outcomes can be
measured by some standardized scores that can be published in newspapers, scores that will help sell houses, scores that will get politicians
elected. And then by determining which schools are achieving above
expectations, the traits and work ethic of that school's leaders can be
identified and then transferred to the leadership of lower-achieving
schools.

Barth rails against the demeaning presumption that student
learning can be measured solely in test scores, the success of which can
only be attributed to effective teaching and dynamic leadership. He
maintains that "the vivid lack of congruence between the way schools
are and the way others' lists would have them be causes most school
people to feel overwhelmed, insulted, and inadequate—hardly building
blocks for improving schools or professional relationships" (39).

Then why do lists persist, even multiply? Barth observes that it is because they are tangible and defensible, and because there are as yet no compelling alternatives. But obvious questions arise: Whose list? What should be on the list? And who decides? Few would deny, however, that schools could be improved and outcomes for kids enhanced if teaching and leadership could be improved. Barth speaks of teachers when he says that some choose to lead for exactly the same reasons others do not. But he could well be speaking of the multifaceted stakeholder leadership when he says,

> They derive respect, if not acclaim, from other teachers for their efforts; they derive energy from leadership activities that fuels, rather than depletes, their classroom activities; by leading, they find they can more fully understand the points of view of other teachers and administrators; . . . they find they learn by leading, that leadership offers profound possibilities for professional development. (132)

Summary. Given the wealth of research on effective leadership and effective schools, it is not surprising that theoreticians and practitioners have as yet to agree on a single definition of effective educational leadership. We have examined the issues of technical skills, personal charisma and deportment, interpersonal skills and attitudes, commitment, energy, and vision. Each measurement reflects the underlying assumptions and beliefs of the author. Van Velsor and Leslie (1991) provide a careful and rigorous description of sixteen leadership assessment tools. Some tests approach educational leadership from the managerial perspective, others from the exceptional qualities perspective. Rarely do such tests or inventories actually measure in-school performance. But they can be used as tools for reflection and self-analysis, drawing attention to a leader's strengths and pointing out weaknesses, for they measure the leader's sense of herself and her role in the school.

Existing measurements of leadership largely ignore how a potential leader's ideological beliefs and attitudes affect decisions and behaviors. As Mitchell (1990) points out, there appear to be two widely accepted views of leadership. The first view argues that leaders behave in ways consistent with their own personal and professional tendencies. Or in Krug's (1990) terms, some people just seem to make better leaders. The second view argues that leadership behavior is contingent on the context and the leadership role that is assumed. Put another way, because some leaders are better able to adapt to situations than others are, there are appropriate leadership styles for a variety of different situations.

CONCLUSION

New Era leadership represents a change in the school mind, a change in how business is conducted. For too long, artificial boundaries of authority and privilege have gone unspoken but not unnoticed. Educators have felt that the classroom is their arena; they were hired to teach. Principals were hired to manage. Families are supposed to quietly but persistently support the work of the school without interference, but with the kind of commitment that prepares and readies their children for learning and makes them anxious to learn. From a removed distance, the school board is to make wise decisions about the community, and the central administration is to offer resources and human support without directly intervening in the individual school. Health, human, and social service agencies, community officials, state departments, and state legislators are to be ready when the school calls upon them. But, unfortunately, this artificial separation relegates talent, commitment, energy, participation, and constructive enthusiasm to a predetermined set of norms that differences out rather than embraces people and their participation. We must ask, Whose school is it? Whose voice has a right to be heard? How can the multitude of voices, beliefs, agendas, and ideologies be blended into a thoughtful, focused vision for the school? Who makes decisions and how are they made? How are success and effectiveness reached, and by what standards are they measured? Whose interests are served? Whose are denied?

New Era leadership, be it transactional, transformational, democratic, or facilitative, is about servant leadership in the purest collective and collaborative sense. Whether this is achieved with sensitivity to domains that have previously been considered private or personal is critical to the success and ongoing growth of the school. The critical examination by designated leaders of their own leadership styles, assumptions, beliefs, norms, and principles that undergird their thinking must precede the task of change. Shared governance cannot be directed or mandated. It must emerge from within the school as the designated leaders nurture others to become leaders, just as they nurture followers to reclaim the dynamic, the powerful construct, of shared beliefs modeled in the relationships and interactions that occur daily in the school.

What makes for an effective leader? Constituent groups answer this question in different ways. The traditionalists are interested in managerial, top-down, centralized authority that standardizes the experiences of all of a school district's students. The tendency of such centralized authority to respond well to federal or state mandates is

outweighed by its cumbersome inability to respond flexibly or creatively in a fast-paced and changing environment. Members of the religious right have their views of leadership and to some extent have removed their children from public schools because of their ideology.
Community leaders, students, parents, teachers, critical theorists, fem-
inists, and those who espouse democratic values for all students—all
have their respective positions on educational leadership. But although
the role expectations and character traits of leaders vary widely, the
single most fundamental attribute of effective educational leadership,
one that is common to all leaders, is an unrelenting focus on students
and their success. And in that gap between attention and success, educational leadership can no longer be reduced to a set of techniques,
traits, procedures, or rules. It should systematically and deliberately
develop leadership skills and attitudes in followers and create opportunities for them.

By collaboratively building New Era learning communities of
support, respect, flexibility, and stakeholder collegiality, the energy and
passion of varied constituencies are channeled into making the school's
vision of itself real. That vision centers on student learning, on creating
possibilities and futures for all of our country's young people. This kind
of New Era educational leadership is a reconstitution of the role of designated leaders. It is a shift from the functionalist paradigm of a leader
as a manager and organizer to a communal paradigm in which the
leader is a reflective, moral, and intellectual leader who converges energy on that which is possible through a collaborative vision that is
mindful of both rights and responsibilities.

The move to New Era thinking about distributed leadership, participatory democracy, shared power, and shared decision making can be
slow, frustrating, and even painful. Yet the rewards that ownership and
responsibility garner are evidenced in the improved academic and social outcomes for all students.

REFERENCES

Adair, J. G. 1983. "Social Artifact Research and Ethical Regulations: Their Impact
on the Teaching of Experimental Methods." *Teaching of Psychology* 10,
no. 3 (October): 159–162.

Adamczyk, J. 2000. "Personalizing the High School." Ph.D. dissertation, Eastern
Michigan University.

Austin, L. M. 2000. Personal Interview. W. K. Kellogg Foundation. Battle Creek,
MI.

Avolio, B. J., and B. M. Bass. 1988. "Transformational Leadership, Charisma, and Beyond." In *Emerging Leadership Vistas,* ed. B. R. Baliga, H. P. Dachter, and C. A. Schriesheim, 64–71. Toronto: Lexington Books.

Barth, R. 1990. *Improving Schools from Within: Teachers, Parents, and Principals Can Make the Difference.* San Francisco: Jossey-Bass.

Bass, B. M. 1985. *Leadership and Performance beyond Basics.* New York: Free Press.

Bell, J., and B. Harrison. 1995. *Vision and Values in Managing Education: Successful Leadership Principles and Practice.* London: David Fulton Publishers.

Bennis, W. G. 1959. "Leadership Theory and Administrative Behavior: The Problem of Authority." *Administrative Science Quarterly* 4: 259–260.

———. 1989. *On Becoming a Leader.* Reading, MA: Addison-Wesley.

Bennis, W. G., and B. Nanus. 1985. *Leaders: The Strategies for Taking Charge.* New York: Harper & Row.

Betts, F. 1997. "ASCD Special Report: Scoreboards for Schools." *Educational Leadership* 55, no. 3 (November): 70–71.

Bhindi, N., and P. Duignan. 1998. "Leadership for a New Century: Authenticity, Intentionality, Spirituality, and Sensibility." In *Policy, Leadership, and Professional Knowledge in Education,* ed. M. Strain, B. Dennison, J. Outson, and V. Hall, 52–59. Thousand Oaks, CA: Sage Publications.

Blaine, D. D., and P. Merrifield. 1986. "Achievement and Proficiency Measures." In *Functional Psychological Testing: Principles and Instruments,* ed. R. B. Cattell and R. C. Johnson, 168–192. New York: Brunner/Mazel.

Blake, R. R., and J. S. Mouton. 1978. "Should You Teach There's Only One Best Way to Manage?" *Training* 15, no. 4 (April): 24–29.

Blase, J., and G. Anderson. 1995. *The Micropolitics of Educational Leadership: From Control to Empowerment.* London: Cassell.

Blase, J., and J. Blase. 1994. *Empowering Teachers: What Successful Principals Do.* Thousand Oaks, CA: Corwin Press.

———. 1998. *Handbook of Instructional Leadership: How Really Good Principals Promote Teaching and Learning.* Thousand Oaks, CA: Corwin Press.

———. 1999. "Principals' Instructional Leadership and Teacher Development: Teachers' Perspectives." *Educational Administration Quarterly* 35, no. 3 (August): 349–378.

———. 2000. "Effective Instructional Leadership: Teachers' Perspectives on How Principals Promote Teaching and Learning in Schools." *Journal of Educational Administration* 38, no. 2: 130–141.

Blase, J., J. Blase, G. L. Anderson, and S. Dungan. 1995. *Democratic Principals in Action: Eight Pioneers.* Thousand Oaks, CA: Corwin Press.

Bolman, L. G., and T. E. Deal. 1997. *Reframing Organizations: Artistry, Choice, and Leadership.* San Francisco: Jossey-Bass.

Brighouse, T. 1986. *Effective Schools.* Oxford: London Education Association.

Brighouse, T., and J. Tomlinson. 1991. *Towards the Effective School: A Policy Paper.* London: Institute for Public Policy Research.

Bryman, A. 1986. *Leadership and Organizations.* Boston: Routledge.

Burns, J. M. 1978. *Leadership.* New York: Harper & Row.

Caldwell, B. J., and J. M. Spinks. 1992. *Leading the Self-Managing School.* Washington, DC: Falmer Press.

Carr, A. 1997. "Leadership and Community Participation: Four Case Studies." *Journal of Curriculum and Supervision* 12, no. 2 (Winter): 67–78.

Conley, D. T., and P. Goldman. 1994. *Facilitative Leadership: How Principals Lead without Dominating.* Eugene, OR: Oregon School Study Council Bulletin Series, August.

Day, C., D. Johnston, and P. Whitaker. 1990. *Managing Primary Schools in the 1990s: A Professional Development Approach.* London: Paul Chapman Publishing.

Dean, J. 1995. *Managing the Primary School.* 2nd ed. London: Routledge.

Dillard, C. B. 1995. "Leading with Her Life: An African-American Feminist (Re)Interpretation of Leadership for an Urban High School Principal." *Educational Administration Quarterly* 31, no. 4: 539–563.

Duignan, P., and R. MacPherson. 1992. *Educative Leadership: A Practical Theory for New Administrators and Managers.* London: Falmer Press.

Dunlap, D., and P. Goldman. 1995. "Power as a System of Authority versus Power as a System of Facilitation." Paper presented at the annual meeting of the American Educational Research Association, Boston, April 21–24. Cited in L. Lashway, "Facilitative Leadership." 1995. *ERIC/CUE Digest* 96 (April): 1–4.

Fink, E., and L. B. Resnick. 2001. "Developing Principals as Instructional Leaders." *Phi Delta Kappan* 82, no. 8 (April): 598–610.

Foster, W. 1986. *Paradigms and Promises: New Approaches to Educational Administration.* Buffalo, NY: Prometheus.

Freire, P. 1972. *Pedagogy of the Oppressed.* New York: Seabury Press.

Fullan, M., and A. Hargreaves. 1991. *What's Worth Fighting For? Working Together for Your School.* Toronto: Ontario Teachers Federation.

Gardner, J. 1990. *On Leadership.* New York: Free Press.

Geijsel, F., P. Sleegers, and R. van den Berg. 1999. "Transformational Leadership and the Implementation of Large-Scale Innovation Programs." *Journal of Educational Administration* 37, no. 4: 309–328.

Glickman, C. D. 1985. *Supervision of Instruction: A Developmental Approach.* Boston: Allyn and Bacon.

———. 1991. "Pretending Not to Know What We Know." *Educational Leadership* 48, no. 8: 4–10.

Grace, G. 1995. *School Leadership: Beyond Education Management.* Washington, DC: Falmer Press.

Griffith, J. 1999. "The School Leadership/School Climate Relation: Identification of School Configurations Associated with Change in Principals." *Educational Administration Quarterly* 35, no. 2 (April): 267–291.

Gronn, P. 1998. "From Transactions to Transformations: A New World Order in the Study of Leadership?" In *Policy, Leadership, and Professional Knowledge in Education,* ed. M. Strain, B. Dennison, J. Outson, and V. Hall, 7–30. Thousand Oaks, CA: Sage Publications.

Guthrie, J. 1990. "The Evolution of Educational Management: Eroding Myths and Emerging Models." In *Educational Leadership and Changing Context of Families, Communities, and Schools,* ed. B. Mitchell and L. Cunningham, 210–231. Chicago: University of Chicago Press.

Hall, V. 1996. *Dancing on the Ceiling: A Study of Women Managers in Education.* London: Paul Chapman Publishing.

Hallinger, P., K. Leithwood, and J. Murphy, eds. 1993. *Cognitive Perspectives on Educational Leadership.* New York: Teachers College Press.

Hallinger, P., and J. Murphy. 1985. "Assessing the Instructional Management Behavior of Principals." *The Elementary School Journal* 86, no. 2: 217–242.

Handy, C. 1993. *Understanding Organizations.* London: Penguin.

Herzberg, F. 1979. "New Perspectives in the Will to Work." *Personnel Administrator* 24, no. 12 (December): 72–76.

Hodgkinson, H. 2000–2001. "Educational Demographics: What Teachers Should Know." *Educational Leadership* 58, no. 4 (December–January): 6–11.

Hodgson, C. P. 1987. "Social and Legal Issues of Biotechnology: An Educational Perspective." *Ohio Journal of Science* 87, no. 5 (December): 148–153.

Hoyle, J. R., F. W. English, and B. Steffy. 1998. *Skills for Successful Twenty-First Century School Leaders: Standards for Peak Performers.* Arlington, VA: American Association of School Administrators.

Hughes, R., R. Ginnett, and G. Curphy. 1993. "Assessing Leadership and Measuring Its Effects." In *Leadership: Enhancing the Lessons of Experience.* Homewood, IL: Irwin (ED 363 927).

Kepner, C. H., and B. B. Tregoe. 1965. *The Rational Manager: A Systematic Approach to Problem Solving and Decision Making.* New York: McGraw-Hill.

Kerchner, C. T. 1993. "The Strategy of Teaching Strategy." In *Cognitive Perspectives on Educational Leadership,* ed. P. Hallinger, K. Leithwood, and J. Murphy, 5–20. New York: Teachers College Press.

Kotter, J. 1988. *The Leadership Factor.* New York: Free Press.

———. 1996. *Leading Change.* Boston: Harvard Business School Press.

Kozol, J. 1991. *Savage Inequalities: Children in America's Schools.* New York: Crown.

———. 2000. *Ordinary Resurrections: Children in the Years of Hope.* New York: Crown.

Krug, S. 1990. *Leadership and Learning: A Measurement-Based Approach for Analyzing School Effectiveness and Developing Effective School Leaders.*

Washington, DC: Office of Educational Research and Improvement (ED 327 950).

Krug, S., S. A. Ahadi, and C. K. Scott. 1990. *Current Issues and Research Findings in the Study of School Leadership.* Washington, DC: Office of Educational Research and Improvement (ED 327 946).

Lashway, L. 1995. "Facilitative Leadership." *ERIC/CUE Digest* 96 (April): 1–3.

———. 1996. "The Strategies of a Leader." *ERIC/CUE Digest* 105 (April): 1–4.

———. 1997–1998. "Measuring Leadership." *National Association of Elementary School Principals* 14, no. 2 (Winter): 1–3.

———. 1999. *Measuring Leadership: A Guide to Assessment for Development of School Executives.* Washington, DC: Office of Educational Research and Improvement (ED 431 209).

Law, S., and D. Glover. 1999. *Educational Leadership and Learning.* Philadelphia: Open University Press.

Leithwood, K. 1992. "The Move toward Transformational Leadership." *Educational Leadership* 49, no. 5 (February): 8–12.

Leithwood, K. A., P. T. Begley, and B. Cousins. 1992. *Developing Expert Leadership in Future Schools.* London: Falmer Press.

Leithwood, K., and D. Jantzi. 2000. "The Effects of Transformational Leadership on Organizational Conditions and Student Engagement with School." *Journal of Educational Administration* 38, no. 2: 112–129.

Leithwood, K. A., and M. Stager. 1986. "Differences in Problem-Solving Processes Used by Moderately and Highly Effective Principals." Paper presented at the annual meeting of the American Educational Research Association, San Francisco, April 21–24.

Leithwood, K., and R. Steinbach. 1990. "Characteristics of Effective Secondary School Principals' Problem Solving." *Journal of Educational Administration and Foundations* 5, no. 1: 24–42.

Leithwood, K., R. Steinbach, and T. Raun. 1995. "Prospects for Organizational Learning in Expertly Managed Group Problem Solving." In *Effective School District Leadership: Transforming Politics into Education,* ed. K. Leithwood, 99–114. Albany: State University of New York Press.

Likert, R. 1967. *The Human Organization: Its Management and Value.* New York: McGraw-Hill.

Lockwood, A. T. 1996. "The Changing Role of Principals: An Interview with Philip Hallinger." *New Leaders for Tomorrow's Schools* 3 (Fall): 30–33.

Lorsch, J. W., and P. R. Lawrence, eds. 1970. *Studies in Organization Design.* Homewood, IL: R. D. Irwin.

Louis, K. S., and M. B. Miles. 1992. *Improving the Urban High School: What Works and Why.* London: Cassell.

McEwan, E. 1998. *Seven Steps to Effective Leadership.* Thousand Oaks, CA: Corwin Press.

Mitchell, D. E. 1990. "Principal Leadership: A Theoretical Framework for Research." In *Advances in Educational Administration,* ed. P. Thurstone and P. Zodiates, 69–83. Vol. 2. Greenwich, CT: JAI Press.

Mitchell, D. E., and S. Tucker. 1992. "Leadership as a Way of Thinking." *Educational Leadership* 49, no. 5 (February): 30–35.

Mohr, N. 1997. "Stages of Developing Facilitative Leadership." In *The Skilled Facilitator,* ed. T. Schwartz, 1–2. New York: Facilitation Institute, NYC Board of Education, September.

Mortimer, P. 1991. "The Nature and Findings of Research on School Effectiveness in the Primary Sector." In *School Effectiveness Research: Its Messages for School Improvement,* ed. S. Riddell and S. Brown, 68–92. Edinburgh: Her Majesty's Stationery Office.

Moss, J., and B. Johansen. 1991. *Conceptualizing Leadership and Assessing Leader Attributes.* Macomb, IL: National Center for Research in Vocational Education.

Murphy, J. T. 1985. *Managing Matters: Reflections from Practice.* Cambridge, MA: Harvard University Graduate School of Education.

Musella, D. 1987. "How CEOs Influence School System Culture." In *Effective School District Leadership: Transforming Politics into Education,* ed. K. Leithwood. London: Croom Helm.

National Forum on Educational Leadership. 1999. *Effective Leaders for Today's Schools.* Washington, DC: U.S. Department of Education.

Ornstein, A. C., and L. S. Behar-Horenstein. 1999. *Contemporary Issues in Curriculum.* 2nd ed. Boston: Allyn and Bacon.

Ortiz, F. I., and R. T. Ogawa. 2000. "Site-Based Decision-Making Leadership in American Public Schools." *Journal of Educational Administration* 38, no. 5: 486–499.

Pajak, E. 1989. *Identification of Supervisory Proficiencies Project.* Alexandria, VA: Association for Supervision and Curriculum Development.

Peterson, K. D., and T. E. Deal. 1998. "How Leaders Influence the Culture of Schools." *Educational Leadership* 56, no. 1 (September): 28–30.

Peterson, K., J. Murphy, and P. Hallinger. 1987. "Superintendents' Perceptions of the Control and Coordination of the Technical Core in Effective School Districts." *Educational Administration Quarterly* 23, no. 1: 79–95.

Ramsey, R. D. 1999. *Lead, Follow, or Get Out of the Way: How to Be a More Effective Leader in Today's Schools.* Thousand Oaks, CA: Corwin Press.

Reynolds, D., P. Sammons, L. Stoll, M. Barber, and J. Hillman. 1996. "School Effectiveness and School Improvement in the United Kingdom." *School Effectiveness and School Improvement* 7, no. 2: 133–158.

Roueche, J. E., G. G. Baker, and R. R. Rose. 1989. *Shared Vision.* Washington, DC: Community College Press.

Sagor, R. 1992. "Three Principals Who Make a Difference." *Educational Leadership* 49, no. 5 (February): 13–18.

Sammons, P., J. Hillman, and P. Mortimore. 1995. *Key Characteristics of Effective Schools: A Review of School Effectiveness Research.* London: Ofsted.

Santeusanio, Richard. 1997. "Using Multi-raters in Superintendent Evaluation." *The School Administrator* 54, no. 3 (March): 12.

Scheerens, J. 1992. *Effective Schooling.* London: Cassell.

Schein, M. W. 1985. "Student Achievement as a Measure of Teaching Effectiveness." *Journal of College Science Teaching* 14, no. 6 (May): 471–474.

Schlechty, P. 1990. *Schools for the Twenty-First Century.* San Francisco: Jossey-Bass.

Seney, B. 2000. "Changing the Way We Think." *Education Update* 42, no. 8 (December): 3.

Sergiovanni, T. 1990. "Adding Value to Leadership Gets Extraordinary Results." *Educational Leadership* 47, no. 8: 23–27.

———. 1991. *Value-Added Leadership: How to Get Extraordinary Performance in Schools.* New York: Harcourt Brace Jovanovich.

Seyfarth, J. 1999. *The Principal: New Leadership for New Challenges.* Upper Saddle River, NJ: Prentice-Hall.

Slenning, K. 2000. *The Future School Manager: Information and Communication Technology Aspects.* New York: International Council for Education Media.

Smith, W., and R. Andrews. 1989. *Instructional Leadership: How Principals Make a Difference.* Alexandria, VA: Association for Supervision and Curriculum Development.

Strain, M., B. Dennison, J. Ouston, and V. Hall, eds. 1998. *Policy, Leadership, and Professional Knowledge in Education.* Thousand Oaks, CA: Sage Publications.

Tannenbaum, R., and W. H. Schmidt. 1973. "How to Choose a Leadership Pattern." *Harvard Business Review* 51, no. 3 (May–June): 51, 162–164, 168, 170, 173, 175, 178–180.

Terry, R. W. 1993. *Authentic Leadership: Courage in Action.* San Francisco: Jossey-Bass.

Tirozzi, G. 2001. "The Artistry of Leadership: The Evolving Role of the Secondary School Principal." *Phi Delta Kappan* 82, no. 6 (February): 434–439.

U.S. Department of Education. 1999. *Effective Leaders for Today's Schools: Synthesis of a Policy Forum on Educational Leadership.* Washington, DC: Education Publications Center, July.

Van Velsor, E., and J. B. Leslie. 1991. "Feedback to Managers." In *A Review and Comparison of Sixteen Multi-rater Feedback Instruments,* vol. 2: 168–201. Greensboro, NC: Center for Creative Leadership (ED 351 391).

Wagner, R. K. 1993. "Practical Problem Solving." In *Cognitive Perspectives on Educational Leadership,* ed. P. Hallinger, K. Leithwood, and J. Murphy, 88–102. New York: Teachers College Press.

Wendel, F., A. Schmidt, J. Loch. 1992. "Measurements of Personality and Leadership: Some Relationships." ED 350 694.

Wilson, M. 1993. "The Search for Teacher Leaders." *Educational Leadership* 50, no. 6 (March): 24–27.

Wirt, F. M. 1990. *The Missing Link in Instructional Leadership: The Superintendent, Conflict, and Maintenance Project Report.* Urbana, IL: National Center for School Leadership.

Wohlstetter, P., and A. van Kirk. 1995. *School-Based Budgeting: Organizing for High Performance.* Washington, DC: Office of Educational Research and Improvement (ED 384 953).

Zaleznik, A. 1977. "Managers and Leaders: Are They Different?" *Harvard Business Review* 55, no. 3 (May-June): 67–78.

Chapter Four

⚭ The Community of Leaders and Learners

SCHOOLS AS COMMUNITIES

Communities are characterized by their vigilance to values, identities, status roles, resources, aggregates, and sanctions. So too are schools. Schools as communities realize the values of intelligence, skills, loyalties, wealth, comfort, and security. Their identities are defined in part by the roles and behaviors of those who participate in them: students are motivated and receptive; parents are supportive, engaged, and nurturing; teachers are intelligent, caring, skillful, and guiding; administrators are responsively facilitative; school boards thoughtfully take into account the wishes of the collective neighborhood when planning the education of its students; and state and federal officials allocate and monitor resources on top of fashioning directives and mandates.

Schools induce role-players or stakeholders to perform tasks and utilize resources, albeit not always in the most productive ways. Schools aggregate stakeholders' roles so that persons who must relate to each other in order to perform common tasks can do so effectively, if not efficiently.

Unfortunately, schools, like communities, at times utilize sanctions to induce conformity and to discourage deviation, sanctions that often promote institutionalized, deeply habitual patterns of behavior that may discourage diversity and are, in fact, resistant to change. Traditionally, schools, like communities, explicitly or implicitly, knowingly or in the name of imparting trust in the dominant culture's "American Dream," negatively strive to reduce diversity by limiting possibilities, by forcing functional compatibility, and by isolating individuals. And in so doing, voices become silenced and the fulfillment of human potential becomes blocked.

Why Is Community Important to Schools? Community is the sense of connectedness to something much larger than the individual, something greater, even, than a single group of stakeholders. It reflects the need of humankind to belong, to hold in common certain values, ideas, and beliefs. Noted French sociologist Emile Durkheim (1964) contended that community is a fundamental human need. He believed that community was, in many ways, a collective conscience that was constructed around issues of attachment, duty, and self-determination. When the collective conscience is lost, so too are the senses of duty and self-determination, leaving the individual disconnected and without a moral base.

This sense of community portrays dimensions of purpose and significance that are uncharacteristic of the educational profession, which tends to be so isolated. Schools that see themselves as communities embrace young people who are increasingly becoming disaffected and alienated from a society that denies them their youth and often does not prize their intrinsic worth, a society that values them not as they are but rather as the productive workers they might become. The explosion of violence and gangs in schools reflects a lack of a sense of belonging among young people who don't feel valued by a group or connected in abiding ways to a deeper moral purpose.

Norman Kunc (1992) observes that this human need, belonging, is no longer an unconditional right. Rather, only a few people may earn it:

> The curricula and the structure of our schools are based on the assumption that children who come to school have had their psychological and safety needs met at home. Students, upon entering school, are immediately expected to learn the curriculum. Successful mastery of schoolwork is expected to foster the children's sense of self-worth, which in turn will enable them to join the community as "responsible citizens." Children are required, as it were, to earn their right to belong. (31)

Schools as communities tie students and stakeholders together, not through constraints or compliance with rules, but through a commitment to ideas and each other, and through a common sense of purpose. Identity is defined in the interdependence of the community members. "The bonding together of people in special ways and the binding of them to shared values and ideas are the defining characteristics of schools as communities," as Sergiovanni (1994, 4) writes. When this relationship is sustained, the health of families and the neighborhood is also enhanced.

Dewey and the Connected Community. New Era educational leadership believes, like John Dewey (1938), who was one of this country's most insightful and influential educational leaders and philosophers, in the regenerative, self-sustaining life of the community of a school. It believes in an intimacy and safety characteristic of earlier communities that helped sort through the collective experiences of the community in the service of growth of and vision for a milieu that was personally connected, culturally and socially responsive, and professionally reflective. This text has viewed educational leadership and shared governance in the context of community. The community we speak of is a place where diversity breeds honesty and critical integrity, where each voice has an active place in the dialogue of humankind, where development is understood as a definite process rather than a single finite event, where conformity gives way to creative transformation, and where making personal sense of one's experiences frees the life-process for its own fulfillment.

Dewey held that schools should be authentic forms of an active community, a place where people worked on the basis of common aims that demanded unity of thought, sympathy of feeling, and commonality of social spirit. Because interaction and communication are the lifeblood of a community, teachers, students, and parents play a vital part in the group, operating from inside the community rather than from outside.

Dewey (1902) saw school as a learning habitat where experiences directed life choices rather than as a place to learn lessons imposed from above. In this type of school, where activity provoked the need for information, kids would acquire both more information and more relevant information. They would gain greater powers of interpretation, learn to draw inferences, make observations, and continuously reflect on their experiences—all cornerstones of a healthy community.

Dewey stated that a community-school, rather than being a place of self-emulation or a place for reciting lessons, should be a social meeting place where members of the community at large converse with each other. It should be a place where people collectively share their experiences and thoughts, where misconceptions are corrected and new possibilities are raised, where the sense of agency is compelled by common responsibility for the future.

The Reawakening of Community. As schools are challenged to respond to the demands of their social milieus and undertake different tasks, the earlier notion of schools as communities becomes less important. However, the research on effective schools in the 1970s and 1980s pointed to the importance of mutually shared values, a common focus on academic standards, and emotional connections that are indicative of communities (Rowan 1990). The emphasis on emotional connections has been subsequently framed as the ethic of caring (Sizer 1984; Lightfoot 1984).

The idea that schools are democratic communities has emphasized mutually shared values and shared responsibility (Larrivee 1999, 78). Sergiovanni (1992a, 1994) and Noddings (1992) applied Dewey's sense of community to the contemporary arena and called for schools to strengthen the lives of fragmented young people by creating communities of caring relationships, meaning, and purpose. And still other educational leaders (Goodlad 1990; Lieberman and Miller 1984) challenged schools to strengthen the emotional as well as the cognitive or academic development of students.

Community and Democracy. Schools in this country were founded on the notion that educated people would become useful contributors to the democracy. They would be critical thinkers, problem-solvers, people responsible to and for each other, people who could think independently while being able to work collaboratively. However, "as many have argued since John Dewey's day, children cannot learn these values in institutions that do not live by them," as Ackerman, Donaldson, and van der Bogert (1996, 141) observe. The school community that celebrates diversity, that practices and teaches social skills, that resolves conflict and differences in respectful and thoughtful ways demonstrates democratic practice. "The ability to appreciate those who are different is a nonnegotiable part of educating for democracy," according to Linda Darling-Hammond (Lockwood 1997, 11).

Educational leaders help create, shape, and sustain a culture in which these principles are deliberately modeled and critically discussed; this is not a task to be accomplished alone. Issues of equity, expectation, and opportunity can confound the school's leaders as the disparities in society loom even larger. Schools need a wide range of support, involvement, engagement, and creative energy. "Returning schools to their public function means making families and communities co-owners in the schools. It means making democracy work through the process of sharing power, providing a democratic vision, and working collectively to create a multicultural and multiracial democracy" (Astuto et al. 1994, 31).

Schools as communities ask such questions as: Whose voice is not represented? Is one voice more dominant than another, and, if so, why? What might be some other frames of understanding or interaction? How are our own values formed, shaped, and represented in the school in general, or in the classroom?

Schools that are democratic communities do not employ the authoritarian, managerial style of educational leadership. Rather, they collaboratively build on the resilience of students, families, faculty, and neighborhood residents. And in doing so they give rise to legitimate forms of shared leadership that help shape the cultivation of values, ownership, empowerment, and possibility. "Democratic communities help students to be as well as to become. They seek to help students meet their needs today as well as become tomorrow's caring and active citizens. Unless today's needs are met, students drift further away from school life" (Sergiovanni 1994, 124).

The community's strength lies in its active citizens as they work for the common good. All members have responsibilities that both connect them to the community and reaffirm their sense of value and belonging.

COMMUNITY OF IDEAS AND RESPONSIBILITY

Sergiovanni (1994) points out that when a school is driven by the sense of a community of responsibility, it is less influenced by hierarchical structures or by the personality of those in leadership positions. "'Follow me' is so much a part of our thinking that we often miss the whole point of leadership. The true leader is one who builds in substitutes for 'follow me' leadership, which enable people to respond from within" (Sergiovanni 1992b, 31).

Even though charismatic "follow me" leadership may well entice people to cooperate, it will not in the long run engender the kind of substantive commitment in followers that systemic reform requires. Because it creates a bifurcated system of subordinates and leaders, commitment to work is neither self-motivated nor enduring.

All stakeholders can follow ideas instead of leaders. In this way the concept of leadership is broadened. Sergiovanni (1992b) contends that idea-based leadership is not only morally defensible but more effective in schools. With idea-based leadership, student success hinges not on a person or persons, but rather on the shared sense of community purpose and responsibility.

When schools embrace the community of responsibility, Sergiovanni observes, the lack of trust that state boards, state legislators, or the general public may have had in the local schools is replaced by a sense of growing communal ownership. And simultaneously this community of ideas enables stakeholders to exercise shared power. It is a leadership of community, which is less about the redistribution of power in a way that

> some gain and others lose, and more about increasing the capacities
> of schools to function more effectively in changing times. Schools are

enabled as they learn more and can do more; as they acquire the passion, moral commitment, and norms to persevere; and as they become communities of responsibility that meet their commitments in ways that win the trust of the people. (Sergiovanni 2000, 19)

When seen as a community rather than an organization, the local school is continuously regenerated by people working together, with shared norms and values, supporting one another and acting with a common purpose. Barth (1990, 9) suggests that this conception of community is twofold: one, a community of learners, a place where all stakeholders are encouraged to engage in meaningful learning and study; two, a community of leaders in which all stakeholders share decision-making opportunities and responsibilities.

Sergiovanni (1994) has identified six forms or identities of schools as communities:

- Caring communities—members are motivated by altruistic love and interdependent commitment.
- Learning communities—members are characterized as thinking, inquiring, growing, and learning, participating in a process and exhibiting a habit of mind that facilitates a shared vision.
- Professional communities—members are committed to ongoing development of professional craft knowledge and professional ideals.
- Collegial communities—members are bound together in pursuit of common goals for mutual benefit; they have mutual obligations and are interdependent.
- Inclusive communities—members from a variety of religious, ethnic, socioeconomic, and other differenced groups are celebrated together as valuable contributors to the community's work.
- Inquiring communities—members are engaged in collective inquiry while reflecting on practice. (71)

Caring Communities. It is important to note that individual teachers, teams, or even individual schools are seen by both students and their families as nurturing and caring, but without overstepping the boundaries and thus becoming intrusive, indulgent, or even intimate. The kind of caring that promotes a sense of community in schools is neither gender-specific nor particular in style. Teachers, administrators, and other community stakeholders vary in how they engage students and relate to them. Deiro's (1996) research demonstrated that caring is neither permissive nor overtly affectionate. Frequently, when middle schools adopt an advocacy program known as the advisor period, a time when an adult works closely with a small group of students, male teachers comment that they are not good with "touchy-feely" stuff, which they feel is better done by the female staff. Nurturing and caring communities should not be reduced to touching students or to allowing students to be "whoever they are"; nor should nurturing and caring be work left only for the women.

In caring communities there is an abiding sense of concern and compassion for students not only as learners but as growing young people who are questioning the world and their place in it, and looking for adult guidance, or at least an adult who will actively listen to them. This is the type of community that builds trust, and without trust little authentic learning ever transpires in the classroom. This kind of community engenders mutual respect among all members of the school family.

In the caring, democratic community, according to Larrivee (1999, 85), everyone "rates," as the interrelationships among the community members are characterized by respect, authenticity, thoughtfulness, and emotional integrity (or, in a word, RATE). Interactions on all levels are honest and open. They are not based on assumed roles but on the integrity of knowing oneself in the service of helping someone else discover himself or herself. And they are based on the accountability of all stakeholders.

In very practical terms, Larrivee observes that when people are committed to creating this type of community, they

- Act authentically by speaking the truth with care and thoughtfulness
- Pay attention to what's being said without interpretation, judgment, or trying to rescue
- Listen beneath the surface, remaining open to discovering something about themselves in the stories of others. (Larrivee 1999, 90)

The community becomes one of cooperation rather than competition, a community of common struggle and common accomplishment.

Stanford's Nel Noddings (1992) persuasively speaks about the link between continuity and caring, and notes four kinds of continuity in schools:

- Continuity in purpose—schools are centers of care.

⟶ Continuity of school residence—students should remain at one school site long enough to develop a sense of belonging.

⟶ Continuity of teachers and students—they should remain together across an extended period of time in order to establish abiding and caring relationships.

⟶ Continuity in curriculum—stakeholders respect and engage the full range of human capacities given opportunities for exploration with a curriculum based on the core theme of caring. (72–73)

Noddings calls into question the ethical ideal of moral conduct and moral community behavior. And she contends that caring is an individual endeavor (1984). To speak of it in collective terms is to attempt to capture in a general sense the intentions of individuals who value caring as a moral action.

Learning Communities. Sergiovanni contends that it is the learning community, in particular, that truly challenges the farthest breadth of the capacity of shared leadership and fundamental relationships. When schools become communities, robust, responsive leadership does more than simply refashion or redefine itself. It continues to evolve in ways that challenge and enable all stakeholders to question their own construction of meaning and those values that are held to be of fundamental consequence. For instance, as a school develops its sense of identity and operation through instructional teams, the designated leader of the building will respond in supportive ways, which challenge the teams to engage in innovative practices with their students. At the same time, the leadership provides a safety net of sorts for risk taking that may be less than successful. On the other hand, work with families and a community roundtable or community stakeholder group may be only in their initial stages. The leadership provided by the building leader or leaders would look very different than that provided by the teaching staff. Yet in all instances the focus is on students and the school's designated goals and purposes.

Lambert (1998) speaks of reciprocal learning processes in learning communities that are engaged in the work of leadership. She suggests that the community is able to renew itself through

⟶ Surfacing, clarifying, and defining community values, beliefs, assumptions, perceptions, and experiences

⟶ Inquiring into the effects of current practice on student learning

⟶ Constructing meaning and knowledge in terms of the discrepancies between expectations and results (i.e., problem analysis)

⇒ Framing action and developing implementation plans (6–7)

Yet it is important to note that all of the above practices take place in an environment of trust and collegiality, one that values risk taking, critical reflection, authentic interactions and relationships, and professional scrutiny in the service of improving practice. But, Lambert points out, "not all learning processes constitute leadership. To be 'leadership,' these processes must enable participants to learn themselves toward a shared sense of purpose—a purpose made real by the collaboration of committed adults" (8).

Peter Senge (2000), MIT senior lecturer and well-known author, reflects a business perspective when he interchangeably uses the terms "learning communities" and "learning organizations." He has identified five disciplines that help address the challenges of contemporary education:

⇒ Personal mastery, a practice that compares one's personal vision with current experience; used in the service of expanding choices

⇒ Shared vision, which creates a mutual purpose; used to nurture a sense of commitment to the school's goals

⇒ Mental models, which shape one's attitudinal and perceptive sensitivity through reflection and inquiry; used to assist in deconstructing and therefore understanding reality

⇒ Team learning, which employs group interaction techniques such as dialogue and skilled discussion, and involves learning to pool group energy to accomplish shared initiatives; used both in the classroom and in various other settings and groups outside the school

⇒ Systems thinking, which instructs people in the more substantive understanding of interdependency, change, and causal and consequential action; used to more critically understand complexity and change in schools across time as well as to assist stakeholders and students in developing a deeper understanding of learning (7–8)

Senge (1990, 68) further observes that systems thinking offers a broader picture of the whole, in this case of the school, allowing for the observation of patterns in change rather than a piecemeal critique of the school organization or attention to only part of it.

San Francisco School Board member Gail Greely recounts the struggles in which her board engaged in attempting to realize their vision of school as community and thereby put Senge's theory into practice:

> We all soon discovered that realizing this vision represented a very complex challenge, because of ingrained policies, practices, and politicking. When I took office on the school board, I assumed I would have a lot to learn about education. But I soon discovered that I needed first to learn how organizations work, how schools are governed, and why the barriers to change exist. (Senge 2000, 433)

Greely goes on to say that during her eight-year tenure on the board, trying to establish a learning community based on Senge's five disciplines was a struggle that yielded great rewards. She describes herself as a "learning school board" member.

Peter Negroni, formerly a principal and superintendent in New York City's public school system, describes himself and his work with the community in much the same way (Senge 2000, 425). When he came to New York's rapidly changing school system, he initiated new ways of involving community stakeholders. But the first three years were brutal ones for him, as people became invested in new relationships and in the process of change were charged with openly confronting their own purposes, commitments, and relationships. Yet the most difficult thing for Negroni was realizing that he could not accomplish alone all that he intended:

> Part of me still holds on to the training that says, "leadership is giving people focus and direction. Tell them what to do and they do it." But genuine leadership is enhancing the opportunity for people to think. That means creating opportunities for people to think together in dialogue. To be a real learner, you have to listen to, and value, what other people say. You have to apply what they tell you to create new approaches together. (Senge 2000, 429)

For Negroni, as well as for Greely, to be an effective leader in a learning community meant first to be willing to learn about learning.

Lambert (1998) examines the concepts of leadership and community in light of the learning processes in which the school community is engaged and the school's connections to its stakeholders. She maintains that leadership involves "an energy flow or synergy generated by those who choose to lead" (5). It is an energy that fuels learning together, constructing meaning and purpose both collectively and collaboratively. It involves opportunities to surface and mediate perceptions, values, beliefs, information, and assumptions through continuing conversations; to inquire about and generate ideas together; to seek to reflect upon and make sense of work in the light of shared beliefs and new information; and to create actions that grow out of these new understandings. (5–6)

Such shared beliefs and norms are the moral values that give guidance and consensual meaning to the school. They are, in essence, the foundation upon which community of mind is built, upon which the struggle to find and construct purpose is founded. And according to Sergiovanni (1992b), a school that functions as a community has at its center an uncompromising sense of moral leadership:

> The heart of the school as moral community is its covenant of shared values. This covenant provides a basis for determining its morality. . . . The virtuous school subscribes to and uses these moralities as a basis for deciding what its values are and how they will be pursued. (108)

In examining the school as a community of mind, as a living organism, educational leaders ask guiding questions such as: What do we believe is the purpose for school? How do we value or view teaching and learning within the context of the school? What do we believe all students should know, be able to do, and value? What do we value about the relationships among the stakeholders, including relationships between teachers and students, relationships that permeate the school community as it learns and grows? What nourishes the community? What gives it life? What is our common purpose? What unifies our action? What are our individual visions for our school? ("Until we have a vision to share, we can't understand anyone else's," Barth [1990, 159] aptly wrote.) What is our collective vision for our school, the jointly constructed compass that will unify and guide our work and point us in the direction of what "can be" for young people? And how do we transform these hopes and aspirations into reality on behalf of students?

Professional Communities. Michael Fullan (1998), a noted leader in school change, contends that all of the energy put into adopting new models of school operation or new ways of providing instruction continually fail and reaffirm teachers' sense of "here comes another fad" because of an ill-placed focus. Rather than focusing on how the school operates, Fullan argues, school leaders should delve a layer deeper and examine the entire process of changing the culture. In other words, they should scrutinize basic assumptions—the norms, values, shared beliefs, and relationships that drive operational decisions.

Wald and Castleberry (2000) point out three basic assumptions about the development of professional learning communities that focus on school culture rather than school structure:

- A shared culture is shaped and bound together through shared philosophy, assumptions, values, and beliefs.
- A community is an interdependent and interlacing network of diverse relationships.
- A community provides the cultural context for the kind of risk taking that helps realize unexpected potential. (13–16)

Likewise, DuFour and Eaker (1998) describe professional communities as those that construct a shared mission, vision, and values; conduct collective inquiry; work as collaborative teams; are driven by action and experimentation; are focused on continuous improvement; and are results-driven.

Professional communities focus on people rather than tasks. And in doing so the school becomes a community of kinship in which all are learners, all feel safe, and all enjoy support and encouragement. In this way the school as a community becomes both an end in itself (it is both just and good) and a means for achieving greater academic success (Sergiovanni 1994).

The school may also become what Parker Palmer (1998) calls a "community of congruence," a place where ideas are challenged and validated, where there are opportunities for mutual reassurance and reaffirmation, where moral persuasions are reinforced, and where skills and dispositions are developed. Palmer indicates that there are five key elements of a supportive professional community:

- Affirmation of personal moral persuasions through mutual reassurance, nurturance and sustenance of beliefs, and validation of democratic ideals
- Development of a common language and the opportunity to practice it with like-minded people
- Refinement of the knowledge that informs transformative leadership practices
- Development of skills necessary for collaborating, criticizing, compromising, dealing with challenge and opposition, strengthening conviction, and resisting co-option by the mainstream
- Experiences that transform moral persuasions into convic-

tions and conviction-based leadership. (As cited in Henderson and Hawthorne 2000, 190–191)

On a practical level, educational leader Seymour Sarason (1993) cautions that adults, and teachers in particular, in the learning community cannot continue to foster the growth and development required in this community unless their own growth and development are nurtured. Wald and Castleberry (2000) present a game plan of sorts for the kind of collegial and collaborative learning indicative of a professional community. They suggest that schools should deliberately identify their current practices and the underlying assumptions that guide them. Then, new ideas that address common goals can be generated, practiced, assessed, and shared.

Collegial Communities. The idea of collegiality is notably absent from the effective schools literature and from many national studies of U.S. education and leadership. Yet in our discussion of distributed leadership and the significance of relationships, collegiality is the touchstone of New Era leadership. Little (1981) speaks of collegiality in four behaviors:

- Adults in schools talk about practice.
- Adults in schools observe each other.
- Adults work together on curriculum planning, designing, implementing, and evaluating.
- Adults teach each other not only about craft knowledge but also about the art of the community of school. (Barth 1990, 31)

Roland Barth, the founder of Harvard University's Principals' Center, looks at educational leadership and observes, "We have engaged in a long and difficult struggle against the belief held by many practitioners that one's success in schools is a private matter, best kept from potential competitors or critics" (1990, 78). Here lies a real indictment of public schools—it is in private that mistrust, isolation, and atrophy flourish. Barth further contends that developing a supportive culture of reflection, learning, cooperation, and professionalism among educators and among the community of stakeholders aids development of this culture in the classroom.

Pointedly, and more profoundly, Barth observes that the "central problem and paradox for public school educators is that we adults try to instill life and excitement and meaning into students' learning while we ourselves are dead as learners" (116). At the center of the character and quality of a school and its students' accomplishments is the quality of adult relationships within the school. These relationships should foster and encourage an atmosphere conducive to risk taking and make it one of the school's chief features.

According to Barth, the collegial community is a healthy culture, a community of learners as well as a community of leaders. But, he observes, it is not the natural order in schools, and it will not happen of its own volition. It must be as deliberate as it is valued, for in many ways it is a kind of professional virtue or disposition.

Barth argues that continuing "self-development is a higher duty than self-sacrifice" in the community of learners (1990, 47). The sixteen habits of mind that Costa and Kallick use to describe leadership also help paint a behavioral portrait of a learning community. The habits of mind they identify are

- Persisting
- Managing impulsivity
- Listening with understanding and empathy
- Thinking flexibly
- Thinking about thinking (metacognition)
- Striving for accuracy
- Questioning and posing problems
- Applying past knowledge to new situations
- Thinking and communicating with clarity and precision
- Gathering data through all senses
- Creating, imagining, innovating
- Responding with wonderment and awe
- Taking responsible risks
- Finding humor
- Thinking interdependently
- Remaining open to continuous learning. (Costa and Kallick 2000, xiii)

In examining these behaviors, we might ask what habits of mind and place are the most productive for the school and for students' learning? What is evidence of a healthy learning community? And what are indicators of the growth of this community of learners? Perhaps all of these questions might best be framed in the context of students, i.e., what habits of mind are the most productive for the kids? What is used as evidence of growth and how is it assessed?

The community of leaders represents the business of shared governance, one of the main themes of this text. We have examined the ideas that contribute to the belief (which is supported by research) that greater investment and ownership brings greater commitment and productivity and more substantive gains for students. The opportunities that designated leaders create in shaping and sustaining a culture of leaders offer multidimensional stakeholders the chance to substitute collective authority and responsibility for the single voice of the principal.

Lambert (1998) points out that this change in roles arises from a change in self-perceptions, one that creates new opportunities for re-defining traditional roles—of teachers, administrators, families, students, school board members, community participants. "As roles evolve, members of a school community reach a point of collective responsibility—a condition demonstrably linked to high student achievement," Lambert writes (94–95). This involves a regeneration of the school not apart from the community but as a microcosm of the community.

With this shift in roles, with this move to shared governance and to schools as communities, will superintendents and school boards lose some of their control? They will lose the kind of control that stifles creativity and sustained change. Lambert observes, however, that "a new form of control emerges, one that invests itself in learning and long-range results. This new form requires that superintendents and board members let go of the need for daily predictabilities, narrow objectives, the development of 'knee-jerk' policies, self-indulgence in crisis, and a paternalistic stance" (98).

The prestigious Annenberg Foundation, which has invested a wealth of resources in low-achieving schools in disadvantaged neighborhoods, applies in a practical way this concept of a community of leaders and learners. Their leadership initiatives use the collaborative concepts of peer observation, team building, consultancy groups, and cooperative protocols to assist in the building of professional learning communities that stimulate transformative leadership and teaching in ways that benefit students (see chapter 5 for specific information on Annenberg's initiatives).

On the school level, this type of community does more than instruct parents in ways to help their children with homework. It increases the number of families who attend meetings or school functions, and even involves them in decisions of the school. Thomas Hatch of Harvard's Project Zero says that community involvement, even to the extent of establishing a school as a community, "is most effective when it serves as a catalyst for improving the physical conditions and resources available, the attitudes and expectations within the school and the community, and the formal and informal learning opportunities for both children and adults" (1998, 19).

Schools as communities transform competitive relationships into collaborative interactions, student learning into community learning, isolation into complex engagement. And as Barth points out, "Communities of leaders beget communities of learners" (1990, 137).

CORE VALUES

Where does a school begin when considering the move to becoming a community? If there were a single answer, it might be to examine the core beliefs that shape both the conduct and meaning of the school. Sergiovanni (1994) points out that core values should infuse every aspect of the school. In educational leadership literature, values refer to enduring or abiding beliefs about the worth of particular actions or means. These pivotal values or ethics become the guiding principles that influence how individuals and the community think, act, and communicate, how choices are made, and how they are morally judged. Wilson asserts, "Only moral leadership with explicit purpose and values provides the possibility for the kind of community dialogue requisite to improving our schools radically" (1993, 220).

Using the idea-based leadership model suggested above, shared values, ideals, and purposes become the forces for shaping school conduct and programs. In effect, this is design from within the community rather than top-down construction based on objectives and instrumental operation. It is the process of translating values into strategies. "What distinguishes effective educational leaders from others is a distinctive set of beliefs about what is possible" (Sergiovanni 1992a, 311).

What Are Core Values? Beliefs in inclusion, the sanctity of the classroom, embracing and celebrating diversity, educating for democracy, and supporting collegial growth may form the foundation of core values upon which the goals and objectives of the school are constructed. Although Clark (1983) identified liberty, social justice, loyalty, and competence as the underpinnings of systems of higher education, they are applicable to core values held by educational leaders and hence are reflected in their schools. Notions of liberty link "choice, initiative, innovation, criticism and variety with democratic values" (McNay 1995, 21).

Other educational leaders have suggested different or additional core values. For instance, Wilson (1993) would add a constructivist view of knowledge that helps to define and shape all relationships within the school in general and those on teaching and learning in particular. It is a view that places the teacher or leader in a facilitator's role while the student derives meaning or constructs knowledge through the activities or opportunities provided. This view contrasts directly with the positivist approach whereby students are told or "given" information, and teachers or other stakeholders are directed to accept a solution rather than examining the problem first and then posing answers together.

Patterson (1993) observes that there is a new openness to the core beliefs in participation, diversity of opinion, learning from conflict, reflection and critique, and acceptance of mistakes. New Era leaders value the direct engagement of stakeholders in all phases of the problem-solving process. They encourage and value differing viewpoints that lead to a richer understanding of the school and its knowledge base. They embrace conflict as opportunity, reflection as a means to making more thoughtful decisions, and mistakes as valuable learning tools.

Patterson poses some perceptive questions that suggest ways schools may develop their own core values and guidelines that help implement them. For instance, if a core value were student success, the school might well ask to what extent the district

- Prized students as valuable human beings, important for who they are and not for who they might become?
- Valued students as inherently curious and active learners?
- Valued doing everything necessary for kids to be successful?
- Valued students being engaged in work that is meaningful, relevant, challenging, motivating, and stimulating? (95)

Can values be learned by students? Some would contend that our country is in an ethical crisis. In one study, 78 percent of students admitted that they had cheated on tests and had difficulty distinguishing right from wrong (Stratton 1995). Phi Delta Kappa (PDK), a prestigious honorary international professional education association, believes values can be developed in students. PDK helps to prepare young leaders through their summer Ethical Leadership Camps in Bloomington, Indiana. They have identified seven core values as learning, honesty, cooperation, service to others, freedom, responsibility, and civility. Some of their young people also attend the League of Value-Driven Schools, an activity sponsored by PDK that grew out of their Study of Core Values. Camp coordinator JoAnn Fujioka contends that students can "turn whole schools and communities around if there are enough of them just saying 'yes' to values" (PDK, 5). This is an example of the kind of leadership that helps young people shape their values, rather than imposing one's will or value system on them. It treats young people with respect—perhaps the ultimate form of moral leadership.

Values and Ethics. Still others speak in broader terms of the "ethic of justice," the "ethic of care," and the "ethic of critique" as ethics that would assist people both in times of crisis and amid the daily interaction of the community's members (Starratt 1994, 46–52). Ethics are frequently defined as the value preferences a group, community, or society shares. When considering educational leadership, discussion and examination of ethics and values are particularly important, given changes—some would say breakdowns—in social structures such as the family, school, and church. If we take into account the effects of the mass media, the increasingly diverse population, and discontinuity in a child's experiences due to transience, socioeconomic factors, or disaffection, it cannot be assumed that there are shared values (Beck and Murphy 1997).

Therefore, educational leaders in all arenas are charged with examining their own notions of the just and good community that they are shaping within the walls of their schools. They are called upon to examine themselves and the integrity and authenticity of their actions as stakeholders. In his book on leadership, Robert Terry (1993) observes, "We can never forget that the conflicts and ambiguities of action reside not just in the world but also within ourselves. No one arrives with pure motives or unambiguous interests" (274).

And if schools are expected to pass on certain societal values and norms to young people, self-examination by the leader and scrutiny of the leader's preparation program seem only reasonable, given the major ethical role that leaders play in shaping the young. If society expects schools to pass on its ethics and values to its young, then leadership preparation programs that focus only on finances, management, and marketing fall short (Grace, 1995). Fullan (1993), a premier voice for educational change, argues that a strong sense of moral purpose and obligation must be recovered in schools if they are to avoid aimlessness and fragmentation.

Research on the role values play in problem solving by educational leaders suggests that, compared with nonexperts, experts

- Are more aware of their values
- Use their values more regularly in solving problems
- Use values as substitutes for knowledge in solving ill-structured problems. (Leithwood 1995, 61)

Values are chosen, and the choices made by educational leaders affect the entire community. Leaders decide what good teaching looks like, how the family should be involved in the work of the school, how choices for instructional materials are made and by whom. They decide what a good school looks like and how that can be implemented. They choose how policy is made, how the school functions as a part of the neighborhood community, and how the community will influence the decisions made in the school. In other words, values permeate every choice and decision an educational leader makes. Hodgkinson (1978, 5) observes that "the intrusion of values into the decision-making process is not only inevitable, it is the very substance of decision." And although values are intrinsic and intangible, they get played out on the public stage of many lives.

Value Changes. Historically, schools have respected and taught the values the society held. An examination of formal educational leadership preparation programs would find prospective leaders were trained to uphold and honor these values. Not surprisingly, across time, schools changed their values in response to changes in the broader culture. For instance, in the early 1900s the values of efficiency and economy were equated with the moral good, and American schools were to emulate them.

With the rise and prominence of John Dewey, by the 1930s efficiency and economy were replaced by the overarching value of democracy, realized in the local school as a cooperative community. And by the 1950s, with the mania for justifying all things as scientific, schools and educational leaders were to be value-free and to emphasize the positivist, scientific emphasis on inquiry. Leadership preparation programs defined and justified themselves as a scientific discipline.

The 1970s continued to reflect the dominant culture's emphasis on scientific validation. However, during the 1980s there was growing interest in the moral and ethical aspects of educational leadership. And by the end of the century, the nuance added to scientific value was witnessed when potential leaders were asked to become self-critical and reflective about their own ethics and values. This became particularly pivotal as shared governance blurred the boundaries between communities and their schools. And as Murphy and Hallinger (1992) observe, the school's underlying values and assumptions were more likely to be contested.

Value-Driven Leadership. Perhaps, as many researchers suggest, leaders are impeded most by their limited and entrenched mind-sets, their denial of possibilities, their failure to reflect on their practices and examine their assumptions and beliefs, and their relegation of values and purpose to the margins of efficient management. Milstein (1993) places value-driven leadership and program development at the opposite end of the continuum from the positivistic, management-driven paradigm that has held prominence in educational leadership during the past forty years.

By its very nature, leadership is built on personal ethics rooted in a sense of purpose and responsibility. Mulkeen, Cambron-McCabe, and Anderson (1994) suggest that the responsibilities of leaders include being

> ➡ A moral exemplar of democratic ideals and principles
> ➡ An advocate for equitable access and allocation of resources
> ➡ A leader knowledgeable of, sensitive to, and willing to ameliorate the gap in achievement between the disadvantaged and the rest of the school population (231)

Educational leader T. B. Greenfield contends that leaders who operate in an ethical manner must "engage in a continuing process of discovery aimed at gaining an understanding of ourselves and of others" (1991, 109). Hodgkinson (1991) concurs, arguing that educational leaders must develop greater sensitivity to values and critically and continuously examine their own values, the values held by the school, and their intersection. Sergiovanni (1992a) charges leaders to examine not only their work but the way of their work. In other words, he challenges them to scrutinize who they are, what they believe, and how they feel, in addition to what they do, how they do it, and how they think.

Mertz addresses the ethical dimensions of preparing her students for leadership roles. She notes her desire to cultivate in them

> ➡ Humility in the face of the influence of their decisions and actions on others
> ➡ A desire to serve something beyond self-interest
> ➡ A sensitivity to their role as moral exemplars. (Cited in Beck and Murphy 1997, 82)

Lynn Beck (1996) stresses the importance of ethical leadership and the struggle to lead a just and caring community in a moral way:

> At least four characteristics of our professional lives compel us to take seriously the challenges at hand: 1) The situations that challenge our moral reasoning are complex. 2) The stakes are high in situations that challenge our moral reasoning. 3) The impact of our moral decisions and actions is enormous. 4) Institutions that traditionally guided our moral reasoning are crumbling. (10–11)

Legislation, Codes, and Standards. Associations, school districts, and various educational boards have proposed codes of ethics for prospective administrators, school board members, and educational leaders. For instance, the Massachusetts Education Reform Act of 1993, in addition to mandating skills and knowledge, required that superintendents, principals, supervisors, and various directors demonstrate the value they placed on equity by

- Understanding "the importance of education in a democratic society, including the need to provide equal education opportunities"
- Accepting and respecting differences in groups and individuals
- Fostering a school culture that addresses the needs of a diverse society
- Recognizing and addressing biased teaching and learning materials as well as biased school practices
- Acting in consort with the profession's ethical principles
- Understanding the legal responsibilities to children with special needs (Beck and Murphy 1997, 162)

The National Policy Board for Educational Administration (1995) cites the National Council for the Accreditation of Teacher Education (NCATE) curriculum guidelines for graduate programs in educational leadership:

Leadership includes an ethical dimension because principals and other leaders are moral agents responsible for the welfare and development of students. Preparation programs should provide opportunities for candidates to formulate and examine an ethical platform upon which to rely for tough decisions. (Quoted in Beck and Murphy 1997, 164)

A Code of Ethics for Minnesota School Administrators, which was adopted by the Minnesota Association of School Administrators (MASA) board of directors, instructs educational administrators to maintain the highest standards of conduct. Among other points, it states that educational leaders must

- Make the well-being of students the fundamental values of all decision making and actions
- Fulfill professional responsibilities with honesty and integrity
- Avoid using positions for personal gain through political,

social, religious, economic, or other influence. (Ramsey
1999, 200)

Wendel, Hoke, and Joekel (1996, 48) cite a high school principal's
code of ethics, which includes being an advocate for students, maintaining integrity, working harder than others, taking risks, treating all
people in a fair and caring way, caring about her own professional development and that of her staff, and creating an environment that stimulates change. Additionally, she felt that building leadership capacity in
the people with whom she worked and adhering to her own principles
were the mainstays of her value system.

It falls upon the shoulders of leaders to advocate on behalf of all
children for the kinds of services that will help realize their creative and
cognitive potential. In the contemporary social milieu, educational leaders are called upon to step into the breach where society has failed its
young, that is, to provide health and human services, to provide physical
and emotional security and safety, and to believe in the potential success of each student. Leaders' values guide their own work and influence
the community. Advocacy is a charge for leaders to act ethically and for
their behavior to be infused with confidence, promise, and hope.

Everyone arrives at the school door with needs—something frequently ignored and seldom talked about in school cultures. If schools
are to become communities of learning and change, they must be
places where

- Learners' needs are understood, appreciated, and attended to
- People are challenged to grow and change, not threatened
  to change
- Learning is accompanied by strong feeling and emotion
- Communication and feedback are frequent, are relevant,
  and suggest next steps
- Collaboration, not competition, characterizes learning activ-
  ities. (Combs, Miser, and Whitaker 1999, 67)

Combs, Miser, and Whitaker (1999) observe that, too often, people's true needs are corrupted by individuals who compete to fulfill only
their own needs—for power, status, favor, protection. And at other
times, those people who are focused on students place other needs (either real or perceived) before their own authentic needs. For example,
during a flurry of state testing, schools often speak of the need to raise
test scores. The more authentic need is to offer equal and more equitable programs across the school district. There is a perceived need to

"cover" material, to get grades done, to have parent conferences, when the more significant focus should be on students and their learning. There is a need to fill out reports, to attend meetings, to prepare budget proposals for the board, to respond to state mandates for titled programs, or to oversee the allocation of district resources, all of which are critical to the operation of the school. Nevertheless, the focus must be on leveraging all the power, status, favor, and protection on behalf of students and their families.

Then there is the need to fashion meaning and purpose in the work of the school and the school curriculum, and as a guideline for the interaction of constituents and for the process itself. Students need to achieve, to learn, to grow. They also need to feel safe, to feel cared for, to feel encouraged to take risks just as adults do. Educational leaders can shape this kind of community, one sensitive and responsive to the feelings, highly charged emotions, energies, and creative imaginations of both students and adult stakeholder-learners.

Summary. Sergiovanni aptly describes the multidimensional character of leadership when he writes,

> Leadership for meaning, leadership for problem solving, collegial leadership, leadership as shared responsibility, leadership that serves school purposes, leadership that is tough enough to demand a great deal from everyone, and leadership that is tender enough to encourage the heart—these are the images of leadership we need for schools as communities. (1996, 184–185)

Educational leaders who view and create schools as communities weave a rich fabric of the world's interests, an amalgam of understood and connected experiences that lessen, through collective struggle, the human suffering born of isolation. Rather than an education trivialized, an experience appropriated and compartmentalized, a human being devalued and dismissed, the community of school in its continual cycle of school-life-school rises like a phoenix from the ashes of fractionalized fragmentation, the artificial separation of the study of academics and the disparate experience of a student lost in the web of overlapping or tardy service delivery—each organization, constituent group, and area broken apart from and competing with all the others. And it becomes a renewing organic, healthy whole. It becomes a family that in order to function successfully demands of each household member a duty, a share of the cooperative work.

In order for schools as communities to thrive, they must have order. They must have physical and mental health. People in them must see meaning and purpose in life and be motivated to perform various tasks. The schools must reproduce culturally and socially. They must share understandings manifested in their artifacts (what they do and what they make) and in their actions. And those involved in them must be ethical and profoundly understand their deeply held beliefs, values, and constructed identity.

Schools must be willing to bare their souls in the service of exposing their spiritual core. Bolman and Deal (1997, 353) warn us that the "signs are everywhere that institutions in many developed nations are at a critical juncture because of a crisis of meaning and moral authority." If schools as communities are to thrive, their educational leaders need to be willing to see themselves as moral exemplars, advocates for the values of a just and caring people. For the very "heart of leadership lives in the hearts of leaders" (Bolman and Deal 1995, 15).

Dewey placed students at the center of all that transpired in schools. So too today, schools as communities help direct the child's innate sense of activity. Educational leaders on all levels help channel such activity through organized materials and equipment, directed discipline, and experience-generated knowledge, which Dewey concluded yielded power.

Dewey held that schools must present the world in relation to human activity, centered and grounded in the practical, the real world, what he called the "enduring earth," which exists quite apart from us and yet sustains us. Perhaps it is through this connection and in direct relation to the endlessly enduring earth that worth and value will be measured. "All studies arise from aspects of the one earth and the one life lived upon it," Dewey (1900, 91) wrote.

CONCLUSION

New Era leadership is a call to renew Aristotle's timeless perceptions of making sense of and in the world. It is a call to embrace his three modes of action: *theoria* (theory), *techne* (technique), and *praxis,* or ethical action as it existed in the political context. It is praxis—"purposeful human conduct, or behavior informed and guided by purposes, intentions, motives, morals, emotions and values as well as the facts or 'science' of the case" (Hodgkinson 1991, 42)—that guides the daily action and reflection of educational leaders. It is praxis that has been ignored in the race to be competitive in the world. Yet it is praxis that may well sustain the world itself.

And it is the leadership of virtue and moral agency rather than position or role. It is leadership that invites the community of steward-ship to act on behalf of the common good. Leaders "nurture the fledg-ling community, and protect the community once it emerges. To do this they lead by following. They lead by serving. They lead by inviting oth-ers to share in the burdens of leadership" (Sergiovanni 1994, 203).

New Era leadership is a craft as well as an art, an intellectual as well as a moral endeavor, a practice of engagement as well as of ethics. It is critical reflection that is cultural, political, moral, professional, and personal. It is power shared and power with. It is participatory democ-racy as well as community connectedness. It is "a noble calling worthy of our most profound commitment. For what we do, in the final analy-sis, rests solely on our faith that our actions in our families, communi-ties, associations, institutions, and the world contribute to the well-being of all those we touch and serve" (Terry 1993, 274).

Schools as communities are ethical agents of integration. It is an integration of all those things that both sustain and stimulate the cul-ture; an integration of the successes as well as the failures of generations past; an integration of mutual confidence, accommodation, and adap-tation; an integration of promises both fulfilled and those never kept; an integration of all of our collective and individual weaknesses and strengths; an integration of all that we hope for and all that we pray will never be.

REFERENCES

Ackerman, R., G. Donaldson, and R. van der Bogert. 1996. *Making Sense as a School Leader: Persisting Questions, Creative Opportunities.* San Fran-cisco: Jossey-Bass.

Astuto, T., D. Clark, A. Read, K. McGree, and L. Fernandez. 1994. *Roots of Reform: Challenging the Assumptions That Control Change in Education.* Bloom-ington, IN: Phi Delta Kappa Educational Foundation.

Barth, R. 1990. *Improving Schools from Within: Teachers, Parents, and Principals Can Make the Difference.* San Francisco: Jossey-Bass.

Beck, L. 1996. "Why Ethics? Thoughts on the Moral Challenge Facing Educa-tional Leaders." *The School Administrator* 9, no. 54 (October): 8–11.

Beck, L. G., and J. Murphy, eds. 1997. *Ethics in Educational Leadership Programs: Emerging Models.* Columbia, MO: The University Council for Educa-tional Administration.

Bell, J., and B. Harrison. 1995. *Vision and Values in Managing Education: Successful Leadership Principles and Practices.* London: David Fulton Publications.

Bolman, L. G., and T. E. Deal. 1995. *Leading with Soul: An Uncommon Journey of*

Spirit. San Francisco: Jossey-Bass.

———. 1997. *Reframing Organizations: Artistry, Choice, and Leadership.* San Francisco: Jossey-Bass.

Clark, B. R. 1983. *The Higher Education System: Academic Organization in Cross-National Perspective.* Berkeley: University of California Press.

Combs, A., A. B. Miser, and K. S. Whitaker. 1999. *On Becoming a School Leader: A Person-Centered Challenge.* Alexandria, VA: Association for Supervision and Curriculum Development.

Costa, A., and B. Kallick, eds. 2000. *Discovering and Exploring Habits of Mind.* Alexandria, VA: Association for Supervision and Curriculum Development.

Deiro, J. 1996. *Teaching with Heart: Making Healthy Connections with Students.* Thousand Oaks, CA: Corwin Press.

Dewey, J. 1900. *The School and Society.* Chicago: University of Chicago Press.

———. 1902. *The Child and the Curriculum.* Chicago: University of Chicago Press.

———. 1938. *Experience and Education.* New York: Macmillan.

DuFour, R., and R. Eaker. 1998. *Professional Learning Communities at Work: Best Practices for Enrichment of Student Achievement.* Bloomington, IN: National Education Service.

Durkheim, E. 1964. *The Division of Labor in Society.* Trans. G. Simpson. New York: Free Press. Original edition, 1893.

Fullan, M. 1993. *Change Forces: Probing the Depths of Educational Reform.* London: Falmer Press.

———. 1998. "Breaking the Bonds of Dependency." *Educational Leadership* 55, no. 7 (April): 4–9.

Goodlad, J. 1990. *Teachers for Our Nation's Schools.* San Francisco: Jossey-Bass.

Grace, G. 1995. *School Leadership: Beyond Education Management.* London: Falmer Press.

Greely, G. 2000. "A School Board That Learns." In *Schools That Learn: A Fifth Discipline Resource,* ed. P. Senge, 432–438. New York: Doubleday.

Greenfield, T. B. 1991. "Reforming and Revaluing Educational Administration: Whence and When Cometh the Phoenix?" *Educational Management and Administration* 19, no. 4: 200–217.

Hatch, T. 1998. "How Community Action Contributes to Achievement." *Educational Leadership* 55, no. 8 (May): 16–19.

Henderson, J. G., and R. D. Hawthorne. 2000. *Transformative Curriculum Leadership.* Upper Saddle River, NJ: Merrill, Prentice-Hall.

Hodgkinson, C. 1978. *Towards a Philosophy of Educational Administration.* Oxford: Blackwell.

———. 1991. *Educational Leadership: The Moral Art.* Oxford: Blackwell.

Kunc, N. 1992. "The Need to Belong: Rediscovering Maslow's Hierarchy of

Needs." In *Restructuring for Caring and Effective Education,* ed. R. A. Villa, J. S. Thousand, W. Stainback, and S. Stainback, 77–92. Baltimore: Brookes.

Lambert, L. 1998. *Building Leadership Capacity in Schools.* Alexandria, VA: Association for Supervision and Curriculum Development.

Larrivee, B. 1999. *Authentic Classroom Management: Creating a Community of Learners.* Boston: Allyn and Bacon.

Leithwood, K., ed. 1995. *Effective School District Leadership: Transforming Politics into Education.* Albany: State University of New York Press.

Lieberman, A., and L. Miller. 1984. "The Social Realities of Teaching." In *Teachers: Their World, Their Work,* ed. A. Lieberman, 1–16. Alexandria, VA: Association for Supervision and Curriculum Development.

Lightfoot, S. 1984. *The Good High School.* New York: Basic Books.

Little, J. W. 1981. *School Success and Staff Development in Urban Desegregated Schools: A Summary of Recently Completed Research.* Boulder, CO: Center for Action Research, April.

Lockwood, A. T. 1997. "Three Views: How Schools Can Educate for Democracy." *New Leaders for Tomorrow's Schools,* North Central Regional Educational Laboratory, Spring: 10–15.

McNay, I. 1995. "Constructing the Vision: Changing the Culture." In *Vision and Values in Managing Education: Successful Leadership Principles and Practice,* ed. J. Bell and B. Harrison. London: David Fulton Publishers.

Mertz, N. T. 1997. "Knowing and Doing: Exploring the Ethical Life of Educational Leaders." In *Ethics in Educational Leadership Programs: Emerging Models,* ed. L. G. Beck and J. Murphy, 77–93. Columbia, MO: The University Council for Educational Administration.

Milstein, M. 1993. *Changing the Way We Prepare Educational Leaders.* Thousand Oaks, CA: Corwin Press.

Mulkeen, T. A., Nelda Cambron-McCabe, and Bruce Anderson. 1993. *Democratic Leadership: The Changing Context of Administrative Preparation.* Interpretive Perspectives on Education and Policy. Norwood, NJ: Ablex.

Murphy, J., and P. Hallinger. 1992. "The Principalship in an Era of Transformation." *Journal of Educational Administration* 30, no. 3: 77–88.

National Policy Board for Educational Administration. 1995. *Monograph.* Arlington, VA: National Policy Board for Educational Administration.

Negroni, P. 2000. "The Superintendent's Progress." In *Schools That Learn: A Fifth Discipline Resource,* ed. P. Senge, 425–432. New York: Doubleday.

Noddings, N. 1984. *Caring: A Feminine Approach to Ethics and Moral Education.* Berkeley: University of California Press.

———. 1992. *The Challenge to Care in Schools.* New York: Teachers College Press.

Palmer, P. 1998. *The Courage to Teach: Exploring the Inner Landscape of a Teacher's Life.* San Francisco: Jossey-Bass.

Patterson, J. L. 1993. *Leadership for Tomorrow's Schools.* Alexandria, VA: Association for Supervision and Curriculum Development.

Phi Delta Kappa. 2000–2001. "Ethical Leadership Camps Nurture Young Leaders." *News, Notes, and Quotes* 45, no. 2 (Winter): 5.

Ramsey, R. D. 1999. *Lead, Follow, or Get Out of the Way: How to Be a More Effective Leader in Today's Schools.* Thousand Oaks, CA: Corwin Press.

Rowan, B. 1990. "Commitment and Control: Alternative Strategies for the Organizational Design of Schools." *Review of Research in Education* 16: 353–385.

Sarason, S. 1993. *You Are Thinking of Teaching.* San Francisco: Jossey-Bass.

Senge, P. 1990. *The Fifth Discipline: The Art and Practice of the Learning Organization.* New York: Doubleday.

———. 2000. *Schools That Learn: A Fifth Discipline Resource.* New York: Doubleday.

Sergiovanni, T. 1992a. *Moral Leadership: Getting to the Heart of School Improvement.* San Francisco: Jossey-Bass.

———. 1992b. "Reflections on Administrative Theory and Practice in Schools." *Educational Administration Quarterly* 28, no. 3 (August): 304–313.

———. 1994. *Building Community in Schools.* San Francisco: Jossey-Bass.

———. 1996. *Leadership for the Schoolhouse: How Is It Different? Why Is It Important?* San Francisco: Jossey-Bass.

———. 2000. *The Lifeworld of Leadership: Creating Culture, Community, and Personal Meaning in Our Schools.* San Francisco: Jossey-Bass.

Sizer, T. 1984. *Horace's Compromise.* Boston: Houghton Mifflin.

Starratt, R. J. 1994. *Building an Ethical School: A Practical Response to the Moral Crisis in Schools.* London: Falmer Press.

Stratton, J. 1995. *How Students Have Changed.* Arlington, VA: The American Association of School Administrators.

Terry, R. 1993. *Authentic Leadership: Courage in Action.* San Francisco: Jossey-Bass.

Wald, P. J., and M. S. Castleberry, eds. 2000. *Educators as Learners: Creating a Professional Learning Community in Your School.* Alexandria, VA: Association for Supervision and Curriculum Development.

Wendel, F., F. Hoke, and R. Joekel. 1996. *Outstanding School Administrators: Their Keys to Success.* Westport, CT: Praeger.

Wilson, P. 1993. "Pushing the Edge." In *Changing the Way We Prepare Educational Leaders,* ed. M. Milstein, 219–235. Thousand Oaks, CA: Corwin Press.

Chapter Five

❧ Competing Models: Leaders Initiating Change

Leaders have a significant role in creating the state of mind that is society.

—John Gardner

A report from the National Commission of Governing America's Schools (Starr 1999) noted the growing demand by the American public to restructure or rethink its schools. The increasing numbers of charter schools (see D. Weil's *Charter Schools* in this series), home-schooled children, schools of choice, schools and districts that have been taken over by CEOs or the state, and private, religious, and magnet schools bear witness to America's discontent with schools as they now exist. Many families believe the nation's public schools have come to mirror the decay and slow death of morality evident in the broader culture. Several 1999 public opinion polls showed that reforming public schools was at the top of the nation's list of concerns. And according to an NPR/Kaiser/Kennedy School survey, Americans are so concerned about public education that they are willing to pay higher taxes if that would improve the schools (Children's Defense Fund 2000, 69).

Moreover, as leaders in the educational, political, and social arenas call for ever higher standards in student learning and achievement and in instructional practice and school accountability, there has been an unprecedented response led by those invested in systemic or all-school reform and restructuring. Such reform addresses all aspects of the school, including school organization and procedures, professional development and resources, and teaching and learning. It is reform that is integrated, focused, and coordinated. Systemic reform also embraces assessment, family involvement, and issues of school governance.

In response to the failed reform efforts of the 1980s, the systemic reform agenda first played out in rather piecemeal form as a reaction to the *A Nation at Risk* report of 1983. The second wave of reform addressed restructuring or the charge to fundamentally change the expectations of student learning, the interaction of the teaching and learning processes, and the organization and management of public schools in general (Elmore 1990, 1).

In many ways, the development of reform models has arisen organically. The models have been constructed within by those educational leaders engaged in the processes of teaching and learning, whether they be researchers, educators, or administrators, leaders who persistently look for more effective ways of educating all of the nation's youth. Can this type of reform succeed? And what initiatives offer the most promise for raising student achievement, offering authentic ways of assessing improvement, and sustaining the viable growth of the entire school as a community? What questions need to be asked to find the appropriate fit between a reform model and a particular school's culture? Each school must seek its own path to reform by first examining itself, its beliefs, and its aspirations for young people.

Questions School Boards Ask. In looking at policies implemented at the district level, school boards may ask (in addition to the above school-level questions) the following questions about how they can promote improved student learning:

- What policies will focus everyone directly on student learning?
- What policies will enlist and gain commitment from all stakeholders?
- What policies will result in all stakeholders having the knowledge and skill to help all students learn well?
- What policies will ensure stability over time so change really happens?
- What policies will make data available and used in decision making throughout the district?
- What policies will focus all resources on student learning?
- What policies will ensure continuous learning and improvement for all stakeholders involved? (Blum 2000, 255)

Change and Educational Leadership. This text has examined the models or styles of leadership and has noted that transformative leadership that moves to facilitative-democratic leadership tends to be the most effective and most sustainable form in the tenuous process of change (Chapman 1988). We have also examined the beliefs and assumptions that shape these styles and express their values. Michael Fullan (1993), a recognized authority on change in schools, pointed out in the preceding chapter that educational leadership bereft of moral purpose would wander undirected and be discontinuous. But he contends, "Without change agentry, moral purpose stagnates" (Grace 1995, 155). Change is endemic to schools given that they are charged with reflecting contemporary culture.

Why Does Change Fail? There are as many reasons why some schools succeed against all odds as there are why others fail. Neither educational leaders nor researchers agree about the process of change. Yet there is a substantial body of research on change, most of which reflects intense ambiguity, conflict, and even failure (Wissler and Ortiz 1988).

While some educational leaders believe the curriculum needs to change first, others believe the principal should initiate and guide the process; still others hold that authentic change happens from within the school, with the support of designated leaders. Yet another camp contends that sustained and substantive change will not happen unless the moral fabric of the school has been examined. The very movement from hierarchical control of school districts to decentralized, shared governance is one fraught with tension and frustration; progress is discontinuous, with multiple stages.

Educational leader Seymour Sarason (1990) claims that failure in school reform is predictable because of the power relationships that exist within the community of stakeholders. Like many other leaders, he contends that most reform initiatives advocate a shift in power relationships and authority. Those initiatives that advocate site-based decision making, shared governance, distributed leadership, and participatory democracy are prime examples. We have examined participatory democracy in terms of shared decision making among students, teachers, parents, administrators, school boards (on the local and state levels), health and human service agencies, government officials, businesspeople, religious leaders, and minority-rights groups. When schools move past assuming that the adoption of some superimposed reform structure or another potential format will, in itself, bring effective changes, and instead at the outset focus on the cultural values of the community and on the relationships and exercise of power, many of the biases and feelings of reluctance that cause reform efforts to fail are mediated.

John Kotter (1995) writes in the *Harvard Business Review* that transformation initiatives fail for several basic reasons:

- ⊷ Failure to establish a communal sense of urgency
- ⊷ Failure to create a strong community base for guiding the reform initiative
- ⊷ Lack of a unifying vision

➻ Failure to adequately communicate the vision; this limits stakeholder involvement

➻ Failure to remove obstacles that will impede the vision

➻ Failure to systematically plan for and create short-term accomplishments, placing the idealized vision beyond reach and visible accomplishment

➻ Declaring victory too soon—a viable and sustainable reform initiative needs at least three years to be effectively implemented

➻ Failure to anchor changes in the school's culture (1–11)

How Change Succeeds. Fullan (1999) responds that those learning communities that manage change the best have constructed collaborative cultures. He contends that these communities will flourish in a shared culture when the following critical connections are forged:

➻ Between parents and other members of the community (in the ways discussed above)

➻ With technology, which is indispensable in the classroom

➻ With corporations—partnerships bring needed resources

➻ With government—using government data and policy for improvement efforts

➻ With professional development that creates an ongoing sense of best practice in schools (1, 4)

Then, Fullan argues, the school community is prepared for the next layer of reform: moral agency. When designated leaders trust moral authority, they place all stakeholders as subordinates to the culture's shared values and ethics and then charge everyone to assume his or her role and fulfill his or her responsibilities or obligations (Sergiovanni 1995, 314).

Louis and Miles (1990) maintain that the five aspects of involvement necessary for successful reform initiatives are

➻ Clarity—everyone shares the same clear information on the initiative

➻ Relevance—the initiative is connected to the reality of stakeholders' experience

➻ Action images that help present visual images of how the initiative will move forward and toward what goal

➻ Will—the commitment to put the knowledge of the initiative into practice

➻ Skill—the physical and behavioral ability to put the vision into practice (198–206)

In other words, without buying into and understanding the initiative, change or new reform efforts will not succeed.

On a more informal but very practical note, Barbara Kellerman (1999) observes that everyone who writes about leadership and change identifies essentially the same elements of effective leadership for reform. They include

➻ Create a vision
➻ Communicate everything—with everyone
➻ Foster diversity
➻ Create networks
➻ Go horizontal
➻ Hang loose
➻ Level with everyone
➻ Rethink motivation
➻ Empower everyone
➻ Form teams
➻ Decentralize
➻ Always learn (125)

Ramsey (1999) adds some twenty-five user-friendly tips and strategies for implementing what he refers to as "real-world" changes in schools. Among them are the following:

➻ Remember that change is built on trust. No trust, no change. Don't even think about it.
➻ Accept the risk. Realize that every change comes with a cost. When things are changed, something is always lost or traded off. Be sure change is worth it before you start.
➻ Concentrate on no more than two changes at a time.
➻ Let everyone in who wants in. Give everyone a job.
➻ Always tie change to making things better for kids.
➻ Provide appropriate training before you start.
➻ Deal with critics early. If you don't, they can sabotage your efforts at any step along the way.
➻ Stay focused.
➻ Radiate confidence.
➻ Don't expect uniform success.
➻ Pay attention to the state of staff approval. (70–74)

Fullan and Miles (1992) suggest there are seven perspectives on successful change initiatives:

- Change is a learning process, ambiguous and uncertain
- Change is a journey, not a road map
- Problems are opportunities rather than troublesome roadblocks
- Change needs a wealth of supportive resources
- Change requires the power to shape, guide, and reshape it
- Change is systemic—it involves the entire school culture
- Large-scale change is implemented on a local or building level (744–752)

Yet because of the great need for resources in systemic reform initiatives, both the central administrative office and the school board play critical roles in creating building-level reform. They support the shared vision and ongoing development of the school as a community. They assist in the acquisition and allocation of resources, creating partnerships with the community and the business sector that supplement limited district or building resources. They initiate and nurture partnerships with other agencies that touch the lives of young people. And they stand to assist and support in the ongoing professional development of the stakeholder-reformers, in the acquisition of needed technology, and in creative budgeting for the school.

And, most particularly, they can exercise an enduring belief in the ability of the school and its stakeholders to engage in meaningful and thoughtful best practices supported by research. In 1997, a team of undaunted and, for the most part, seasoned teachers from East Middle School in Ypsilanti, Michigan, along with parents, the school's principal, Janice Sturdivant (a person pivotal to the success of the initiative), a representative from Michigan's State Department of Education, this writer, and a colleague (the last two serve as technical assistant partners and professors of education at Eastern Michigan University just minutes from the school) stood before the local school board and asked for their support. This writer was told that, in the preceding fifteen years, three previous attempts in front of the school board had failed. East Middle School was a Title I school whose state test scores were below the state average; it had not been considered one of the district's best schools. In fact, realtors were quick to point out that families moved out of the district when it came time to attend middle school.

The volunteer leadership team that came to the board that spring evening had spent an entire school year preparing, researching, studying, and shaping a common vision. That evening we asked the school board and the central administration to take a step of faith and allocate the school $500,000 in new funding to implement the Middle Start model (spoken of below). Wisely, they took that step. A year later, we came again and asked them to take a step of reason and continue to support our burgeoning efforts for the next two years. Again, they thoughtfully and astutely agreed.

Today, East Middle School is visited by teams from other middle schools from across the state, teams who come to see how systemic reform can really happen. East has been nominated as one of the four schools in the nation that are outstanding examples of comprehensive school reform. Families now move into East Middle School's district. More importantly, students are achieving at higher levels, attendance has increased, and tardiness, class disruptions, and truancy have significantly decreased. It was and continues to be a community effort, one born of belief, of trust, of hope, of talent, of hard work, and of vision.

Corporate/Philanthropic Influence. The leadership of the corporate world and the nonprofit philanthropic sector has played a key role in both initiating large-scale educational reform and in supporting the hopes and dreams of those whose work would otherwise go unsupported and therefore ignored in the country's schools. However, at the same time, schools must be particularly mindful and watchful of the ways they can gain resources without compromising their own values. George Kaplan, a Washington policy analyst, observes that the heart of corporate vision for school reform is accountability, standards, and high-stakes testing (2000, K4). Many schools have been able to negotiate these requisite behavioral reforms while making the affective changes that are so important to the social growth and development of responsible young citizens.

In considering the rush by schools to access sorely needed corporate resources, Kaplan challenges them to note such events as the 1996 National Education Summit, which was chaired not by an educator but by the CEO of IBM, Louis Gerstner. The small number of educators who were invited to the follow-up summit chaired by Gerstner were, not surprisingly, pro-business and supportive of private school choice (Kaplan 2000, K5). The challenge to protect the thoughtful attention to the moral discourse of ethics and values quietly endures. It is the province of all those engaged in change, and in particular that of designated leaders, to mediate an ethical vision of working and thinking with young people, with the technical mandates of reform and reformers.

Federal Support for Systemic Reform. In 1997, the U.S. Congress appropriated monies (Obey-Porter Comprehensive School Reform

Demonstration competitive grants) to fund schools that were ready to embrace "proven," comprehensive, research-based programs. These schools were predominantly in economically depressed areas and their levels of student achievement were low.

The congressional report on the funding recognized several national reform models and the emergence of other high-profile, research-based initiatives that had proven effective. Some of the more widely adopted models are listed below as systemic or comprehensive school models, instructional models that address teacher-student engagement, and curricular models that emphasize what the student should learn and the most effective ways to learn it.

NATIONAL REFORM MODELS

Systemic or Comprehensive Reform Models

Accelerated Schools (K–8)
National Center for the Accelerated Schools Project
University of Connecticut
Neag School of Education
2131 Hillside Road, Unit 3224
Storrs, CT 06269-3224
(860) 486-6330
(860) 486-6348 (fax)
http://www.acceleratedschools.net
Developer: Henry Levin, Stanford University

Begun in San Francisco Bay Area elementary schools in 1986, the Accelerated Schools Project is now in over 1,000 schools. Its main goal is to bring all students to grade level in performance by the end of their elementary school experience. This improves the performance of the lower-achieving at-risk students while continuing to challenge other students. The initiative's emphases are on enrichment rather than remediation; on offering motivating, challenging, relevant, and problem-solving instructional techniques rather than "drill-and-practice"; on embracing the family as a viable resource for the student's education; and on engaging the faculty in solving problems and posing solutions. Accelerated Schools are based on the following three core principles:

- Unity of purpose—a collaborative focus on achievement among parents, teachers, students, and administrators
- School-site empowerment and responsibility—collabora-

tively posing solutions to problems, implementing them, and evaluating the outcomes
•• Building on strengths—assessing and constructing teaching and learning based on the strengths of teachers and students (Accelerated Schools 1994)

This emphasis on participatory learning and teaching processes for all students in the model, processes that were once reserved for the "gifted and talented," reflects the value the initiative places on equity, participation, communication, collaboration, community spirit, reflection, experimentation, discovery, trust, risk taking, and the school as the center of expertise. The project has satellite centers in eleven states that are considered to be certified training and support sites for local work.

Sample schools: Roanoke Academy Elementary School, Roanoke City, Virginia; North Middle School, Aurora, Colorado.

America's Choice School Design (K–12)
National Center on Education and the Economy
700 11th Street, NW, Suite 750
Washington, DC 20001
(202) 783-3668
(202) 783-3672 (fax)
http://www.ncee.org
Contact person: Pat Harvey
Developer: National Center on Education and the Economy

America's Choice began in 1989 as the National Alliance for Restructuring Education; there are currently over 300 America's Choice schools in fourteen states. The model focuses on meeting benchmarks in English, mathematics, and science; mastering concepts; and applying those concepts. It identifies students whose achievement level is below average early in their academic careers and provides them with the necessary resources to raise their level of achievement, particularly in reading, writing, and mathematics. The goal is high levels of achievement in academic core courses so as to prepare all students for college. Key features of this initiative's design include

•• Standards and assessments
•• Learning environments
•• Community services and support
•• High performance management
•• Parent and public engagement

The model designs a series of systems that include

- An accountability system for districts; rewards and consequences for schools are based on performance
- Allocation of control over funding
- Performance monitoring and review
- Focused assistance for low-achieving schools (National Center on Education and the Economy 1998)

The model stresses continuous technical assistance on site, a "class teacher" who follows students for three years, a literacy and math block, a small "house" system, college preparation for all students, and a work-based technical preparation program.

Sample schools: Gage Park High School, Chicago, Illinois; Ray Kroc Middle School, San Diego, California; John F. Kennedy Elementary School, Louisville, Kentucky.

ATLAS Communities (PreK–12)
55 Chapel Street
Newton, MA 02158-1060
(617) 618-2401
(617) 969-3440 (fax)
http://www.edc.org/ATLAS/
Contact person: Reggie Silberg

ATLAS Communities, designed by Harvard's Project Zero, the School Development Program, the Coalition of Essential Schools, and the Education Development Center, coherently links elementary, middle, and high schools as partners in creating "pathways" to teaching and learning. Its emphasis on the construction of concepts, reasoning skills, practical applications, and the importance of self and others is built on five basic principles:

- Authentic teaching and learning driven by questions; focuses on understanding; provides challenging, purposeful, and sustained work
- Effective teaching, learning, and organizational change shaped by continuous cycles of planning, action, and reflection
- Social relationships that prepare students to learn
- Collaborative learning culture built on shared leadership, commitment, and communication

➣ Participatory membership by all schools in a larger, more integrated learning community through study groups and networking (Yale Child Study Center 1998b)

ATLAS teachers emphasize active, inquiry-based learning while intentionally structuring learning experiences around students' strengths and weaknesses. Additionally, particular attention is paid to internal decision-making processes, the engagement of family and communities, ongoing focused and sustained professional development, the improved learning of all students, and the evaluation of student work through a variety of assessments.

Sample schools: Narragansett Elementary, Gorham, Maine; Norview High School, Norfolk, Virginia.

Coalition of Essential Schools (K–12)
1814 Franklin Street, Suite 700
Oakland, CA 94612
(510) 433-1451
(510) 433-1455 (fax)
http://www.essentialschools.org
Contact persons: Theodore Sizer, founder and chairman; Amy Gerstein, executive director

CES is a national network of schools and centers engaged in comprehensive school reform built on ten common principles that promote more effective student learning:

1. The school should focus on helping adolescents learn to use their minds well.
2. The school's goals should be simple: that each student master a limited number of essential skills and areas of knowledge.
3. The school's goals should apply to all students.
4. Teaching and learning should be personalized.
5. The governing practical metaphor of the school should be student-as-worker.
6. Students entering secondary school studies are those who can show competence in language and elementary mathematics.
7. The tone of the school should explicitly and self-consciously stress values of unthreatened expectation.
8. The principal and teacher should perceive themselves as generalists in content knowledge.

9. Ultimate administrative and budget targets should include, in addition to total student loads per teacher of eighty or fewer pupils, substantial time for collective planning by teachers, competitive salaries for staff and an ultimate per pupil cost not to exceed that at traditional schools by more than 10 percent.

10. The school should demonstrate nondiscriminatory and inclusive policies, practices, and pedagogies. (CES, n.d.)

The model emphasizes a sense of community, graduation by exhibition (students share portfolios of their accumulated work), personalized learning, and mastery of a few essential skills and content areas.

Sample school: Tyner High School, Hamilton County, Tennessee.

Community for Learning (K–12)

Laboratory for Student Success
Temple University
Center for Research in Human Development and Education
1301 Cecil B. Moore Avenue
Philadelphia, PA 19122-6091
(800) 892-5550
(215) 204-5130 (fax)
http://www.temple.edu/LSS
Contact person: Frederick McCoy
Developer: Margaret C. Wang

CFL was developed in 1990 as a coordinated team approach to student success. CFL's instructional component, the Adaptive Learning Environments model, was developed through the National Follow Through Project and has been adopted in over 200 schools in twenty-two states. Based on the belief that students learn in multiple and often overlapping environments or communities, CFL links the school to other institutions such as the home, workplaces, social service and health agencies, and cultural and religious centers. This coordinated system fosters community-wide ownership and commitment to the local school and student success. CFL describes its goals for students as

- Readiness for school
- High standards of academic achievement
- Completion of high school
- School to work
- Citizenship
- Adult literacy and lifelong learning

➥ Safe, disciplined, and drug-free schools
➥ Use of technology (Community for Learning 1998)

Full school restructuring encourages shared responsibility, the use of a strategic plan to integrate the school with other environments, and the use of multiple instructional techniques to address and meet students' diverse needs and abilities. CFL accomplishes this through a focused plan that encompasses

➥ Curriculum standards, instruction, and assessment
➥ Classroom management and student development
➥ Organizational structure
➥ Schoolwide practices and policies
➥ Implementation planning
➥ Delivery system
➥ Staff development
➥ Family involvement and community connections
➥ School-linked service coordination (Community for Learning 1998)

Sample schools: Stetson Middle School, Philadelphia, Pennsylvania; Eighth Avenue Middle School, Houston, Texas; Walker-Jones Elementary School, Washington, DC.

Co-NECT Schools (K–12)

1770 Massachusetts Avenue, #301
Cambridge, MA 02140
(617) 995-3100
(617) 955-3103 (fax)
http://www.co-nect.net
Contact person: Heather Corbitt

Developed in 1992 by the Educational Technologies Group at BBN Corporation for New American Schools, Co-NECT emphasizes academic achievement for all students in mathematics, reading, writing, science, and the social sciences based on five benchmarks:

➥ High expectations for all students, and schoolwide accountability for results
➥ Schoolwide emphasis on practical application of content knowledge to problems relevant to students
➥ Authentic assessments that measure both school and student performance

- → School organization into clusters or small learning communities
- → Integrated use of technology (Co-NECT Schools 1998)

It is a standards-based K–12 reform model that pays particular attention to on-line and on-site technical training, assistance, and instruction.

Sample schools: Alton Elementary, Memphis, Tennessee; the ALL School, Worcester, Massachusetts.

Edison Schools (K–12)
Human Resources Department
521 Fifth Avenue
New York, NY 10175
(212) 309-1600
(212) 309-1604 (fax)
http://www.edisonschools.com
Developer: Chris Whittle and Edison Project design team

A privately sponsored for-profit initiative begun in 1992 in schools in Texas, Kansas, Michigan, and Massachusetts, Edison now has contractual partnerships with local school districts or charter schools in 113 sites in eight states. The project describes its ten fundamental design principles as

- → Schools organized for every student's success based on smaller communities of school-within-a-school
- → Better use of time, employing a longer day and a longer year
- → Rich and challenging curriculum based on what is described as world-class standards in the humanities, arts, mathematics, science, ethics, practical skills, and physical health and fitness
- → Teaching methods that motivate by using multiple instructional techniques
- → Careful assessment based on accountability rather than standards; evaluation through the use of multiple assessments
- → A professional teaching environment that provides every teacher with a portable computer and fosters their professional development
- → Technology for an information age that places a computer in every student's home; well-equipped schools

●● New partnership with parents, with regular communication between teachers and parents

●● Schools tailored to meet local curricular and community needs

●● Backed by a system that serves students, offering support, guidance, and resources from the national Edison headquarters (Edison Schools n.d.)

Sample schools: Dodge-Edison Elementary School, Wichita, Kansas; Phillips-Edison Partnership School primary and elementary academies, Napa, California.

High Schools That Work (9–12)
Southern Regional Education Board
592 Tenth Street, NW
Atlanta, GA 30318-5790
(404) 875-9211
(404) 872-1477 (fax)
http://www.sreb.org
Contact person: Gene Bottoms, senior vice president
Developer: Southern Regional Education Board, Atlanta, Georgia

Begun in 1987, this systemic research- and assessment-based reform initiative merges academic and vocational education to raise the achievement of career-bound high school students. HSTW describes its schools as sites that

●● Set high expectations and help students meet them

●● Enroll more youth in an upgraded academic core and a major; close down the general track; and require all students to finish an academic or career concentration

●● Increase access to academic studies that teach the essential content of college preparatory curricula and actively engage students in the learning process

●● Use national, state, and local academic and industry skill standards and the requirements of postsecondary schools (including community and technical colleges) and employers to review and improve their academic and vocational curricula

●● Provide students with a carefully planned sequence of challenging academic courses

●● Offer technical programs of study that are rich in high-level academic concepts

- Change school organization from a system that isolates teachers to one that supports them in a collegial, collaborative environment
- Create a climate in which district and school teachers work together to examine and respond to assessment data
- Revise guidance systems to make parents partners with students and schools in planning high school programs of study
- Use the world of work to situate academic concepts, making them more accessible to many students (High Schools That Work 1998)

Three guiding ideas of HSTW are reflected in these sites:

- Vision setting, reorganization, and implementation are carried out by academic and vocational teachers, principals, and counselors
- Teachers and school leaders accomplish goals through the collegial sharing of expertise
- Assessment, evaluation, and feedback power the implementation of the model (High Schools That Work 1998)

Sample schools: Hoke County schools, Raeford, North Carolina; Lexington School District 4, Swansea, South Carolina.

High/Scope (K–8)
600 North River Street
Ypsilanti, MI 48198
(734) 485-2000
(734) 485-0704 (fax)
http://www.highscope.org
Contact person: Charles Wallgren
Developer: David Weikart

The High/Scope model, currently in use in over 100 elementary schools, is based on active learning and an understanding of the student's physical, social, intellectual, and emotional development. The model presents learning as an interactive social experience among adults and students. Unique to High/Scope is the "plan-do-review" process in which students choose, organize, evaluate, and share with peers daily learning experiences. Key to the model is the emphasis on student responsibility and opportunity that facilitate lifelong learning and a positive self-image.

Sample schools: Bessie Hoffman Elementary School, Belleville, Michigan; West Point School, West Point, California.

Middle Start (6–8)
W. K. Kellogg Foundation
One Michigan Avenue East
Battle Creek, MI 49017-4058
(616) 968-1611
(616) 968-0413 (fax)
http://www.wkkf.org
Contact person: Steve Hoelscher, state coordinator
Developer: W. K. Kellogg Foundation (Leah Mayer Austin, program officer), in collaboration with other groups

The Middle Start initiative, a data-driven, research-based, comprehensive reform model for middle-grades education, was initiated in 1994 by the W. K. Kellogg Foundation and Leah Meyer Austin, program officer, in collaboration with the Academy for Educational Development (AED) in New York, the Center for Prevention Research and Development at the University of Illinois, Michigan-based organizations and agencies including state universities and public schools, and other initiatives. Developed in consort with the National Forum to Accelerate Middle-Grades Reform, Middle Start's three major goals for high-performing middle-grades schools are

- Academic excellence for all students
- Developmental responsiveness
- Social equity

The model attempts to meet these three goals through work in ten areas:

- Curriculum—connected to state standards and benchmarks; relevant, integrative, exploratory, and challenging
- Student assessment—diverse in construct and based on the varying stages of student learning
- Program evaluation—ongoing
- School climate—student-centered, collegial, caring, nurturing, and collaborative, with high expectations and commensurate resources for all students
- Family involvement—active investment in the student's learning and the school

- Instruction—varied in strategy with emphasis on cooperative learning and differentiation among students in flexible, heterogeneous groupings
- Professional development—intentional; focused on goals and informed by data
- School organization—flexible, small, mutually respectful learning communities of adults and students
- Internal and external communications
- School-community partnerships—securing access to comprehensive health education and services for young adolescents (W. K. Kellogg Foundation 1998)

Through focused professional development and the collaboration of technical assistance partners with higher education and community organizations, Middle Start has expanded its work with Michigan middle schools in impoverished neighborhoods to include the Mid-South Middle Start initiative and the Kansas-Missouri initiative.

Sample schools: East Middle School, Ypsilanti, Michigan; Grayling Middle School, Grayling, Michigan.

Modern Red School House Institute (K–12)
208 23rd Avenue North
Nashville, TN 37203
(615) 320-8804
(615) 320-5366 (fax)
http://www.mrsh.org
Contact person: Brian Spears, vice president
Developer: Hudson Institute

Sponsored by the New American Schools, this nonprofit model emphasizes high academic standards for all students, character education, integrated technology, and a compact individual education for each student. Its guiding principles are

- All students can learn and attain high standards in core subjects, given understanding of the variance in learning speed and methodology
- Schools should transmit the democratic values of a shared culture in a pluralistic society
- Principals and teachers exercise professional freedom in making instructional decisions and in acquiring resources to fulfill student needs

- Schools should have flexibility in setting and accomplishing their mission and be held accountable through assessments of student progress
- Advanced technology is fundamental to achieving a cost-effective, quality education
- Schools are places teachers and students should choose to be (Modern Red School House 1998)

Built on these beliefs is a shift not only in expectations, but in the use of time, parental responsibilities, community involvement, professional development, and assessment. Teachers vary their uses of time and instructional techniques to ensure that all students pass "watershed" assessments that enable them to move from primary to intermediate to upper divisions. Additionally, technology specialists are added to the faculty; parents agree to share responsibility for student performance through Individual Education Compacts; and the community helps define instruction in character development.

Sample schools: Maverick Elementary School, San Antonio, Texas; Robert Lee Frost Elementary School, Indianapolis, Indiana.

School Development Program (K–12)
53 College Street
New Haven, CT 27401
(203) 737-4008
(203) 737-4001 (fax)
http://www.info.med.yale.edu/comer
Contact person: Beverly Crowther
Developer: James Comer

Developed in 1968 by Dr. Comer at the Yale Child Study Center, this preK–12, holistic, all-school reform model has been implemented in eighteen states and more than sixty at-risk schools. Based on the development of the child, the adolescent, and the adult, this model seamlessly joins administrators, parents, and other concerned adults in the support of students' academic growth and achievement as well as their personal, moral, and social development. The model is based on three guiding principles:

- No-fault approach to problem solving—teams enjoy total support as they analyze problems and propose solutions
- Consensus decision making promotes communication and common understanding

•• Collaboration that authentically joins administration and teams in school management (Yale Child Study Center 1998b)

The operation of the school is built on three plans:

•• Comprehensive school plan that gives particular direction to school improvement from a total environmental perspective such as school climate, content knowledge, staff development, public relations
•• Staff development plan that focuses teacher professional development on the school's goals and priorities
•• Monitoring and assessment plan that provides direction for school improvement based on formative data (Yale Child Study Center 1998a)

Both the principles and plans are implemented through the following teams:

•• School planning and management team, consisting of administrators, teachers, support staff, parents, and other interested personnel; constructs and monitors the comprehensive school plan
•• Student and staff support team, consisting of social workers, counselors, special education educators, and staff with child development and mental health expertise; focuses on improving the school's social climate
•• Parent team, which engages parents in all facets of the school (Yale Child Study Center 1998a)

Other features of this model include Teachers Helping Teachers (THT), which arranges for teachers to meet in pairs or small groups to examine and reflect on individual student development and learning and teacher responsiveness; Essentials of Literacy, which targets students who have reading problems and provides them with the necessary instruction and environment; and a balanced curriculum that addresses content standards and a student's performance on standardized tests.

Sample schools: Guilford County schools, Greensboro, North Carolina; Prince George County public schools, Bowie, Maryland.

Talent Development School Program (6–12)
Center for Research on the Education of Students
Placed at Risk (CRESPAR)
Johns Hopkins University
3003 North Charles Street, Suite 200
Baltimore, MD 21218
(410) 516-8829
(410) 516-8890 (fax)
http://www.jhu.edu
dmaciver@csos.jhu.edu
Contact person: Douglas MacIver, co-director

Developed by Johns Hopkins University and Howard University, the Talent Development model is built on basic elements that transform an at-risk school into an effective learning community. The model focuses on a core curriculum that prepares students for college attendance, and includes a four-period day that emphasizes in-depth instruction and project learning. Basic components of the model include

- Facilitated instructional programs in math, science, U.S. history, reading, English, and language arts that integrate effective instructional practices with authentic assessments, focused and ongoing staff development, and in-class support
- Student Team Literature, a cooperative learning approach to instructional and acquisition skills in reading, English, and language arts
- Standards-based math curriculum that integrates skill building and problem solving, built on the University of Chicago School Mathematics Project
- Inquiry-based, interactive science curriculum designed to meet national science standards and benchmarks
- U.S. history constructed around Joy Hakim's multicultural narrative *A History of US* series
- School organization and staffing that permit smaller learning communities that foster interdependence, close relationships, and partnerships among students, families, and staff
- Heterogeneous groupings of students
- Intensive additional help in math and reading for lower-achieving students
- Career exploration courses
- Culturally relevant curriculum and instructional support (MacIver 1999)

Talent Development schools become part of the National Network of Partnership schools, which bring together schools, families (using Epstein's family involvement model), and members of the community in focused activities.

Sample school: Central East Middle School, Philadelphia.

Curricular Models

Core Knowledge (K–8)
Core Knowledge Foundation
801 East High Street
Charlottesville, VA 22902
(804) 977-7550
(804) 977-0021 (fax)
http://www.coreknowledge.org
Contact person: Constance Jones, director of school programs
Developer: E. D. Hirsch, Jr.

Developed in 1990, the Core Knowledge curriculum is currently used in over 700 schools. The program is based on the basic concepts, skills, and knowledge that the developer considered necessary for being a member of a culturally literate society. Its emphasis is on increased academic performance as evidenced through scores on standardized national and state examinations. It provides a specific progression of grade-level content in mathematics, language arts, fine arts, science, history, and geography; teachers are also expected to teach reading. The model involves the family and community in acquiring resources, developing a school-wide plan, and planning various school activities (Core Knowledge Foundation 2001).

Sample schools: Ridge View Elementary School, Kennewick, Washington; Three Oaks Elementary School, Fort Myers, Florida.

Different Ways of Knowing (K–8)
6053 West Century Boulevard, 3rd floor
Los Angeles, CA 90045-6434
(310) 645-1960
(310) 645-1915 (fax)
http://www.dwoknet.galef.org/
Contact person: Sue Beauregard
Developer: The Galef Institute

Different Ways of Knowing (DWoK) is a combination of professional development and curricular reform based on an overriding assumption about how students learn. DWoK is currently used by over 500 elementary schools, and as of the fall of 2001 the Galef Institute will pilot the model in fifteen middle-level sites. The institute describes the model as interdisciplinary, student-centered, standards-driven, and comprehensive. The emphasis on people's use of multiple types of intelligence combines several elements: inquiry-based teaching and learning through the understanding of students' verbal and math skills; creative arts; social skills; and logical thinking. DWoK describes its philosophy as embracing

- Positive expectations for the academic and social achievement of all children
- Thematically integrated instruction across disciplines
- Active student participation
- Early intervention
- Parent participation in the classroom and at home (Galletti 2000)

The initiative's three-year course of professional development and community building offers leadership training, technical assistance, periodicals, and other culturally diverse reading materials. The integrated approach to curriculum, instruction, and assessment includes nongraded modules that integrate the visual and aural arts with science, mathematics, history, and social studies themes.

Sample schools: Anderson Elementary School, Lawndale, California; Harvey Milk Civil Rights Academy, San Francisco, California.

National Writing Project (K–16)
University of California
2105 Bancroft, #1042
Berkeley, CA 94720-1042
(510) 642-0963
(510) 642-4545 (fax)
http://writingproject.org/
Contact person: Richard Sterling, executive director
Developer: James Gray, University of California, Berkeley

Begun as the Bay Area Writing Project in 1974, the National Writing Project has been replicated in nearly 200 sites in forty-six states. Teachers attend a rigorous summer institute in which they examine their approaches to the teaching of writing, consider strategies for writing across the curriculum, actively learn about the teaching of writing (through both personal engagement and the study of best practices), and then become mentors in professional development programs in their own schools. This collegial teaching model fosters continuity throughout the school and establishes active local and national networks. NWP states that its three major goals are

- •• To improve the teaching of writing in all grades
- •• To improve the quality of professional development
- •• To improve the professional position of the classroom teacher as an effective mentor (National Writing Project 1998)

The model also embraces and promotes responsiveness to the local culture of the school and the neighborhood, crafting its workshops to the particular needs of individual sites. The model works with teachers in a series of workshops rather than in a single institute, seminar, or workshop.

Sample schools: Campostella Elementary School, Norfolk, Virginia; Writing Improvement Network, Columbia, South Carolina.

Paideia
National Paideia Center
University of North Carolina, Greensboro
School of Education
P.O. Box 26171
Greensboro, NC 27402-6171
(336) 334-3729
(336) 334-3739 (fax)
http://www.paideia.org/
Contact person: Terry Roberts, director
Developer: Mortimer Adler

Built on Adler's 1984 text *Paideia Proposal: An Educational Manifesto*, the National Paideia Center works with over ninety schools in fourteen states. Paideia is based on the democratic principle that society has an inherent responsibility to provide a quality education and that every individual has a right to one. Its guiding precepts are to prepare young people for their place in the work world, for a life of continual learning, and for assuming the national and international responsibilities of citizenship. Paideia focuses on developing a conceptual understanding of ideas and values, cognitive skills, and content knowledge. These objectives are achieved through using the following instructional strategies:

➤ Direct or didactic instruction whereby the teacher lectures and provides knowledge
➤ Socratic seminars in which students question and examine ideas in an in-depth manner
➤ One-on-one coaching of students at their individual level and pace (National Paideia Center n.d.)

Sample schools: Pueblo School for the Arts and Sciences, Pueblo, Colorado; Madison Elementary School, McLeansville, North Carolina.

Reading Recovery (first grade)
Reading Recovery Council of North America
1929 Kenny Road, Suite 100
Columbus, OH 43210-1069
(614) 292-7111
(614) 292-4404 (fax)
http://www.readingrecovery.org/
Contact person: Jean Bussell, executive director
Developer: Marie Clay

Developed by New Zealand educator and psychologist Marie Clay, Reading Recovery came to the United States in 1984; over 10,000 schools currently use the program. It is an intensive early intervention literacy program for first-grade children who score in the lowest 20 percent of their class. The program provides thirty-minute, one-to-one daily tutoring outside of the classroom. It is based on accelerated learning expectations and builds on the student's interest in books and stories. Students remain in Reading Recovery until they can read at or above grade level (Reading Recovery Council of North America 2000).

Sample schools: Fort Bend Independent School District (ISD), Sugarland, Texas; Lawrence Public Schools, Lawrence, Kansas.

Roots & Wings (preK–6)
3505 North Charles Street
Baltimore, MD 21218
(410) 516-8896
(800) 548-4998
(410) 516-8890 (fax)
http://www.successforall.net
Developers: Robert Slavin and Nancy Madden, Johns Hopkins University

Although Roots & Wings is a comprehensive reform model, its emphasis is on the importance of basic skills, problem solving, creativity, and critical thinking. Roots & Wings is a collaboration among Johns Hopkins

University, the Maryland State Department of Education, and St. Mary's County School District in Maryland. The model is used in over 700 schools in forty states. The model focuses on the success of every child by using well-structured curricular and instructional approaches and evaluation methods in all elementary content areas. It also stresses sound classroom management, student motivation, and professional development. Additionally, the model emphasizes one-to-one tutoring, cooperative learning, on-site facilitation, the use of a site advisory team, and the integration of a family support team.

> •• *Roots* refers to sound health and language and reading skills necessary for preparing all children, and early intervention for at-risk students, one-to-one tutoring, extensive professional development, and the integration of health and social services
> •• *Wings* refers to curricular and instructional strategies designed to challenge students to soar (Universal Excellence in Elementary Education n.d.)

Roots & Wings builds on the model's reading component, Success for All.

Sample schools: Springdale Memphis Magnet School, Memphis, Tennessee; Hardy Elementary School, Hamilton County, Tennessee.

Success for All
3505 North Charles Street
Baltimore, MD 21218
(800) 548-4998
(410) 516-0543 (fax)
sfa@csos.jhu.edu
http://www.successforall.net
Developers: Robert Slavin and Nancy Madden, Johns Hopkins University

Success for All contains the elements that are the foundation of Roots & Wings and is being used in over 200 schools in fifty-nine districts. Implemented primarily in low-income, Title I schools, this reading program emphasizes early detection and intervention. It shares Roots & Wings' emphasis on one-to-one-tutoring, family support, integrated services, intensive professional development, and on-site facilitation. It is a school-wide reading program that groups students by reading level for a large part of the day, and then returns them to their grade level, where cooperative learning techniques are stressed. Features of the program include

•• Ongoing formative assessment of students' reading progress and necessary changes in grouping

•• Family support team—encourages parents to read to their children, to become involved in the activities of the school, and to intervene when home problems interrupt student learning

•• Full-time, on-site facilitator who provides ongoing support and professional development

•• Advisory committee—principal, facilitator, faculty and parent representatives, and family support staff who assess ongoing progress of the program (Slavin and Madden 1998)

The curriculum is layered into the Early Learning program for prekindergarten and kindergarten, which emphasizes oral language development; Reading Roots, the beginning reading program that emphasizes phonics and meaning; and Reading Wings for readers in the second through sixth grade levels, which uses literature, anthologies, and basal readers.

Sample schools: P.S. 159, Brooklyn, New York; Lakeland City Elementary School, San Antonio, Texas.

Instructional Model

Foxfire Fund (K–12)
P.O. Box 541
Mountain City, GA 30562
(706) 746-5828
(706) 746-5829 (fax)
Contact person: Christy Stevens, coordinator of Teacher Support Services
Developer: Eliot Wigginton

Initiated in 1966, the Foxfire approach is now used by teachers in over thirty states. The Foxfire Fund is an independent nonprofit organization that disseminates its work through regional networks, local alliances, and professional development workshops. The approach is learner-centered in that it helps students become creative, productive, and engaged citizens. It is also interactive, as it provides academically rigorous experiences that promote ongoing active dialogue between students and members of the community. Foxfire's core principles are

•• The work teachers and students are engaged in is shaped by learner choice and design

- ➡ The role of the teacher is a constructivist one, that of a facilitator, collaborator, or coach
- ➡ The academic engagement of teachers and students is rigorous and respectful
- ➡ Student learning is active
- ➡ Classroom experiences involve peer teaching, small group work, and teamwork
- ➡ Relevance of classroom work to the larger world is fundamental
- ➡ Student work is shared beyond the classroom
- ➡ Learning activities naturally flow out of previous lessons and experiences
- ➡ Imagination and creativity are valued
- ➡ Reflection is an ongoing part of student work and necessary for authentic growth
- ➡ Assessment of teacher-student work is rigorous (Foxfire Foundation n.d.)

Unlike other systemic reform models, the Foxfire approach is reflected in the individual classroom as the teacher responds to the particular cultural, curricular, and student needs as exhibited in the neighboring community. In this model, the teacher is viewed as the key agent for creating sustained changes over time.

Sample schools: Elk City Elementary School, Elk City, Idaho; Calexico High School, Calexico, California.

FOUNDATIONS AND CORPORATIONS

During 1999 corporate funding of education increased 22 percent, to $3 billion. Public K–12 and higher education remained the dominant foci, with added interest in new technology, minority education, and collaborative partnerships. Some of the more aggressive and influential foundations are listed below.

The Annenberg Foundation
St. Davids Center, Suite A-200
150 Radnor-Chester Road
St. Davids, PA 19087
(610) 341-9066
info@whannenberg.org
http://www.whannenberg.org

This private foundation's funding specifically addresses K–12 systemic reform and restructuring in program development, pilot projects, and program replication. Some of the professional development initiatives that it has funded include Teach for America, Teachers as Leaders, and leadership institutes for principals in Philadelphia. Additionally, in 1993 the foundation made the largest single gift to public education, $500 million, in the form of the Annenberg Challenge Grant. The grant provided funds to sites in Los Angeles, Philadelphia, San Francisco, Chicago, South Florida, New York City, Detroit, Boston, Salt Lake City, Chattanooga, Atlanta, Baltimore, and Chelsea, Massachusetts. In addition, it funded the Rural School and Community Trust.

Annie E. Casey Foundation
701 St. Paul Street
Baltimore, MD 21202
(800) 222-1099
(410) 547-6600
wwebmail@aecf.org
http://www.aecf.org/index.htm
Contact person: Douglas W. Nelson, executive director

The Casey Foundation funds projects that address child welfare, leadership development, minority education, and family services. Though it does not fund individuals, the foundation gives grants for research, conferences, seminars, and special projects. It also provides technical assistance for disenfranchised families and children, assistance that promotes comprehensive reform, school/community partnerships, school-based accountability, and smaller class sizes. Through its educational reform initiatives, the foundation funds a limited number of sites in distressed communities (Kentucky, Maryland, New York, Pennsylvania, Texas) for a significant length of time. Additionally, the foundation's Children and Family Fellowship program develops leaders and leadership skills.

Publications: The foundation publishes yearly a *Kids Count* report, which presents in statistical form the status of the nation's children, as well as the national report *Families Count.*

BellSouth Foundation
1155 Peachtree Street, NE, #7H08
Atlanta, GA 30309-3610
(404) 249-2396
(404) 249-5696 (fax)
http://www.bellsouthcorp.com/bsf/
Contact person: program manager

Since its inception in 1986, the BellSouth Foundation has awarded over $43 million in grants to schools throughout nine southeastern states. Having specifically targeted middle-grades schools and teachers, as well as some higher education content areas, the foundation is now targeting prekindergarten–12 system reform initiatives, which focus on improving individual learning, creating appropriate learning environments, and promoting partnerships through technology that improve learning.

Bill & Melinda Gates Foundation Education Programs
P.O. Box 23350
Seattle, WA 98102
(206) 709-3607
(206) 709-3280 (fax)
edinfo@gatesfoundation.org
http://www.gatesfoundation.org/learning/education

The foundation's Millennium Scholarship program, which will provide $1 billion in scholarships to 1,000 minority high school students during the next twenty years, is open to all ethnic minorities, although it primarily targets blacks, Latinos, and American Indians. Through other initiatives such as State Challenge Grants for Leadership Development, the Alliance for Education, and the Teacher Leadership Project, the foundation focuses on developing district, school, and classroom leadership, and on encouraging the development of high-performance models infused with technology.

Carnegie Corporation of New York
437 Madison Avenue
New York, NY 10022
(212) 371-3200
(212) 754-4073 (fax)
http://www.carnegie.org
Contact person: Vartan Gregorian, president

This foundation awards nearly $60 million annually to nonprofit organizations and institutions that it feels will have national or international impact. It sponsors study groups, commissions, and task forces in addition to funding such initiatives as the Carnegie Corporation's Scholars Program, the Starting Points State and Community Partnerships for Young Children, the Child Care Action Campaign, and the Council on Adolescent Development. It also disseminates material on best practices in higher education for the preparation of teachers who are proficient in content areas, technology, and appropriate developmental practices for elementary and secondary students. The corporation has also funded the work of the National Governors Association and the Council for Basic Education, which works to establish national education goals.

Publications: Carnegie commissions, councils, task forces, and initiatives have produced many important research reports, including those of the Carnegie Task Force on Learning in the Primary Grades; the Carnegie Task Force on Meeting the Needs of Young Children; the Carnegie Council on Adolescent Development; the Carnegie Commission on Science, Technology, and Government; and New York's Starting Points State and Community Partnerships for Young Children. All of these publications are available free of charge through the commission's offices at 1779 Massachusetts Avenue, NW, Suite 715, Washington, DC 20036-2103.

The David and Lucile Packard Foundation
300 Second Street, Suite 200
Los Altos, CA 94022
(650) 948-7658
http://www.packard.org
Contact person: Susan Packard Orr, chairperson

The foundation supports nonprofit organizations that focus on the healthy development of children, the economic security of families, and the reduction of violence in homes and communities. These organizations include the Prudential Youth Leadership Institute; Communities in Schools, which helps children access the necessary community resources to stay in school; the Challenge Learning Center, a unique outdoor experiential learning program; and the Children's Defense Fund (CDF), whose president and founder is Marian Wright Edelman. CDF's national headquarters is at 25 E Street, NW, Washington, DC 20001, (202) 628-8787. CDF has twelve regional and affiliate offices. Begun in 1973, it provides funding for such programs for low-income children and families as Healthy Start, Head Start, Fair Start, Moral Start, and Safe Start. CDF has exercised an effective voice on legislative and governmental issues that touch the lives of children and families.

CDF is one of over 1,000 public and private nonprofit member agencies that fund the Child Welfare League of America (CWLA), the nation's oldest and largest nonprofit organization, which promotes the well-being of children and the strengthening of the family.

Publications: The foundation's biannual journal, *The Future of Children,* includes research-based articles bearing on the well-being of children.

DeWitt Wallace–Reader's Digest Fund
Two Park Avenue, 23rd floor
New York, NY 10016
(212) 251-9780
(212) 679-6990 (fax)
wrdf@wallacefunds.org
http://www.wallacefunds.org
Contact person: Lee Mitgang

The Wallace–Reader's Digest Fund describes their support of education as helping to develop effective educational leaders who will help improve student learning, particularly in low-achieving schools. In the first decade of the twenty-first century, their initiative Leaders Count will concentrate on ways to attract, train, and support more effective principals and superintendents. Some of their national partners include the Academy for Educational Development, the Adult Literacy Media Alliance, the Education Trust, and the Urban Institute. Recipients of foundation funds for leadership projects include the Big Picture Company and the Aspiring Principals' program, in Providence, Rhode Island; a project cosponsored with the RAND Corporation to critically analyze leadership preparation and career progression; the Council of Chief State School Officers to help create a five-state consortium that addresses policy issues affecting leadership preparation and achievement and establishes criteria for leadership; the American Association of School Administrators to create a recruitment and preparation program for potential leaders in urban school districts; and Teachers College of Columbia University to create and sustain a National Center on Education Leadership.

Publications: Publications that present the fund's projects and initiatives may be purchased or acquired on-line.

Edna McConnell Clark Foundation
250 Park Avenue
New York, NY 10177-0026
(212) 551-9100
(212) 986-4558 (fax)
http://fdncenter.org/grantmaker/emclark/index.html
Contact person: Michael A. Bailin, president

The foundation offers support to nonprofit organizations and public agencies that are committed to bettering the lives of children and families. The Program for Children, Program for Student Achievement, and Youth Development Program direct support and technical assistance, in a community-based framework, to middle schools that are striving to collaboratively design curricular and professional development programs and to develop partnerships and family/community investment in schools.

Publications: Four reports authored by Anne C. Lewis examine the Clark Foundation–supported initiatives implemented in six school districts (*Figuring It Out: Standards-Based Reform* [1999]; *Believing in Ourselves: Progress and Struggle in Urban Middle School Reform, 1991–1995* [1996]; *Changing the Odds: Middle School Reform in Progress, 1991–1993* [1994]; and *Gaining Ground: The Highs and Lows of Urban Middle School Reform, 1989–1991* [1992]). A booklet written by Anne MacKinnon, *Working Together: Harnessing Community Resources to Improve Middle School* (1997), examines the ways citizens can mobilize community resources on behalf of local schools.

Ewing Marion Kauffman Foundation
4801 Rockhill Road
Kansas City, MO 64110-2046
(816) 932-1000
http://www.emkf.org
Contact person: grant administrator

The foundation funds initiatives in education at all levels, family support, school-to-career, entrepreneurship, and youth development. The JumpStart effort partners the Center for the Study of Community Colleges with the Kauffman Center in providing entrepreneurial education for African Americans, Hispanic Americans, Native Americans, and women. Project STAR is the foundation's youth development initiative aimed at the prevention of drug, alcohol, and tobacco use and abuse. At the forefront of the foundation's leadership efforts are the Youth Advisory Board, which helps to develop youth leaders in the metropolitan Kansas City area, and the Kauffman Center for Entrepreneurial Leadership.

Publications: Among its reports and papers, the most notable are *A Partnership for Quality and Access: School-Based Health Centers and Health Plans* (1996), available through School Health Policy Initiative, Albert Einstein College of Medicine, Montefiore Hospital and Medical Center, 111 East 210th Street, Bronx, NY 10467-2490; and *Service Learning: What It Offers to Students, Schools, and Communities* (1997), available through the Council of Chief State School Officers, Homer Building, Suite 400N, 601 Thirteenth Street, NW, Washington, DC 20005.

Ford Foundation
320 East 43rd Street
New York, NY 10017
(212) 573-5000
(212) 351-3677 (fax)
http://www.fordfound.org
Contact person: secretary

In the educational arena, the foundation funds initiatives that particularly target low-income and chronically underrepresented groups through the design and implementation of interdisciplinary and collaborative approaches. The Leadership for a Changing World program recognizes and supports emerging individual and group leaders and represents the foundation's sustained commitment to leadership. The foundation also awards grants to various universities, such as Tuskegee, Howard, Southern, Tennessee State, Clark Atlanta, Florida A&M, Texas, and North Carolina A&T, as well as the United Negro College Fund. Ford continues to expand collaborative programs such as the Detroit area Pre-College Engineering program and the Minority Engineering Scholarship program.

The Joyce Foundation
Three National Plaza
70 West Madison Street, Suite 2750
Chicago, IL 60602
(312) 782-2464
(312) 782-4170 (fax)
info@joycefdn.org
http://www.joycefdn.org
Contact persons: Warren Chapman and Peter Mich, education program officers

In Chicago, Cleveland, Detroit, and Milwaukee, the foundation funds public school reform efforts that address quality teaching, improved measures for assessing student performance, community engagement, and equitable allocation of resources in the Great Lakes region.

Milken Family Foundation
1250 Fourth Street
Santa Monica, CA 90401-1353
(310) 998-2800
(310) 998-2828 (fax)
http://www.mff.org

Contact person: Lowell Milken, chairman

The foundation focuses on strengthening the teaching profession through acknowledging and rewarding outstanding educators; through challenging and developing their leadership skills; through family and community revitalization and involvement initiatives; and by encouraging young people to become involved in the teaching profession. Among the projects funded by the foundation are the Milken Scholars Program, which honors outstanding high school graduates; an annual National Education Conference, which assembles educators, policy makers, and business leaders; and the Teacher Advancement Program, which examines all facets of the teaching profession, including entrance to it.

Publications: Many of the most widely read publications address the foundation's interest in learning and technology. They include *The Impact of Education Technology on Student Achievement, Technology in American Schools: Seven Dimensions for Gauging Progress, Will New Teachers Be Prepared to Teach in a Digital Age?* and *Online and Electronic Research by Middle School Students.*

The Pew Charitable Trusts
One Commerce Square
2005 Market Street, Suite 1700
Philadelphia, PA 19103-7077
(215) 575-9050
(215) 575-4939 (fax)
http://www.pewtrusts.com
Contact person: Susan K. Urahn, director of educational programs

In 1999 the trusts awarded thirty-one education grants that totaled over $38 million. Two of the trusts' goals aimed at academic leaders and others with a stake in schools address K–12 reforms in both teaching and the overall work of the school. The trusts provide funding to *Education Week*'s "Quality Counts" report, the National Board for Professional Teaching Standards, and the Pew Forum on Standards-Based Reform at the Harvard Graduate School of Education. Additionally, they support higher education initiatives such as the Higher Education Policy Institute and the National Survey of Student Engagement at Indiana University's School of Education.

The Posse Foundation
14 Wall Street, 7th floor
New York, NY 10005
(212) 571-2087

(212) 571-2083 (fax)
http://www.possefoundation.org

High school students who show signs of potential leadership but are underrepresented in leadership positions, and who are from nontraditional or minority backgrounds, are identified while in public high schools. They are assembled in multicultural teams and supported with a variety of resources through college. Scholarships and other support from corporate sponsors are awarded to students from New York and Boston public schools to attend Bowdoin, Wheaton, and Middlebury colleges, and Brandeis and Vanderbilt universities.

The Rockefeller Foundation
420 Fifth Avenue
New York, NY 10018-2702
(212) 869-8500
(212) 852-8273 (fax)
http://www.rockfund.org
Contact person: Alice Stone Ilchman, chair

The foundation allocates funds for various school development and community-building efforts in urban districts. It also supports the building of districtwide infrastructure for professional development and reform that have a direct effect on teaching and learning. Grants-in-aid are given to such initiatives as the After-School Corporation based in New York, which fosters support for parents in schools; Children Now; and the Chapin Hall Center for Children in Chicago.

W. K. Kellogg Foundation
One Michigan Avenue East
Battle Creek, MI 49017-4058
(616) 968-1611
(616) 968-0413 (fax)
http://www.wkkf.org
*Contact person: Leah Meyer Austin, program director
for Youth and Education*

Through all of its initiatives, the foundation focuses on building the capacity of communities, institutions, and individuals to be problem-solvers. Its initiatives include Community Voices, Engaging Latino Communities for Education, Managing Information with Rural America, Turning Point, and the Middle Start initiative, a model for systemic middle-grades school reform that focuses on fostering social equity, developmental practice, and academic rigor.

Publications: Among its many print and video resources, *Leadership Reconsidered: Engaging Higher Education in Social Change* and *Middle Start: Revitalizing Middle-Grades Education for Students, Teachers, Schools, and Communities* are of particular note.

True reform is about realizing the potentials, possibilities, hopes, and opportunities of all young people. A focus on anything else is simply an exercise in change. We end where we began—with the kids.

REFERENCES

Accelerated Schools. 1994. "Frameworks for Learning." *Accelerated Schools* 3, no. 3 (Spring): 2001.

Blum, R. 2000. *Building Capacity for Change.* Portland, OR: Northwest Regional Educational Laboratory.

Chapman, J. 1988. "Decentralization, Devolution, and the Teacher: Participation by Teachers in the Decision Making of Schools." *Journal of Educational Administration* 26, no. 1: 39–72.

Children's Defense Fund. 2000. *The State of America's Children: A Report from the Children's Defense Fund Yearbook.* Boston: Beacon Press.

Coalition of Essential Schools. n.d. "The Ten Common Principles of the Coalition of Essential Schools." Public information packet. Oakland, CA.

Community for Learning. 1998. "Building on Diversity." Public information packet. Philadelphia, PA: Temple University Center for Research in Human Development and Education.

"Co-NECT Schools." 1998. Public information packet. Cambridge, MA: Co-NECT Schools.

Core Knowledge Foundation. 2001. "Core Knowledge." http://www.coreknowledge.org.

Edison Schools. n.d. "The Ten Fundamentals behind Edison's School Design." Public information packet. New York, NY.

Elmore, R. 1990. "Introduction: On Changing the Structure of Public Schools." In *Restructuring Schools: The Next Generation of Educational Reform,* ed. R. F. Elmore, 1–28. San Francisco: Jossey-Bass.

The Foxfire Foundation. n.d. "Foxfire Fund." Public information brochure. Mountain City, GA.

Fullan, M. 1993. *Change Forces: Probing the Depths of Educational Reform.* London: Falmer Press.

———. 1999. "Leading Change in Professional Learning Communities." *Education Update* 41, no. 8 (December): 1–4.

Fullan, M., and M. Miles. 1992. "Getting Reform Right: What Works and What Doesn't." *Phi Delta Kappan* 73, no. 10 (June): 744–752.

Galletti, S. 2000. "Different Ways of Knowing." Public information packet. Los Angeles, CA.

"High Schools That Work." 1998. Public information packet. Atlanta, GA: High Schools That Work.

Kaplan, G. R. 2000. "Friends, Foes, and Noncombatants." *Phi Delta Kappan* 82, no. 3 (November): K1–12.

Kellerman, B. 1999. *Reinventing Leadership: Making the Connection between Politics and Business.* Albany, NY: State University of New York Press.

Kotter, J. 1995. "Leading Change: Why Transformation Efforts Fail." *Harvard Business Review* (March–April): 1–11.

Louis, K., and M. Miles. 1990. *Improving the Urban High School: What Works and Why.* New York: Teachers College Press.

MacIver, D. 1999. "The National Field Test of the Talent Development Middle School." Information packet. Baltimore: Johns Hopkins University.

Modern Red School House. 1998. "MRSH Implementation." Public information packet. Arlington, VA.

National Center on Education and the Economy. 1998. "The National Alliance for Restructuring is America's Choice for School Design." Public information packet. Washington, DC.

National Paideia Center. n.d. "Philosophy and Methodology: The Three Columns of Instruction." http://www.paideia.org/.

"National Writing Project." 1998. Public information brochure. Berkeley: University of California.

Ramsey, R. 1999. *Lead, Follow, or Get Out of the Way: How to Be a More Effective Leader in Today's Schools.* Thousand Oaks, CA: Corwin Press.

Reading Recovery Council of North America. 2000. "Reading Recovery: Executive Summary, 1984–1999." Public information packet. Columbus, OH.

Sarason, S. 1990. *The Predictable Failure of Educational Reform.* San Francisco: Jossey-Bass.

Sergiovanni, T. 1995. *The Principalship: A Reflective Practice Perspective.* Boston: Allyn and Bacon.

Slavin, R., and N. Madden. 1998. "Success for All." Public information packet. The Success for All Foundation. Baltimore, MD.

Starr, L. 1999. "Governing America's Schools: Changing the Rules." *Education World* (December): 1–5.

Roots and Wings. n.d. "Universal Excellence in Elementary Education: Roots & Wings." Public information packet. Baltimore: Johns Hopkins University.

Wissler, D. F., and F. I. Ortiz. 1988. *The Superintendent's Leadership in School Reform.* London: Falmer Press.

W. K. Kellogg Foundation. 1998. *Starting Again in the Middle: Executive Summary.* Battle Creek, MI: W. K. Kellogg Foundation.

Yale Child Study Center. 1998a. "School Development Program: Atlas Communities." Public information packet. Newton, MA.

———. 1998b. "School Development Program: New District Presentation." Public information packet. New Haven, CT.

Chapter Six

⁓ Directory of Organizations, Institutes, Associations, Government Agencies, and Leadership Academies

> Leadership is action, not position.
> —Donald H. McGannon

The directory presented below offers a wealth of contact information for educational leaders in all arenas. Professional associations and organizations address the concerted work and focus of educators, administrators, families, concerned citizens, policy makers, and students. Various institutes offer professional development and training through a variety of courses, workshops, seminars, annual conferences, and print and nonprint resources. Institutions of higher learning offer preparation and licensure programs for formal study in addition to research and dissemination of material on best practices. The associations and alliances listed here reflect the diverse texture of our country as they speak to cultural, social, political, and individual needs and talents.

ORGANIZATIONS

Bureau of Indian Affairs (BIA)
Office of Indian Education Programs (OIEP)
1849 C Street, NW
Washington, DC 20240
(202) 208-6123
(202) 208-3312 (fax)
http://www.oiep.bia.edu/toc.htm

BIA and OIEP exercise leadership roles in providing and ensuring quality educational opportunities that are culturally consistent with tribes' needs and economic well-being. OIEP funds twenty-two innovative early childhood programs through its Family and Child Education initiative; twenty-six tribal colleges or universities; and up to thirty projects that increase student academic achievement. It encourages family and community involvement in all facets of Indian education. Additionally, the following associations focus on education for indigenous people.

National Indian Education Association (NIEA)
700 North Fairfax Street, Suite 210
Alexandria, VA 22124
(703) 838-2870
(703) 838-1620 (fax)
http://www.niea.org
John W. Cheek, executive director

NIEA supports traditional native cultures and values through enabling native students to be contributing members of their communities; promoting self-control of educational institutions; and improving the educational opportunities, resources, and experiences of American Indians and Alaskan natives. NIEA publishes a newsletter and sponsors an annual national conference.

National Indian Impacted Schools Association
Wapato School District, Box 38
Wapato, WA 98951
(509) 877-4181
(509) 877-6077 (fax)
Rick Foss, associate superintendent

This association describes itself as a national organization whose focus is raising educational funding. The association sponsors a summer conference, provides technical services, and offers a quarterly newsletter.

National Indian School Board Association (NISBA)
P.O. Box 770
Polson, MT 59860
(406) 883-3603
(406) 675-4801 (fax)
Carmen Taylor, director

In conjunction with the Bureau of Indian Affairs, NISBA trains school members and conducts annual regional workshops for teachers, administrators, students, and members of the community.

Publication: The periodical *Hoofbeats*, which is published three times a year.

Center for Educational Leadership Services
Kent State University
Northeast Regional Satellite of the National Center
for Effective Schools at Phi Delta Kappa International
Research One Building
1100 East Summit Street
Kent, OH 44146
(330) 672-2280
Judith March, director

The center provides services and resources for area school districts and their leaders, and serves as a focal resource for schools involved in the national Effective Schools reform effort.

Publications: *Developing High-Performance Schools* describes the components of the instructional design model used in the Effective Schools movement. The *Phi Delta Kappan,* often referred to simply as the *Kappan,* is the Phi Delta Kappa journal.

The Council for Exceptional Children (CEC)
1920 Association Drive
Reston, VA 20191-1589
(703) 620-3660
(703) 264-9494 (fax)
http://www.cec.sped.org

CEC is the largest international professional organization that focuses on improving educational outcomes for students with exceptionalities and disabilities. It advocates for appropriate legislation, resources, professional standards, and ongoing professional development. Special projects include the National Clearinghouse on Professions in Special Education, the ERIC Clearinghouse on Disabilities, and Gifted Education and the Culturally and Linguistically Appropriate Services Early Childhood Research Institute. CEC is a partner of CASE and places particular emphasis on legislation and research.

The Council of Administrators of Special Education (CASE)
The Council for Exceptional Children
1920 Association Drive
Reston, VA 20191-1589
(877) 232-4332
(703) 264-1637 (fax)
http://members.aol.com/casecec
Jo Thomason, executive director

This international professional educational organization, affiliated with the Council for Exceptional Children, describes its mission as providing leadership and support for its members by shaping policy and practice on the dignity and worth of all individuals in educational settings. It is the recognized advocacy voice for children with special needs.

Publications: Position paper on the least restrictive environment for special needs students, "Position Paper on Delivery of Services to Students with Disabilities" (1997).

The Council of Chief State School Officers (CCSSO)
One Massachusetts Avenue, NW, Suite 700
Washington, DC 20001-1431
(202) 408-5505
(202) 408-8072 (fax)
http://www.ccsso.org

CCSSO is a nonprofit organization whose constituents are department heads responsible on a state level for elementary and secondary education. CCSSO sponsors several national conferences that address various leadership issues throughout the year. It also sponsors nearly forty projects, including the Interstate School Leaders Licensure Consortium, Policymaker Partnership for Special Education, and State Action for Education Leadership. The council exercises its impressive authority on issues of leadership on a variety of levels, from the classroom to the boardroom.

Publications: CCSSO offers over 200 working papers, reports, and studies on a full range of issues affecting K–12 public education.

Council of the Great City Schools
1301 Pennsylvania Avenue, NW, Suite 702
Washington, DC 20004
(202) 393-2427
(202) 393-2400 (fax)
http://www.cgsc.org/

The council is comprised of fifty-seven of the nation's largest urban public school systems. Its authority to stimulate services for urban schools is growing, as is its ability to initiate dialogue. It serves as a national advocate for urban education through lobbying; research; dissemination of special reports, videos, and papers; professional development; provision of technology; and special projects.

Education Commission of the States (ECS)
707 17th Street, #2700
Denver, CO 80202-3427
(303) 299-3600
(303) 296-8332 (fax)
ecs@ecs.org
http://www.ecs.org
Christie McElhinney, public relations director

ECS is the most recognized nonprofit organization that assists governors, legislators, and state education officials in the identification, development, and implementation of policies that help improve student learning. ECS works in conjunction with corporate leaders and Fox River Learning, Advantage Learning Systems, and Voyager Expanded Learning. ECS provides an information clearinghouse; convenes leadership development workshops, courses, and conferences; holds state, regional, and national policy seminars (including a national forum and an annual meeting); and offers a variety of publications, videos, and audio materials, including *State Education Leader,* which is published three times a year.

Hispanic Association of Colleges and Universities (HACU)
8415 Datapoint Drive, Suite 400
San Antonio, TX 78229
(210) 692-3805
(210) 692-0823 (fax)
http://www.hacu.net/contact_us/contact.htm

HACU is active in more than 260 colleges and universities that have concentrated Hispanic populations. The association advocates for federal funding and support; provides financial assistance in the form of internships, scholarships, and research grants; and holds annual national conferences, capitol forums, and meetings.

International Center for Leadership in Education
1587 Route 146
Rexford, NY 12148
(518) 399-2776
(518) 399-7607 (fax)
http://www.daggett.com
Dr. Willard R. Daggett, president

The center offers a well-respected menu of services and resources, ranging from publications for administrators, teachers, and students to data-collection instruments and systemic school reform models.

Publications: The center's Leadership Press publishes work directed at improving teaching and learning, such as *Educational Improvement Trilogy, Defining Excellence for American Schools,* and *Testing and Assessment in American Schools.*

National Association of State Boards of Education (NASBE)
277 South Washington Street, Suite 100
Alexandria, VA 22314
(703) 684-4000
(703) 836-2313 (fax)
boards@nasbe.org
http://www.nasbe.org
Brenda Welburn, executive director

NASBE is the nonprofit association that represents state and boards of education, their attorneys, and their executive secretaries. The association's primary focus is strengthening state leadership on educational policy making and promoting excellence and equality of opportunity for all of the nation's children. The association provides effective training and technical assistance both to members and to the larger education community. It sponsors regional and national conferences, publishes resource materials for policy makers, and briefs business leaders, members of Congress, and executive agencies. NASBE holds an annual conference focusing on the professional development of board members, and an annual legislative conference that brings state board members together with congressional leaders and administration officials in Washington. It convenes study groups, task forces, and commissions, and conducts the yearly New State Board Member institute. In addition, the association undertakes management studies on state education leadership, offers action networks, and serves as a policy information clearinghouse whose database addresses current issues and policy implications.

Publications: *The State Education Standard* is NASBE's quarterly education policy journal.

The National Board for Professional Teaching Standards (NBPTS)
26555 Evergreen Road, Suite 400
Southfield, MI 48076
(810) 351-4444
(810) 351-4170 (fax)
http://www.nbpts.org

NBPTS is an independent, nonpartisan organization focused on establishing and ensuring rigorous standards for classroom teachers. The National Board's vision is to recognize outstanding teachers from across the country, raise the standards of practice, and stimulate best-practice dialogue in all schools.

National Center for Education Statistics (NCES)
1990 K Avenue, NW
Washington, DC 20006
(202) 502-7300
http://www.governmentguide.com/research/Statistics.adp

NCES describes itself as the primary federal body that collects and analyzes education data. It disseminates the data through its website, which includes links to K–12 practitioners, to postsecondary education data, to the "Nation's Report Card," to conferences and training, and to online postings of college opportunities.

National Center for Educational Alliances
Bronx Community College
Bronx, NY 10453
(718) 289-5163
http://www.thenationalcenter.org
Richard Donovan, director

The center organizes teams consisting of educators, community leaders, and corporate and political constituents, who assist underrepresented and underprepared urban students in the completion of higher education degrees. Among the center's initiatives are the Urban Partnership program, GEAR UP, and Merrill Lynch Scholarships. The center has an interactive on-line forum on leadership and partnerships.

Publications: *The Collaborative Advantage in Educational Reform: The Case for the K–16 Partnership, The Role of Family Resource Centers,* and a variety of articles.

National Center for Learning Disabilities
381 Park Avenue, South
Suite 1401
New York, NY 10016
(212) 545-7510
(212) 545-9665 (fax)
http://www.ncld.org/

The center offers national leadership in support of all citizens with learning disabilities through providing referral services, information, and resources, and through public advocacy, congressional lobbying, workshops, programs, and seminars. The center is another respected voice and initiator of policy on exceptionalities. Its workshops and seminars are timely and state of the art.

The National Center for Public Policy and Higher Education
1001 Connecticut Avenue, NW, Suite 310
Washington, DC 20036
(202) 822-6720
(202) 822-6730 (fax)
center@highereducation.org
Patrick M. Callan, president
Governor James B. Hunt, Jr., founder and chairman

Supported entirely by foundations such as the Ford Foundation and the Pew Charitable Trusts, the center describes itself as providing action-oriented analyses and stimulating leadership on state and federal policies that affect higher education opportunities for all young people. The center provokes discussion on controversial issues and effectively stimulates discussion on the policy level about leadership.

Publications: Position paper entitled "The Context: Higher Education Policy in the 1990s"; reports; and the journal *National Crosstalk.*

National Center on Educational Outcomes (NCEO)
University of Minnesota
350 Elliott Hall
75 East River Road
Minneapolis, MN 55455
(612) 626-1530
(612) 624-0879 (fax)
http://www.coled.umn.edu/NCEO
Martha Thurlow, director

NCEO describes itself as providing national leadership on the issue of the participation of students with disabilities and limited English proficiency in public schools by helping to identify outcomes, indicators, and assessments that help monitor the development of students with disabilities. The center provides training, resource materials, consulting services, and technical assistance to organizations across the country. It offers a broad list of publications, technical reports, and self-study guides, as well as a directory of assessment projects. It boasts a national network on assessment issues.

National Council for Accreditation of Teacher Education (NCATE)
2010 Massachusetts Avenue, NW
Washington, DC 20036-1023
(202) 466-7496
(202) 296-6620 (fax)
http://www.ncate.org

NCATE is the most influential performance-based accrediting body for teacher education programs in higher education. NCATE holds higher education programs to very specific standards and benchmarks. One of the intents of NCATE accreditation (besides the recognition gained) is that students may move from institution to institution and experience equivalent program quality and content. NCATE offers on-line publications, policy briefs, and research studies.

National School Boards Association (NSBA)
1680 Duke Street
Alexandria, VA 22314
(703) 838-6722
(703) 683-7590 (fax)
info@nsba.org
http://www.nsba.org
Clarice Chambers, president

NSBA describes its mission as fostering equity and excellence in public education through school board leadership and advocacy for public schools in the local community. This is the recognized association of school boards. It holds an annual leadership conference and the annual Urban Boards of Education conference. Its support for local boards is not only practical but shows foresight.

Publications: Among the numerous periodicals NSBA offers are the *American School Board Journal, Education Vital Signs,* and *Technology Leadership News.* On-line publications include "Exploring New Directions: Title I in the Year 2000."

North Central Regional Educational Laboratory (NCREL)
1900 Spring Road, Suite 300
Oak Brook, IL 60523-1480
(630) 571-4700
(630) 571-4716
cscdwww@ncrelsgi.ncrel.org
http://www.ncrel.org
Gina Burkhardt, executive director

NCREL conducts research and evaluations and provides research-based training, technical assistance, and resources to education professionals. NCREL is one of ten regional educational laboratories across the country; its research, professional development, and distribution of educational and leadership materials is the most extensive.

Publications: *Urban Audio Journal; Urban Education Program.*

Teachers College
Columbia University
525 West 120th Street
New York, NY 10027
(212) 678-3000
http://www.tc.columbia.edu

The prestigious Teachers College engages in research and dissemination of educational leadership studies through a variety of centers at the college. Some of them are:

The Center for Young Children and Families sponsors summer policy programs, internships, workshops, and practica on the interrelationship between education and the development of children and families. Contact person: Jeanne Brooks-Gunn, director, Teachers College, Box 39, (212) 678-3904.

The Elbenwood Center for the Study of the Family as Educator engages in research on the relationship between the family and other educative institutions. Contact person: Hope Jensen Leichter, director, Teachers College, Box 123, (212) 678-3187.

The Center for Technology and School Change assists schools as they integrate technology into their curricula. Contact person: Howard Budin, director, Teachers College, Box 8, (212) 678-3773.

The Hechinger Institute on Education and the Media assists journalists who cover education. Contact person: Gene Maeroff, director, Teachers College, Box 127, (212) 678-4197.

The Institute on Education and the Economy is an interdisciplinary policy research center that examines the interrelationship between education and the economy. Contact person: Thomas Bailey, director, Teachers College, Box 174, (212) 678-3091, (212) 678-3699 (fax), iee@columbia.edu.

The Institute on Education and Government provides support specifically to the nation's governors and other leaders committed to an education agenda. Contact person: Gaston Caperton, director, Teachers College, Box 34, (212) 678-8402, ieg@columbia.edu.

The Institute for Urban and Minority Education is engaged in the research and dissemination of improved diverse experiences for urban and minority populations. The institute provides professional development, youth programs, and technical assistance and spurs public awareness of minority challenges. Contact person: Dr. Erwin Flaxman, director, Teachers College, Box 75, (212) 678-3780.

The Institute of Higher Education conducts research on state systems of higher education and on policies and problems, administration, and financing of educational institutions. Contact person: L. Lee Knefelkamp, coordinator, Teachers College, Box 101.

The National Center for Restructuring Education, Schools, and Teaching (NCREST) supports restructuring efforts by researching successful initiatives, creating reform networks, and linking policy to practice. Contact person: Betty Whitford, director, (212) 678-3432.

The Klingenstein Center offers a master's degree in Private School Leadership aimed at department heads, deans, division directors, and school heads. Contact person: Dr. Pearl Kane, Teachers College, Box 126, (212) 678-3156.

TRAINING

Annenberg Institute for School Reform
Brown University, Box 1985
Providence, RI 02912
(401) 863-7990
(401) 863-2390 (fax)
http://www.aisr.brown.edu/leadership
Mary Neuman, director of leadership

At various sites across the country, this prestigious institute holds meetings and programs that focus on developing learning communities through fostering collaborative leadership. The institute defines educational leaders as including teachers, principals, superintendents, and members of the community. Its projects and initiatives include the Annenberg Superintendents group, the Annenberg Senior Fellows in Urban Education, and School Communities That Work, as well as research on designs for comprehensive school reform. Additionally, Annenberg's public television channel offers a wide variety of professional development workshops for K–12 educational leaders. The "Principles for Principals" series, in particular, focuses on improving student achievement in K–12 math and science. The institute is recognized as one of the key players in working with urban schools and districts, and influencing them.

Publications: "The Promise of Urban Schools."

Aspiring Principals Academy
Educate Indiana & Region 8 ESC
P.O. Box 592
Markle, IN 46770
(800) 669-4565
http://www.r8esc.k12.in.us/apa/
Linda Michael

The academy challenges teacher-leaders who aspire to the principal-ship through administrator shadowing, network and web resources, and project-based research.

The Aspiring Principals Program
The Big Picture Company
275 Westminster Street, Suite 500
Providence, RI 02903
(401) 456-0600
(401) 456-0606 (fax)
http://www.bigpicture.org/aspirinc.htm
Dennis Littky, co-director

Founded in 1998, this national training and certification program creates a cadre of creative and innovative leaders for the nation's schools. Aspiring Principals (APs) apprentice one year with Distinguished Principals (DPs) selected from outstanding small urban and rural schools. Graduates are awarded certificates from partner higher education institutions.

The Association of California School Administrators
Principals and Superintendents Academies
Lompoc High School
515 West College Avenue
Lompoc, CA 93436
(805) 735-2371 ext. 401
(805) 735-1411 (fax)
http://www.acsa.org/
Roberta Heter, president

The Association of California School Administrators (ACSA) boasts a faculty of nationally recognized educational leaders who offer courses designed for coadministrators, mentor teachers, and other school leaders who aspire to become principals, administrators, and other educational leaders. Additionally, ACSA disseminates research through a variety of position papers and periodicals, and through lobbying.

Publications: *Thrust for Educational Leadership.*

Center for Creative Leadership
One Leadership Place
P.O. Box 26300
Greensboro, NC 27438-6300
(336) 545-2810
(336) 282-3284 (fax)
info@leaders.ccl.org
http://www.ccl.org
Governor William Friday, chairman

Established thirty years ago, the center focuses on undertaking and disseminating research on leadership and leadership development. Although it directs much of its work at the business sector, seminars and papers on human resources discuss services relevant to the educational sector. The center provides feedback; evaluates the impact of programs; develops leadership in women and people of color; fosters global leadership, teams, and team-based organizations; and provides systemic leadership development and new lenses on leadership.

LEADERSHIP ACADEMIES AND INSTITUTES

Curry School of Education–Leadership Institutes
University of Virginia
Ruffnor Hall
P.O. Box 400275
Charlottesville, VA 22904-4275
(434) 924-3334
Dr. Brenda Turner
The Curry School offers several leadership institutes throughout the summer, including the Leadership Institute for Principals; the annual Leadership Institute for Assistant Principals and Those Aspiring to Become Assistant Principals; and the Institute for School Leaders Intervention, Prevention, and Remediation: Alternatives to School Failure, which is sponsored by the Center for State and National Programs for Educators.

Gabbard Institutes
Center for Professional Development and Services
Phi Delta Kappa
408 North Union Street
P.O. Box 789
Bloomington, IN 47402-0789

(800) 766-1156
(812) 339-1156, ext. 2500
(812) 339-0018 (fax)
cpds@pdkintl.org

Every summer at the Phi Delta Kappa (PDK) international headquarters in Bloomington, Indiana, the institutes conduct sessions that run from one to five days in length and address a range of educational issues faced by leaders from all sectors. Scholarships are awarded to PDK members to help defray the expenses of the sessions, which are regarded as premier professional development workshops.

The Institute for Educational Leadership (IEL)
1001 Connecticut Avenue, NW, Suite 310
Washington, DC 20036
(202) 822-8405
(202) 872-4050 (fax)
http://www.policy
James Renier, chairman

The institute bridges gaps between the civic, business, and educational sectors by training leaders who serve children and families. It offers a "Directory of Leadership Development Training Resources," which lists a variety of leadership development programs across the country. Also, it identifies organizations and initiatives that jointly focus on leadership preparation. Topics of its publications include governance and leadership, collaboration and effective services, workforce development, and demographic policy. IEL works with an impressive team of other organizations in the development and operation of the National Clearinghouse for Comprehensive School Reform, which offers a computerized database and website dedicated to state and national school reform (http://www.goodschools.gwu.edu/index.htm).

The Principals' Training Center for International School Leadership
P.O. Box 458
Cummaquid, MA 02637
(508) 362-6550
(508) 362-0285 (fax)
theptc@aol.com
http://www.members.aol.com/theptc
Bambi Betts, director

Established in 1989, this well-regarded center provides training programs and contracted services to administrators and teachers on an international scale. Summer institutes and regional seminars address leadership and group dynamics, finance, law and policy, and curriculum and instruction.

Professional Development Center
P.O. Box 46609
Tampa, FL 33647
(800) 332-2268
Mkatzen383@aol.com

For teachers and administrators, the center offers training programs such as Leadership Development for Teachers and Improving Student Outcomes. It also offers leadership instruments such as the "Teacher Leadership School Survey," "Assessing Readiness for Teacher Leadership," and the "School Culture Quality Survey."

Publications: *Awakening the Sleeping Giant: Leadership Development for Teachers,* by M. Katzenmeyer and G. Muller.

STATE AND NATIONAL INITIATIVES OF NOTE

California School Leadership Academy
300 Lakeside Drive, 18th floor
Oakland, CA 94612
(510) 302-4261
(510) 302-4270 (fax)
macguru@csla.org
http://www.csla.org

The California School Leadership Academy is recognized both statewide and nationally for providing professional development for administrators and teacher-leaders. The academy offers three training programs in addition to housing the Executive Leadership Center, which cosponsors a seminar series with the Association of California Administrators and the California Department of Education. Some of the training modules include the Superintendent's Leadership Role in Accountability and Assessment, Sustaining Transformation: Taking the Long View, Leading for Results: The Superintendent's Role, and Building a Learning Organization in Tough Times. (Other school leader programs across the country include Kentucky's Identifying and Developing Educational Administrators for Schools [IDEAS], Oklahoma's New Principal Assistance program, Virginia's Principal Leadership in Urban Schools, Illinois' Leadership Academy and Urban Network for Chicago [LAUNCH], the California

School Boards Association's Curriculum and Instructional Leaders Academy and leadership institutes for board members, and New Mexico's Extra Support for Principals [ESP].)

The International Network of the Principals' Center
Harvard Graduate School of Education
336 Gutman Library
Harvard University
Cambridge, MA 02138
(617) 495-9812
(617) 495-5900 (fax)
inpc@gse.harvard.edu
http://www.gse.harvard.edu/~principals/about/international.htm
Mildred Collins Pierce, director

Throughout the year, this distinguished center sponsors institutes, small meetings of interest groups, lectures, and forums that examine the relationship between effective leadership and student achievement. The center offers an invaluable international directory of contact persons, activities, and evaluation tools. It also provides support to member centers and serves as a network of information and practitioners. Although the International Center is housed at Harvard, it is a distinct entity from the Harvard Principals' Center, whose sole focus is on the community of principals.

The Maine School Leadership Network
45 Memorial Circle
Augusta, ME 04330
(207) 622-6345
(207) 622-6346 (fax)
mdf@mdf.org
http://www.mdf.org/msln
Leanne Greeley Bond

The Maine network describes its mission as building and developing the leadership capacity of teachers, principals, and school-based educators. The network is an exemplary and intensive two-year program open to teachers, principals, and developing school leaders.

Minnesota Elementary School Principals Association (MESPA)
2380 Wycliff Street, Suite 104
St. Paul, MN 55114-1257
(651) 917-4286

(651) 917-4288 (fax)
info@mespa.net

MESPA provides instructional leadership programs through annual leadership conferences, professional development, national conventions, and annual state leadership institutes.

School of Leadership and Lifelong Learning
University of Georgia
129 River's Crossing
Athens, GA 30602
(706) 542-3891
(706) 542-3893 (fax)
Dave Wynne

The school includes the departments of adult education, educational leadership, and occupational studies at the university. It prepares leaders in a variety of educational capacities; disseminates research on leadership; and offers technical assistance through institutes and professional development. It also helps leaders shape policy.

The South End Principals' Organization: Urban Leadership Center
University of Illinois Extension
10244 South Vincennes Avenue
Chicago, IL 60643
(773) 233-2900
urbanleader@mail.aces.uiuc.edu
Ward Weldon, director

The South End Principals' Organization builds collegial support networks for educational leadership on school improvement. It provides professional development and resources on transformational leadership, collaborative communities, and urban school leadership.

Texas Principals Leadership Initiative
400 West 15th Street, Suite 305
Austin, TX 78701
(512) 473-8754
(512) 473-8814 (fax)
www.tpli.org
Bobbie Eddins, executive director

This is a clearinghouse for information on the professional development of principals in Texas. It provides in-service assessment of the principal's role in facilitating teaching and learning. The initiative presents a three-tiered model of leadership with appropriate development opportunities. It also provides multimedia resources and references.

Publications: Articles, books, and website pieces on such topics as the values and ethics of leadership, human resources in leadership and management, organization, community integration, and curriculum planning.

ASSOCIATIONS

American Association of Colleges for Teacher Education (AACTE)
1307 New York Avenue, NW, Suite 300
Washington, DC 20005-4701
(202) 293-2450
(202) 457-8095 (fax)
www.aacte.org

AACTE exercises recognized national leadership as an association of colleges and universities that prepare professional educators on the undergraduate and graduate levels. It disseminates research and materials on a variety of educational topics, including best practices, governmental relations, multicultural diversity, and its state chapters to schools, colleges, and departments of education.

Publications: *The Journal of Teacher Education.*

American Association of School Administrators (AASA)
1801 North Moore Street
Arlington, VA 22209
(703) 528-0700
(703) 841-1543 (fax)
http://www.aasa.org

AASA is a 14,000-member professional organization that focuses on preparing schools and school systems for higher student achievement through improved leadership expertise while connecting schools with communities.

Publications: "Leadership News Online" and the *Rural, Small Schools Weekly Newsletter,* which focuses on small rural schools.

American Association of University Women (AAUW)
1111 16th Street, NW
Washington, DC 20036

(202) 728-7602
(202) 872-1425 (fax)
http://www.aauw.org

AAUW is a national organization that promotes educational equity for girls and women. It is composed of three corporations: the association itself, a 150,000-member organization; the Educational Foundation, which funds innovative research on girls and education; and the Legal Advocacy Fund, which provides outstanding resources and support for women in higher education who are seeking legal counsel. The work of the AAUW is widely recognized as cutting edge on gender equity issues.

Association of American Colleges and Universities (AACU)
1818 R Street, NW
Washington, DC 20009
(202) 387-3760
(202) 265-9532
info@aacu.nw.dc.us
http://www.aacu-edu.org/
Carol Geary Schneider, president

AACU describes its purpose as advancing liberal learning through the coordination of curriculum and standards. Its Diversity Web coordinates lobbying for group preferences, and its grant projects are intended to increase the responsiveness of curricula to race, ethnicity, and gender. The Knowledge Network is an electronic resource that presents best practices in undergraduate education. AACU's Institute on Collaborative Leadership for Academic Change offers projects, publications, and training aimed at leaders and geared toward fostering systemic change.

Publications: The *Liberal Education* journal and the quarterly newsletter *On Campus with Women,* which focuses on women in leadership.

Association for Supervision and Curriculum Development (ASCD)
1703 North Beauregard Street
Alexandria, VA 22311-1714
(800) 933-2723
(703) 578-9600
(703) 575-5400 (fax)
http://www.ascd.org

ASCD is an international, 160,000-member, nonprofit association of professional educators from all disciplines and all levels that provides professional development, promotes equity in education, and offers internationally recognized best-practice resources. The association sponsors widely attended and high-caliber forums, seminars, and conferences. It disseminates studies through print and nonprint resources.

Publications: *Classroom Leadership* newsletter, *Educational Leadership* journal, *The Journal of Curriculum and Supervision,* and *Education Update.*

National Alliance of Black School Educators (NABSE)
2816 Georgia Avenue, NW
Washington, DC 20001
(202) 483-1549
(202) 483-8323 (fax)
http://www.nabse.org

The alliance consists of black educators and community leaders dedicated to promoting equitable education of black youth. NABSE lobbies legislators, advances public awareness, builds networks, and provides professional preparation of educators.

National Association of Elementary School Principals (NAESP)
1615 Duke Street
Alexandria, VA 22314-3483
(703) 684-3345
(703) 548-6021 (fax)
naesp@naesp.org
http://www.naesp.org/network.htm/
Samuel G. Sava, executive director

This 27,000-member association provides outstanding administrative and instructional leadership for elementary schools worldwide, and is the elementary school counterpart to the NASSP. Advocating for the country's 33 million children in prekindergarten through eighth grade, the association sponsors national and regional meetings, offers a wealth of thoughtful resources, and along with its fifty state affiliates is a public voice for children and their leaders. NAESP sponsors the principal on-line forum, which offers additional resources and workshops including the book *Previewing the Principalship.*

Publications: *Principal* magazine, the *Communicator* newsletter, "Research Roundup," "Here's How," "Middle Matters," and other professional on-line resources.

National Association of Partners in Education (NAPE)
901 North Pitt Street, Suite 320
Alexandria, VA 22314

(703) 836-4880
http://www.napehq.org/3.html

NAPE offers leadership resources for establishing and supporting partnerships between schools and communities. These resources include the newsletter *Partners in Education,* partnership guides, kits, and manuals.

National Association of Secondary School Principals (NASSP)
1904 Association Drive
Reston, VA 20191-1537
(703) 860-0200
(703) 476-5432 (fax)
nassp@principals.org
http://www.nassp.org
Thomas F. Koerner, interim executive director

This is the most recognized and respected association of secondary school principals. It serves 46,000 members in middle schools and high schools, including administrators, teachers, and students. Although it provides a wide array of resources, the NASSP lists its primary sources on school leadership as the *NASSP Bulletin,* a widely read educational journal; a magazine entitled *Principal Leadership;* and *CASE,* which offers a state-of-the-art evaluation and planning system for schools. Additionally, the NASSP publishes a newsletter entitled *Legal Memorandum* four times a year. The association sponsors the National Alliance of High Schools and the National Alliance of Middle Level Schools. It also initiated the National Honor Society, the National Association of Student Councils, and the Middle Level Student Activities Association, among other groups.

National Coalition of Advocates for Students
100 Boylston Street, Suite 737
Boston, MA 02116
(617) 357-8507
ncasmfe@mindspring.com

The coalition is a national, nonprofit educational and advocacy organization focused on achieving equal and equitable access to quality education for those students who may be most vulnerable to school failure. On-line, it provides legal support; sponsors a variety of national projects such as the Clearinghouse for Immigrant Education and Mobilization for Equity; posts a newsletter and flyers; and provides links to other education advocacy organizations and resources.

National Education Association (NEA)
1201 16th Street, NW
Washington, DC 20036
(202) 833-4000
http://www.nea.org
John Wilson, executive director

NEA is the country's oldest, largest, and most influential educational organization dedicated to the advancement of public education. With a
membership of 2.5 million, NEA is an advocate for quality education nationally, in individual states (with affiliates in each state), and locally. It
coordinates innovative projects; offers workshops, seminars, and national and state conferences; and maintains a broad print library and a
wealth of outstanding on-line sources and videos.

**National Foundation for the Improvement
of Education (NFIE)**
1201 16th Street, NW
Washington, DC 20036
(202) 822-7840
(202) 822-7770 (fax)
http://www.nfie.org
Judith Renyi, executive director

This NEA foundation thoughtfully encourages innovation and risk taking through impressive competitive leadership grants open to all public
school teachers, education support personnel, and higher education
faculty. Additionally, it offers on-line news, publications, and reports on
professional development and leadership topics.

National Middle School Association (NMSA)
4151 Executive Parkway, Suite 300
Westerville, OH 43081
(800) 528-6672
info@NMSA.org

NMSA is a 20,000-member, internationally recognized professional organization of teachers, administrators, parents, educational consultants, and community leaders focused on the needs of the young adolescent. It sponsors an annual national conference, state conferences and
workshops, and several networks such as the National Forum for Middle Grades Reform. It provides outstanding professional development,
consultant services, and a wealth of resources, from books and periodicals to web links and newsletters. The association sets national stan-

dards for higher education teacher preparation programs and is the leading international voice for middle-grades education.

Publications: *National Middle School Journal* and *Middle Ground.*

National Parent-Teacher Association (PTA)
National PTA Headquarters
330 North Wabash Avenue, Suite 2100
Chicago, IL 60611
(800) 307-4782
(312) 670-6783 (fax)
info@pta.org
http://www.pta.org
Patricia Yoxall, director of public relations

The PTA's website offers links to the national and all fifty state PTA offices as well as other pertinent information.

National Rural Education Association (NREA)
246 Education Building
Colorado State University
Fort Collins, CO 80523-1588
(970) 491-7022
(970) 491-1317 (fax)
http://www.colostate.edu/Orgs/NREA
Joseph Newlin, executive director

NREA is a national advocate for all levels of rural education. It provides leadership for rural education through workshops, conventions, conferences, lobbying, and the dissemination of research on best practices.

Publications: *The Rural Educator* and *NREA News.*

National Staff Development Council (NSDC)
P.O. Box 240
Oxford, OH 45056
(513) 523-6029
nsdcoffice@aol.com
http://www.nsdc.org

NSDC is an 8,000-member, nonprofit professional association committed to ensuring the success of all students through school improvement and staff development. The council's influence is growing, as is its provision of high-quality professional development. It offers useful audio recordings that include talks by such reform leaders as Michael Fullan and Anthony Alvarado; a video library that addresses such current topics as the high-quality school, assessment and scoring, and professional learning communities; and books and manuals.

Publication: *Journal of Staff Development.*

Partners in School Innovation
1060 Tennessee Street
San Francisco, CA 94107
(415) 824-6196
(415) 824-6198 (fax)
admin@partnersinschools.org

The Partners initiative assists school leadership teams in managing both the process of change and the implementation of best-practice reforms. An Americorps initiative, Partners focuses on developing leadership skills, promoting equity and diversity, exploring themes in education, aiding career development, and providing teaching and learning skills.

Pi Lambda Theta
P.O. Box 6626
4101 East Third Street
Bloomington, IN 47407-6626
(800) 487-3411
(812) 339-3462 (fax)
root@pilambda.org
http://www.pilambda.org/

This international honor society and professional association champions leadership skills and intellectual values, convenes an international conference, and provides research and publications in addition to scholarships, grants, professional awards, and print and nonprint resources.

Publications: The *Educational Horizons* journal.

Urban Superintendents Association of America (USAA)
P.O. Box 1248
Chesapeake, VA 23327-1248
(757) 436-1032
info@usaa.org
C. Fred Bateman, executive director

USAA functions as an informational network on urban public school systems. It holds an annual urban superintendents' academy and an annual conference.

STUDENT LEADERSHIP

Note: Information on each organization listed below is available on its website.

The Jepson School and Youth Leadership Education
School of Leadership Studies
University of Richmond
28 Westhampton Way
Richmond, VA 23173
(804) 287-6478
aperkins@richmond.edu
http://www.richmond.edu
Suzanne Morse, executive director

The Jepson School of Leadership Studies, funded in part by the Pew Charitable Trusts, offers rigorous study in the history, theory, ethics, and techniques of leadership/followership. The youth program seeks to develop K–12 leadership through summer course work, school-based projects, conferences, and the annual Jepson Leadership Forum.

Student Leadership Network
202 South State Street, Suite 1400E
Chicago, IL 60604-1904
(312) 922-5180
info@studentleaders.net
http://www.studentleaders.net

Formerly the Student Alliance Organization, the network is a national, nonprofit, student-led youth leadership development organization for middle and high school students who serve on student councils or school boards, and who are activists. The network offers five development programs, including a student leaders convention and programs on student and youth rights and on students on school boards. It offers on-line community service projects, ideas, and team-building suggestions in addition to providing technical assistance through message boards, e-mail, and the National Youth Yellow Pages.

GROUPS THAT ADDRESS THE FAMILY
IN A LEADERSHIP ROLE

Canadian Association of Student Activity Advisors (CASAA)
821 9th Avenue North
Lethbridge, Alberta T1H1E8
Canada
(403) 328-0250
George Takashima, executive director

Center for Youth as Resources
1700 K Street
Washington, DC 20006
(202) 785-0698
www.yar.org

This is a community-based initiative that offers grants to students to design and implement service projects that address social concerns and contribute to community improvement.

Connecticut's Parent Leadership Training Institute (PLTI)
Commission on Children
18–20 Trinity Street
Hartford, CT 06106
(860) 240-0290
(860) 240-0248 (fax)
http://www.wesleyan.edu/mtsd/presentation/parent.html
Stacy Leeds and Ruth Sales

Family Involvement Sources
America's Promise. The Alliance for Youth
909 N. Washington Street
Suite 400
Alexandria, VA 22314-1556
(703) 684-4500
(703) 535-3900 (fax)
http://www.americaspromise.org

America's Promise is a collaboration to support local efforts that encourage family and community involvement.

Center on School, Family, and Community Partnerships
Johns Hopkins University

3505 North Charles Street
Baltimore, MD 21218
(410) 516-8800
(410) 516-8890 (fax)
http://www.csos.jhu.edu/p2000/center.htm
Joyce Epstein, director

Family, Career, and Community Leaders of America
1910 Association Drive
Reston, VA 20191-1584
(703) 476-4900
www.fcclainc.org

National Coalition for Parent Involvement in Education
1201 16th Street, NW
Box 39
Washington, DC 20036
(202) 822-8405
(202) 872-4050 (fax)
Sue Ferguson, director

National Parent Information Network
ERIC Clearinghouse on Elementary and Early Childhood Education
University of Illinois
805 West Pennsylvania Avenue
Urbana, IL 61801-4897
(217) 333-3767
(217) 333-3767 (fax)
http://www. npin.org/
Anne R. Robertson

National Parent Leadership Network
1135 Tremont Street
Suite 420
Boston, MA 02120
(800) 493-2338
(617) 572-2094 (fax)
http://www.iccparent.org/contacts.htm

The National Parent Leadership Network, part of the National Parent Leadership Support Project, provides databases, networking, leadership development training, and resources to parent leaders across the country.

The Partnership for Family Involvement in Education
U.S. Department of Education
400 Maryland Avenue, SW
Washington, DC 20202-8173
(800) USA-LEARN ([800] 872-6327)
partner@ed.gov

The Florida Student Leader
Oxendine Publishing
P.O. Box 14081
Gainesville, FL 32604-2081
(888) 547-6310
(352) 373-8120 (fax)
http://www.floridaleader.com

Kentucky's Parents and Teachers Talking Together
Prichard Committee for Academic Excellence
P.O. Box 1658
Lexington, KY 40592-1658
(606) 233-9849
(606) 233-0760 (fax)
www.prichardcommittee.org

Leadership High School
300 Seneca Avenue
San Francisco, CA 94112
(415) 841-8910

Learn and Serve America Exchange
Exchange National Center
National Youth Leadership Council
1910 West County Road B
St. Paul, MN 55113
(877) LSA-EXCH
lsaexchange@nylc.org; www.lsaexchange.org
Carole Klopp, project director

Learn and Serve America Exchange has five regional centers and provides technical assistance to schools, community organizations, and higher education institutions.

Learning in Deed: Making a Difference through Service-Learning
W. K. Kellogg Foundation

One Michigan Avenue East
Battle Creek, MI 49017-4058
(202) 778-1040
www.LearningInDeed.org

Learning in Deed encourages and works with national leaders, policy makers, teachers, administrators, parents, and students on involvement in service-learning.

National Indian Youth Leadership Project
814 South Bourdman
Gallup, NM 87301-4711
(505) 722-9176
(505) 722-9794 (fax)
niylp@cia-g.com.

Service-Learning Resources: Learn and Serve America National Service-Learning Clearinghouse
University of Minnesota
1954 Buford Avenue, Room R460
St. Paul, MN 55108
(612) 624-4758
www.umn.edu/~serve
Rob Shumer, director

This is a clearinghouse for K–12, higher education, community-based, and national service programs.

Vietnamese American Youth for the Future
Asian Family Resource Center
625 Woolcreek Drive
San Jose, CA 95122
(408) 299-8900
http://www.acwp.org/vayf

Wisconsin's Statewide Parent-Educator Initiative (WSPEI)
800 Wisconsin Street
Suite 420, Building D-2, Mailbox 65
Eau Claire, WI 54703
(877) 844-4925
Mary Skadahl and Barb Breen, directors

Chapter Seven

● Selected Print and Nonprint Resources

People educate each other through the mediation of the world.
—Paulo Freire

SELECTED PRINT RESOURCES

Books

Barth, R. 1991. *Improving Schools from Within*. San Francisco: Jossey-Bass.

Barth contends that school change occurs given the dynamic, collegial leadership within the school, among students, teachers, principals, and parents.

Beck, L., and J. Murphy. 1997. *Ethics in Educational Leadership Programs: Emerging Models*. Columbia, MO: The University Council for Educational Administration.

This is a landmark on the subject of ethics. It examines the attention given to ethical and moral values in administrative preparation in higher education and in professional development programs.

Cantarella, Gina-Marie, ed. 1999. *National Guide to Funding for Children, Youth, and Families,* 5th ed. Portland, OR: Book News, Inc.

This directory lists over 5,100 foundations and corporate programs that fund nonprofit organizations who serve the needs of children, youth, and families. Included are the grant-maker's full contact information, general synopses of the foundations' giving perspectives, and application and submission information. Available through the Foundation Center (listed above).

Combs, A. W., A. B. Miser, and K. S. Whitaker. 1999. *On Becoming a School Leader*. Alexandria, VA: Association for Supervision and Curriculum Development.

The text argues for person-centered leadership built on the relationships between faculty, staff, students, administrators, parents, and community members. It is a practical guide to developing the skills necessary for constructing and interpreting data that is relevant to the development of healthy self-concepts and interrelationships that build effective learning communities.

Covey, S. R. 1989. *The Seven Habits of Highly Effective People*. New York: Simon & Schuster.

Covey suggests a stepwise process of effective personal and professional leadership based on fundamental moral principles.

Doyle-Walton, K. 1996. *Against the Tide*. Bloomington, IN: Phi Delta Kappa.

This book is a collection of autobiographical essays by American and British women who are leaders of colleges and universities. It examines the conflict women in leadership face in a male-dominated career. Available through Phi Delta Kappa at (800) 766-1156.

Leithwood, K., ed. 1996. *International Handbook of Educational Leadership and Administration*. Norwell, MA: Kluwer.

Leithwood's handbook is an international review of contemporary theory and research on leadership and administrative practice. It focuses on cognitive and critical perspectives, conceptions of practice, and leadership development.

National School Boards Association. 1997. *Education Leadership Toolkit: A Desktop Companion.* Alexandria, VA: National School Boards Association.

This is a collection of case studies, discussion guides, and research reports bearing on the effective use of technology in the classroom.

Phi Delta Kappa offers a variety of leadership videos and books of note:

Leadership beyond the Seventh Generation II: A Tool for Everyone Reforming Schools to Be More Effective So All Children Will Learn. $13 ($11.95 for members).

Produced by the National Indian School Board Association and the Bureau Effective Schools Team, the book is a guide for reform training and for the professional support of students, staff, parents, school board members, and other educational leaders.

The Elementary Principal Series (1989). $3 each ($2 for members) and $23 for the entire set.

The entire series was written by field-based principals who address issues such as leadership, learning about the school and community, supervision, fiscal management, strategic planning, the law, and school-based professional development. There are nine books in the series.

Readings on Leadership in Education and Profiles of Leadership in Education (2000). $22 ($16.50 for members).

Both volumes are new publications by PDK and present thoughtful essays and character sketches on aspects of leadership and those who hold leadership positions.

Walling, D. R., ed. 1994. ***Teachers as Leaders.*** $21 ($15.75 for members).

Twenty of the nation's leading educators present their positions on leadership issues such as professional development, recruitment and retention of quality educators, and what it means to achieve excellence in the profession.

Rogers, J. 1992. ***On Board: A Survival Guide for School Board Members.*** $12 ($10 for members).

This text examines the full range of board members' responsibilities, from hiring a superintendent to managing finances to addressing controversy.

Prince, J. D. 1989. ***Invisible Forces: School Reform versus School Culture.*** $12 ($10 for members).

This short text is basically a handbook for the administrator on curricular and instructional changes in the world of translating theory into practice.

Ramsey, R. 1999. *Lead, Follow, or Get out of the Way: How to Be a More Effective Leader in Today's Schools*. Thousand Oaks, CA: Corwin Press.

Ramsey presents a how-to manual for developing a solution-oriented, collaborative environment through professional leadership and ethical practice.

Schlechty, P. C. 1990. *Schools for the Twenty-First Century.* San Francisco: Jossey-Bass.

Mindful of the close relationship between culture and school change, the text describes an educational leader as one who not only purposefully gets others to act in moral ways, but also possesses the social and intellectual skills necessary for influencing and engaging people in more comprehensive ways to achieve greater competence.

Sparks, D. 1998. *Leader's Guide to Staff Development.* Oxford, OH: National Staff Development Council.

This guide and kit describes the National Staff Development Council's work on such issues as time management, resources, data-based decision making, technology, and learning.

Spillane, R., and P. Regnier. 1999. *The Superintendent of the Future: Strategy and Action for Achieving Academic Excellence*. Aspen, CO: Aspen Publishers.

The authors view the superintendent in the next century as a visionary and practical chief academic officer.

Takanishi, R. 1997. *Preparing Adolescents for the Twenty-First Century: Challenges Facing Europe and the United States.* Cambridge, MA: Cambridge University Press for the Carnegie Corporation.

Commissioned by the Carnegie Corporation of New York, this book examines the public school preparation of youth in light of the impending changes characteristic of the information-based era. Available through Cambridge University Press at (800) 872-7423 or at http://www.carnegie.org/sub/research/index.html.

Zirkel, P. 1995. *A Digest of Supreme Court Decisions Affecting Education,* 3rd ed. Bloomington, IN: Phi Delta Kappa.

This is a reference book that succinctly presents summaries of cases up to December 1994. Available through Phi Delta Kappa at (800) 766-1156.

Authors of Note

Terrence E. Deal

Shaping School Culture: The Heart of Leadership. San Francisco: Jossey-Bass, 1998. Deal challenges school leaders to capitalize on the power of the school culture in building a cooperative community. He includes exemplary practices representing a variety of school cultures.

Leading with Soul: An Uncommon Journey of Spirit, with Lee G. Bolman. San Francisco: Jossey-Bass, 1995. Deal uses the form of a parable to explore the bonds between spirituality and leadership and examines the integration of social sciences, poetry, philosophy, and theory of organizations as it impacts current educational leaders.

The Leadership Paradox: Balancing Logic and Artistry in Schools, with Kent Peterson. San Francisco: Jossey-Bass, 1994. Deal looks at the challenges facing leadership from a field-based perspective and argues that the art and craft of leadership should be able to meet the increasing demands of both technical and symbolic problems.

Michael Fullan

Change Forces. London: Falmer Press, 1993. Fullan urges educators guided by a moral imperative to see themselves as advocates for children in the process of change.

What's Worth Fighting for in the Principalship? New York: Teachers College Press, 1991. This text serves as a plan of action for positive change for principals and teacher-leaders.

What's Worth Fighting for Out There? New York: Teachers College Press, 1998. Fullan challenges leaders in administration, teaching, and policy making, as well as those in the community, to think broadly about possibilities for future education.

Ann Leiberman

The International Handbook on Educational Change, with Andy Hargreaves, Michael Fullan, and David Hopkins. New York: Kluwer, 1998. This is a compilation of articles written by the most widely acclaimed researchers in educational leadership and school reform. The text examines the full context of the process of change, such as resistance to change, implementation of effective and sustained change, innovation, and reform.

Peter Senge

The Dance of Change: The Challenges to Sustaining Momentum in Learning Organizations. Garden City, NY: Doubleday, 1999. Senge examines the challenges that systemic change will present and describes field-based learning initiatives and experiences of leaders of change.

Schools That Learn: A Fifth Discipline Fieldbook for Educators, Parents, and Everyone Who Cares about Education. Garden City, NY: Doubleday, 2000. Senge presents vignettes and case studies of schools and programs from across the country that are applying the tenets of learning systems to school reform and reconstitution.

Thomas Sergiovanni

Leadership for the Schoolhouse: How Is It Different? Why Is It Important? San Francisco: Jossey-Bass, 1996. Sergiovanni places systemic school reform in the context of the democratic community that is responsive to human needs, teacher growth, and student development.

Building Community in Schools. San Francisco: Jossey-Bass, 1994. In this book, Sergiovanni examines the beliefs, philosophy, structure, and processes of the culture of community.

Moral Leadership: Getting to the Heart of School Improvement. San Francisco: Jossey-Bass, 1992. In this book, Sergiovanni argues for the legitimation of moral values and beliefs as a context in which to nurture collegiality, common objectives, and organic teacher interdependence, which compel schools to become virtuous communities.

Selected Articles

Fullan, Michael. 1992. **"Visions That Blind."** *Educational Leadership* 49, no. 5 (February): 19–20.

Fullan suggests that principals who are more successful at creating the capacity for effective sustained change in schools do so through establishing collaborative cultures rather than through exercising charismatic leadership.

Lambert, Linda. 1998. **"How to Build Leadership Capacity."** *Educational Leadership* 55, no. 7 (April): 17–19.

Lambert defines leadership as collaboratively promoting learning by adults and students. She examines the basic ideas that support leadership as learning and the ways in which a capacity for such leadership may be developed.

Lashway, Larry. 1997–1998. **"Measuring Leadership."** *Research Roundup* 14, no. 2 (Winter): 1–5.

Lashway reviews current publications that address measuring and evaluating leadership from a variety of viewpoints.

Leithwood, Kenneth A., and Mary S. Poplin. 1992. **"The Move Toward Transformational Leadership."** *Educational Leadership* 49, no. 5 (February): 8–10.

Leithwood and Poplin argue that the image of the instructional leader has been replaced by that of a transformational leader who empowers those who are engaged in collective action.

Lewis, Phyllis H., and Sharon A. McDade. 1995. **"Creating and Implementing a Culture of Leadership."** *CUPA Journal* 46, no. 4 (Winter): 19–24.

Lewis and McDade review leadership development programs and the attendant issues of a learning organization, the benefits of a leadership culture, the need for one, and the ways in which that culture may be created and nurtured.

Murphy, Jerome T. 1988. **"The Unheroic Side of Leadership: Notes from the Swamp."** *Phi Delta Kappan* 69, no. 9 (May): 654–659.

Murphy points to the development of a shared vision rather than a hierarchical dictate as the organizing force undergirding successful schools, and suggests characteristics of effective leaders and effective strategies.

Sergiovanni, Thomas. 1994. **"Organizations or Communities? Changing the Metaphor Changes the Theory."** *Educational Administration Quarterly* 30, no. 2 (May): 214–226.

Sergiovanni examines the critical differences between schools as organizations and schools as communities, and suggests the shifts in perspective and process necessary for schools to become communities based on shared ideas. He also analyzes the differences between authority and leadership that the two models present.

Wilson, Meena. 1993. **"The Search for Teacher-Leaders."** *Educational Leadership* 50, no. 6 (March): 15–21.

Wilson presents vignettes of exemplary high school teacher-leaders as a foundation for understanding who leaders are and how they are characterized.

Research Reports

American Association of University Women
The AAUW Report: How Schools Shortchange Girls (1992) is a stark examination of how girls in K–12 public schools receive an inferior education compared to boys.

Shortchanging Girls, Shortchanging America (1991) is a nationwide poll that examines the impact of gender on self-esteem, career aspirations, educational experiences, and interest in math and science among children aged 9–15.

These reports can be obtained from the American Association of University Women at 1111 Sixteenth Street, NW, Washington, DC 20036; (202) 728-7602, (202) 872-1425 (fax); http://www.aauw.org.

The Carnegie Corporation of New York
Great Transitions: Preparing Adolescents for a New Century (1995, $10.00) and *Turning Points: Preparing American Youth for the Twenty-First Century* (1989, $9.95) are among the seminal studies that have helped guide appropriate developmental practice for middle schools.

Similarly, two Carnegie Corporation reports have helped set the agenda for program development in the appropriate grade levels: *Years of Promise: A Comprehensive Learning Strategy for America's Children* (1996, $10.00), for the primary grades; and *Starting Points: Meeting the Needs of Our Youngest Children* (1994, $10.00).

These four reports are available from the Carnegie Corporation of New York at P.O. Box 753, Waldorf, MD 20604.

Council of the Great City Schools
Teaching and Leading in the Great City Schools (1988) examines the challenges of recruiting, retaining, and training urban teachers and administrators. It provides vignettes from exemplary large urban programs. The report can be obtained from the Council of the Great City Schools at 1301 Pennsylvania Avenue, NW, Suite 702, Washington, DC 20004; (202) 393-2427, (202) 393-2400 (fax); http://www.cgsc.org/.

Institute for Educational Leadership (IEL)
The Policy Exchange of the IEL published the CRS report for Congress entitled *Children and Their Families: Federal Programs and Tax Provisions* (1999). Written by Joe Richardson and Sharon House, the report summarizes and examines a variety of facets of education and training, including block grants, Indian education, the job corps, education for the homeless, school-to-work, and systemic school reform. The report is available from the Institute for Educational Leadership at 1001 Connecticut Avenue, NW, Suite 310, Washington, DC 20036; (202) 822-8405, (202) 872-4050 (fax); http://www.policyexchange.iel.org/pubs/Federal_Programs_for_Children.html.

The Joyce Foundation
The Joyce Foundation, in company with the Education Commission of the States, sponsored an ongoing work entitled *Spotlight on School Governance, Minority Achievement.* Begun in January 2000, the report calls for policy makers to aggressively adopt the "affirmative development" of promising strategies for reaching, identifying, and supporting potential high achievers from early childhood education through higher education. The report calls for providing scholarships to students in science and engineering. Additionally, the report challenges decision makers to look to governance as a focus of school reform. The report is available from the Joyce Foundation at 3 National Plaza, 70 West Madison Street, Suite 2750, Chicago, IL 60602; (312) 782-2464, (312) 782-4170 (fax); http://www.joycefdn.org.

National Association of Elementary School Principals
The National Association of Elementary School Principals, in collaboration with the National Association of Secondary School Principals and the Educational Research Service, wrote a report entitled *Is There a Shortage of Qualified Candidates for Openings in the Principalship? An Exploratory Study* (1998). Through a rigorous literature review and a national survey, the report examines the discrepancy between openings and candidates for principalships across the country. It suggests inhibiting factors, possible steps that could be taken to address the shortage, and some long-range planning for training and recruitment. Its reference list cites many of the leading authors on educational leadership. The report can be obtained from the National Association of Elementary School Principals at 1615 Duke Street, Alexandria, VA 22314-3483; (703) 684-3345, (703) 548-6021; http://www.naesp.org.

National Association of Secondary School Principals

Commissioned by the National Association of Secondary School Principals in conjunction with the Kauffman Foundation, the report written by Harry Hodgkinson entitled *Secondary Schools in a New Millennium: Demographic Certainties, Social Realities* examines the diverse demographics of the world and of U.S. schools, focusing on age, race, ethnicity, wealth, educational level, national origin, and religion. The report presents trends, social realities, and complexities that must be understood in order to authentically transform schools. The report can be obtained from the National Association of Secondary School Principals at 1904 Association Drive, Reston, VA 20191-1537; (703) 860-0200, (703) 476-5432; http:www.nassp.org/press_releases/dfclts_chlngs.htm.

National Association of State Boards of Education (NASBE)

Principals of Change: What Education Leaders Need to Guide Schools to Excellence (1999) examines the changing role of the principalship and provides recommendations on the reforms needed to ensure that all schools have well-qualified administrators. Topics covered include the growing shortage of qualified principals, recruiting high-quality candidates, developing a standards-based vision for the principalship, and training and retaining good principals.

A Motion to Reconsider: Education Governance at a Crossroads (1996) describes the essential attributes of sound governance found to be critical to high-performance policy making and leadership at both the local and state levels. It emphasizes the link between perceptions of good education governance and today's serious problem of public alienation from government in general.

Public Accountability for Student Success: Standards for Education Accountability Systems (1998) develops ten standards that policy makers should use in designing education accountability systems.

These three reports can be obtained from the National Association of State Boards of Education at 277 South Washington Street, Suite 100, Alexandria, VA 22314; (703) 684-4000, (703) 836-2313; http://www.nasbe.org.

National School Boards Association

The report *Leadership Matters: Transforming Urban School Boards,* which was funded by BellSouth, Ford, Motorola, and the W. K. Kellogg Foundation, focuses on strategies that school boards may use to increase student achievement. The report can be obtained from the National School Boards Association at 1680 Duke Street, Alexandria, VA 22314; (800) 950-6722; http://www.nsba.org.

Policy Brief

Effective Leaders for Today's Schools: Synthesis of a Policy Forum on Educational Leadership. June 1999.

This brief was prepared by the U.S. Department of Education's Office of Educational Research and Improvement and the National Institute on Educational Governance, Finance, Policymaking, and Management. The brief examines the preparation and ongoing development necessary for effective twenty-first-century schools (given the changing definitions of educational leaders—principals, superintendents, school board members), and the attendant policy implications.

SELECTED NONPRINT RESOURCES

World Wide Web Sites

Annenberg Institute for School Reform
http://www.learner.org/channel/workshops

Annenberg's public television channel offers some fourteen interactive workshops on-line. The "Principles for Principals" series offers eight interactive workshops that critique documentary footage from schools across the country. The series also challenges educational leaders to meet state and national standards, to pursue effective teaching and learning strategies, and to develop effective professional development models.

The Annie E. Casey Foundation
http://www.aecf.org

The Casey Foundation's "ADVOCASEY Online" presents the foundation's work, an update of its print articles, AEC financial and grant reports, and full information on initiatives, sites, and grant application forms.

Center for Creative Leadership
info@leaders.ccl.org
http://www.ccl.org

The center generates and disseminates information on leadership and leadership development worldwide. They describe themselves as developers of models of managerial practice and providers of training programs, products, research, and on-line information on leadership programs. As a nonprofit educational institution, the center offers services to the educational world and the business, philanthropic, and nonprofit sectors.

Center on Education Policy

http://www.ctredpol.org
John Jennings, director

Supported entirely by charitable foundations, the center serves as a communicator between educators and the general public. It offers on-line publications; sponsors conventions and community forums; and provides technical assistance to the education, business, state, and civic sectors.

Publications: Topical research papers that cover a wide variety of issues relevant to overlapping communities, such as vouchers, violence and crime in schools, Title I, public engagement, standards-based education reform, student achievement, and national assessments of educational progress. In conjunction with Phi Delta Kappa, the center also presents yearly the results of the Gallup poll on education.

Council on Foundations

webmaster@cof.org

The council is a nonprofit membership association of grant-making foundations and corporations. Its website lists more than 1,700 member foundations and corporations that offer educational grants. It also lists other foundation resources and publications; links to legal and governmental activities that affect both funding and education; and links to other networks such as the regional Metropolitan Association for Philanthropy, the Forum of the Regional Association of Grantmakers, the national Independent Sector, and the Foundation Center.

DeWitt Wallace–Reader's Digest Funds

http://www.wallacefunds.org
M. Christine DeVita, president

The website of DeWitt Wallace–Reader's Digest Funds presents studies on various educational issues, such as pathways to teaching; preparing and retaining effective teachers for the United States's schools; and leadership and partnerships. It also provides links to its national partners, such as the Academy for Educational Development (AED), the Urban Institute, and the National Institute on Out-of-School Time.

The Edna McConnell Clark Foundation
http://fdncenter.org/grantmaker/emclark/index.html

The foundation lists grants awarded for that quarter and the annual report of the foundation's president. The foundation's "Clearinghouse Bibliography" can be accessed at http://www.cssp.org/cpcbib.html. All publications can be obtained free of charge by writing or faxing the foundation's Office of Communications.

Federal Government Internet Educational Resources
http://www.ed.gov/EdRes/EdFed/index.html

This website presents government internet resources for education, including resources funded by the U.S. Department of Education. It offers access to grant projects and programs; the Comprehensive Regional Assistance Centers; the Educational Resources Information Center (ERIC); the ten Eisenhower Regional Consortia, which provide technical assistance in math and science education; and all Regional Educational Laboratories.

The Foundation Center
fdonline@fdcenter.org
http://www.fdncenter.org

The Foundation Center is the self-described "gateway to philanthropy on the World Wide Web." It publishes the weekly *Philanthropy News Digest*, sponsors writing seminars on effective funding, and lists career opportunities in foundations, charities, and nonprofit organizations. Its on-line library provides links to nonprofit resources, offers common grant application forms, and provides literature from the nonprofit sector. The foundation offers training and outreach, computer searches, books and periodicals, grant-maker files, bibliographic databases, and libraries. A monthly subscription to its web database, "The Foundations Directory Online," which accesses 10,000 of the largest funders in the United States, costs $19.95. A monthly subscription to the new "Foundation Directory Online Plus," which lists 10,000 foundations and 100,000 available grants, costs $29.95.

The Global Schoolhouse
http://www.gsn.org

The Global Schoolhouse specializes in on-line collaborative learning. It offers access to projects; communication tools such as conferencing, discussion boards, and mailing lists; and professional development. In company with Lightspan.com, this website offers a rich variety of resources through its "School Leaders" link, including information on organizations, grants, fund-raising, research, evaluation, school reform, state and national standards, and teacher certification. The website also provides links to information on education legislation through three major sources: American Association of School Administrators (AASA): Advocacy (http://www.aasa.org/Advocacy.htm), which examines issues surrounding rural and small-school funding; Education World: Education Legislation (http://db.education-world.com/perl/browse?cat_id=3), which includes over twenty articles on Goals 2000 and other legislative issues; and the U.S. Department of Education: Legislation, Regulations, and Policy Guidance, which presents resources in the areas of legislation, regulations, and policy guidance.

House Committee on Education and the Workforce
http://edworkforce.house.gov/

The committee's website presents daily congressional legislation and committee activity in addition to offering links to such facilities as the Library of Congress. It also offers internet access to information on educational topics, including the need to improve educational research, teacher quality and empowerment, classroom modernization, and programs for the disadvantaged. The committee's projects include "Education at a Crossroads: What Works and What's Wasted?" which examines both quality education in the United States and the federal role in education.

International Electronic Journal for Leadership in Learning
http://www.ucalgary.ca/~iejll/

The Electronic Journal presents on-line a refereed academic journal, with full text articles on educational leadership.

The Middle Web Index
http://www.middleweb.com

Middle Web offers links to material on school leadership and the professional development of principals; middle-grades curriculum and instruction; assessment and evaluation; the professional development of teachers; parents and the public; standards-based school reform; and students and school life.

The Milken Family Foundation
http://www.mff.org/contact/contact.taf

This website has a Milken Educator Virtual Workspace site, which is a free on-line resource for both students and teachers. It presents an array of internet tools, such as bulletin boards, information on web publishing, calendars, document sharing, evaluation applications, e-mail, chat rooms, and project management information.

National Center for Learning Disabilities
http://www.ncld.org/

The center offers a variety of on-line publications of both general interest and special interest to teachers, adults with learning disabilities, and parents of children with learning disabilities.

National Center on Educational Outcomes
http://www.coled.umn.edu/NCEO

This center offers a variety of special and technical reports on issues such as special education outcomes, accountability for educating students with disabilities, the appropriate ways of assessing special-needs learning and standards, and it offers Data Links, which is an open forum for assessing students with disabilities, exchanging information, and presenting news briefs and information on conferences, clinics, and meetings.

National Governors Association
http://www.nga.org
Contact person: Kristin Conklin

This on-line source, which focuses on education, offers the Education Policy Studies Division's best-practice resources such as *State Strategies for Incorporating Technology into Education* and *Third International Mathematics and Science Study (TIMSS): Findings and Implications for State Policymakers*. Other print resources on educational reform include *A Back to School Special Report on the Baby Boom Echo: Growing Pains*, as well as press releases, policy papers, and a complete listing of all on-line documents.

National Parent-Teacher Association
info@pta.org
http://www.pta.org
Patricia Yoxall, director of public relations

This website offers links to the national and all fifty state PTA offices. Additionally, it offers an historical photo archive, biographies of the PTA's founders, PTA history and milestones, practical information on fundraising, copyrighted PTA materials, and National PTA program sponsors and partners.

North Central Regional Educational Laboratory (NCREL)
cscdwww@ncrelsgi.ncrel.org

NCREL offers a wealth of full-text articles that can be downloaded from its website Leadership Learning, the Center for School and Community Development. Additionally, it offers useful internet links to other leadership centers and organizations.

Publications: *New Leaders for Tomorrow's Schools* is a periodical that examines critical leadership issues, ranging from systemic school reform to the integration of technology, and controversial issues such as vouchers, charter schools, leadership skills, and partnerships.

Urban Education Web
http://eric-web.tc.columbia.edu

The Urban Education Web is a site focused on urban students, their families, and the educational population that serves them. It offers access to the National Parent Information Network; serves as a clearinghouse for the ERIC system on urban education; and presents bibliographies, parent guides, abstracts, digests, and additional resources on a variety of urban education issues, including administration, finances, and leadership on equity and cultural diversity. Additionally, it provides links to the national ERIC database, other urban education resources, conferences, workshops, the Institute for Urban and Minority Education, and the U.S. Department of Education.

Publications: Its most recent works address the issues of school safety, comprehensive school reform, and challenges facing the country's diverse student population.

U.S. Department of Education
http://www.ed.gov/

The Department of Education offers a wealth of on-line information about the government's work in education in the United States. Its site provides the full texts of "A Teacher's Guide to the U.S. Department of Education," "A Researcher's Guide to the U.S. Department of Education," as well as publications for parents. Information on initiatives such as the Twenty-First Century Community Learning Centers can be fully downloaded, along with information on annual conferences and institutes.

Publications: *Bringing Education into the After-School Hours* (1999) and the report *Safe and Smart: Making After-School Hours Work for Kids* (1998).

Databases

American Association of School Administrators (AASA)
www.aasa.org

Through its on-line "Leadership Forum," AASA posts updated information about workshops, conferences, and job openings; a searchable database; and articles of interest to the educational leadership community. AASA provides links to the School Administrators' Center and to *Education World* (http://www.education-world.com/), an on-line compilation of papers on issues critical to educational leadership.

The Annie E. Casey Foundation
http://www.aecf.org

This additional website is an interactive on-line database with state and national profiles, graphs, maps, and rankings bearing on the status of the well-being of children. The material can be downloaded.

Child Welfare League of America (CWLA)
http://www.cwla.org

CWLA provides free on-line access to all states' child abuse and neglect data in both text and statistical formats. Additionally, it provides links to each state's website and other research sources.

Children's Defense Fund (CDF)
http://www.childrensdefense.org

CDF has a national headquarters in Washington; regional offices in California, Colorado, Minnesota, Mississippi, New York, Ohio, South Carolina, Tennessee, and Texas (where there are two); and an affiliate, Stand for Children, in Washington. This website has a CDF listserv; links to similar organizations; publications, news, and reports, which can all be downloaded free of charge; and a job opportunity databank.

Institute for Educational Leadership
http://www.policyexchange.iel.org/pubs/Federal_Programs_for_Children.html

The institute's Policy Exchange website offers not only the notable special report, "Federal Programs for Children and Families: A Tool for Connecting Programs to People," which can be downloaded, but links to other federal agencies, legislative committees and subcommittees, the Indian Education Act, and the Twenty-First Century Community Learning Centers document.

National Center for Education Statistics (NCES)
http://nces.ed.gov/

NCES provides a searchable bibliographic database of U.S. Department of Education publications funded or written since 1980.

Philanthropy News Network (PNN)
http://pnnonline.org

PNN has an interactive on-line database with links to foundations, education grants, news summaries on corporate funding and educational initiatives, a free newspaper, and a free e-mail alert for Requests for Proposals (RFPs).

School Administrator News
editor@schooladministrator.net
http://www.schooladministrator.net/

The News's weekly presents notable articles to school leaders, in addition to offering quick links to other sites, a news bulletin board, job listings, a chatline, and a bookstore.

U.S. Department of Education Award Databases
ocfoweb@ed.gov
http://www.ed.gov/offices/OCFO/gcsindex.html

The Department of Education presents grant and contract award information on-line. Each database link is listed by fiscal year and offers specific information (as well as its search function). Some of the links provided through this database are to the following offices:

The Office of Educational Research and Improvement (OERI)
edpubs@inet.ed.gov
http://www.ed.gov/pubs/edpubs.html

This office provides information on grants and competitions.

Office of Elementary and Secondary Education (OESE)
AldaGiusti@ed.gov

This office lists all funded initiatives, application notices, and deadlines for competitions.

Office of Postsecondary Education (OPE)

JaneWrenn@ed.gov

This office also lists all funded initiatives in higher education, application notices, and deadlines for competitions.

Videotapes

Advocates for the Public Schools. 1997.

In this set of videocassettes, Phi Delta Kappa presents the views of four of the nation's outstanding educational leaders. The talks examine the conflict between the nation's initial commitment to the democratic good and the prevalent commitment to economic good. The set includes *Education for Democratic Character,* John Goodlad, 49 minutes (product code APSJG); *Public Schools and the Future of the Democracy,* John Stanford, 34 minutes (product code APSJS); *The Manufactured Crisis? Realistic Plans for Improving Education,* Bruce Biddle, 56 minutes (product code APSBB); and *Hearts of Children and the Obligations of Our Nation's Schools,* Jonathan Kozol, 77 minutes (product code APSJK). The product code for the set is APSSET.

Available from Phi Delta Kappa, 408 North Union, P.O. Box 789, Bloomington, IN 47402–0789; (800) 766-1156; (812) 339-0018; www.pdkintl. org. The videocassettes cost $21.95 each ($19.95 for members), and $76.95 for the set ($69.95 for members).

Further Thoughts.

Each of the thirty-minute video and program guides in this eight-tape series by Phi Delta Kappa examines a critical educational issue, such as civil behavior, the impact of Goals 2000, the ongoing science and religion debate, school reform as a movement, and dangerous schools. The videocassettes cost $29.95 each ($19.95 for members). Available from Phi Delta Kappa at 408 North Union, P.O. Box 789, Bloomington, IN 47402-0789, (800) 766-1156, (812) 339-0018, www.pdkintl.org.

Satellite Town Meeting #62: School Leadership: Principals at the Center. 1999.

In this videocassette by the National Parent-Teacher Association of an interactive teleconference, nationally recognized experts, local educators, and community leaders share their views on how to improve schools and reach national educational goals. The videocassette focuses on principals and their role as school leaders. Available from National

Parent-Teacher Association (PTA), 330 North Wabash Avenue, Suite 2100, Chicago, IL 60611, (800) 307-4782, (312) 670-6783 (fax), http://www.pta.org.

Town Hall Meeting on School Safety and Violence. 1993.

This was taped at the fall 1993 conference of the Council of the Great City Schools in Houston, Texas. It features a panel, moderated by Dan Rather, of education leaders, including Cornel West, Thomas Payzant, Lee Brown, Joseph Fernandez, Florence Cox, Edward Olmos, Lou Harris, and Aqueelah Ahmed. The tape costs $19.95. Available from the Council of the Great City Schools, 1301 Pennsylvania Avenue, NW, Suite 702, Washington, DC 20004, (202) 393-2427, (202) 393-2400 (fax), http://www.cgsc.org/.

Audiotapes

All the audiotapes listed here are available from the National Staff Development Council (NSDC), P.O. Box 240, Oxford, OH 45056; (513) 523-6029; nsdcoffice@aol.com.

Building Effective Leadership for Quality Professional Development. 1999.

John Bonstingl examines professional development that is both practical and effective in building leadership. Three cassettes (#9060-F05). $30.00.

Intuitive Leadership: Out of Survival and into Thriving. 1999.

Geraldine Flaherty describes a style of leadership based on thriving that is built on three levels of intuitive intelligence. Two cassettes (#9060-D34). $20.00.

Quantum Leadership: Educational Leadership and the New Sciences. 1999.

Suzanne Gilmour bases leadership in schools on the parallels in the research of new organizational perspectives as evidenced in new sciences. Two cassettes (#9060-H06). $20.00.

Spirited Leadership—Building a Culture of Care and Continuous Improvement. 1998.

Joan Vydra suggests ways to create and build dynamic communities. Two cassettes (#8040-K01). $20.00.

Teacher-Leaders: Change Agents for Growth and Renewal. 1999.

Sharon Graves presents a plan of action for identifying, nurturing, and supporting teacher leadership. One cassette (#9060-K08). $12.50.

Teachers Leading Teachers: Changing the Way We Do Business. 1999.

Marrietta Castle and Douglas Whisker examine the ways a district can use teacher-leaders to initiate and sustain change in teaching and learning. One cassette (#9060-C34). $12.50.

◆◆ Index

◆ About the Author

Pat Williams-Boyd is an Associate Professor of Education at Eastern Michigan University. She is a member of the Kellogg Foundation State of Michigan Advisory Board for the Middle Start Initiative. She has received an Office of Research and Development Fellowship for Project Middle Vision, a fellowship to the University of California, Berkeley's Developmental Studies Center for social justice in middle-grades education, a Knox Scholarship to study at Harvard, a Kellogg Foundation grant for Project Middle Vision, and three federal Comprehensive School Reform Initiative Grants for systemic reform initiatives with Title I schools.

She has presented her research at the annual meetings and conferences of numerous scholarly and professional organizations, including most recently the National Middle School Association's annual meeting and the American Educational Research Association's annual meetings, and she has forthcoming work in *Critical Thinking and Critical Pedagogy* (ed. Dan Weil and Joe Kinchloe). She has presented workshops throughout the United States on differentiated instruction and heterogeneous grouping, student-led conferences, portfolio assessment, teaming, educational leadership, suicide prevention, and full-service schools.

She is a reviewer for and has been cochair of the Nominations Committee for the Qualitative Special Interest Group for the American Educational Research Association. She is also a developer and director of Middle Vision: The Center for Dynamic Middle Level Education at Eastern Michigan University. She has worked closely with an Ypsilanti middle school that recently received an award from the U.S. Department of Education as a "Promising Site" for whole-school reform. During her twenty-eight years of public school experience, she has won numerous awards, including Teacher of the Year, Outstanding Young Educator from the Jaycees, and the Governor's Award for Exceptional Service to Kansas Public Education. She is also listed in *Who's Who in American Secondary Education*. She holds two doctoral degrees, one in ethnomusicology and the other in curriculum and instruction.